THE 4MM WAGON PART THREE

by GEOFF KENT

Conflats & Containers, Wagons for long loads & steel, Brake Vans and Finishing touches

Banbury. 5th August 1943. NATIONAL RAILWAY MUSEUM

CONTENTS

XP
WB 16'0"
19-7
PALBRICK A.
13 T
B461668
XP
WB 10'0"
6-18
SHREWSBURY
(COTON HILL)
R.U.
NOT IN
COMMON
13 T
B461900
PALBRICK A

13 T
B461900
PALBRICK A

PREFACE

The publication of this, the third part of *The 4mm Wagon*, completes a project which I first took on nearly fifteen years ago. At that time neither I nor Wild Swan expected it to develop in the way that it has. A single slim volume describing the construction of half-a-dozen kits of one sort or another was, as I recall, the intention, but, like Topsy, it just growed.

When I began, I set myself the objective of examining a series of wagon types that might be expected to be seen in an ordinary pick-up goods train in the middle decades of the twentieth century. Whilst a few of the ones I've included may be a touch esoteric, by and large I have, I believe, stuck to this aim.

In doing this, I would like to think that I've approached the study of goods wagons in a way that no-one else has, at least on the same scale. Other writers have demonstrated a far more encyclopaedic knowledge of wagons built by and for individual railway companies than I could hope to achieve, generally backed up by a lifetime's research, and I must acknowledge myself heavily dependent on their efforts. What to the best of my knowledge no-one has done before, however, is to draw together enough information from a range of these sources to help the modeller produce a representative selection of stock typical of goods trains up and down the country in the fifteen to twenty years either side of Nationalisation.

While this has involved me in comparatively little original research, the need to present things in a way that will be of value to modellers had led me to examine perhaps more closely than other writers a good many details that have gone largely unrecorded elsewhere: container fittings, and tank wagon impedimenta, for example. Ferreting out information of this kind on grounded bodies and preserved vehicles has occupied a good deal of my time in recent years, and continues to do so. All modellers with an interest in such details have good reason to be grateful to those who, whether intentionally or otherwise, have saved these relics of a railway system that has now changed out of all recognition.

Even so, most of the information I have transmitted in these pages has come from other published sources, and happily the last few years have seen a resurgence of interest in goods wagons, with the re-publishing of a number of standard texts on the subject and the appearance of several new works as well; a supplementary bibliography to the one in Part Two is included here. The ever-increasing contribution of the internet as a source of original information is another positive development.

The growing number of kits that continues to appear on the market is also a welcome trend, as is the marked improvement and expansion of some ranges of ready-to-run equipment. Some of these developments have, not surprisingly perhaps, rendered superfluous a few of the modifications and conversions I've described. All the same, the techniques used in these adaptations can hopefully be applied in other related areas. But there are still some wagon types that remain largely unexploited by any manufacturer: hoppers and tank wagons, to name but two.

In conclusion, may I repeat my grateful thanks to all who have helped me in my efforts (to those named in Part Two I should add in particular Steve Banks, Paul Bartlett, David Geen, Eric Gent, Doug Hewson, John Marsh, Don Rowland, Peter Smith and Graham Thomas), and especially to everyone who has been kind enough to say that they've found the books useful and interesting. That is, after all, why they were written.

Geoff Kent
Hemswell, Lincs.
2004

Two types of insulated container. The AF type, seen new in 1951 mounted on a refurbished ex-LNER Conflat S, was to a design built in many hundreds by BR after small batches of similar containers had been produced by the LMS and GWR. The AFP type, larger and equipped with dry ice bunkers, numbered only 142, but is well-known by virtue of its Birds Eye livery. This 1958 example, AFP 66412B, shows evidence of a second, later livery, having been re-allocated to Macfisheries and repainted accordingly in blue with yellow and white markings. By the time it was seen grounded in Grimsby in 1991, the older colours were emerging again.

NATIONAL RAILWAY MUSEUM and AUTHOR

CHAPTER ONE

CONFLATS AND CONTAINERS

Containerisation is not a new phenomenon, though the large metal boxes we call containers nowadays weren't in general use much before the 1970s. The basic idea of putting things in big boxes to enable larger quantities to be transhipped at a time, thus speeding up the operation and reducing the risk of damage, has been around at least since the canal age.

From the inception of the principle until well into the twentieth century, however, its application was essentially localised and small-scale, designed to overcome special problems in an ad hoc fashion, such as transhipment between canals and feeder tramways, or differences in levels as an alternative to locks or inclined planes. Later on, the railways adopted the idea in much the same sort of parochial way: in Flintshire, for example, the Buckley Railway carried clay products in wheeled 'shipping boxes' which were loaded bodily onto coasting vessels to avoid breakages. Elsewhere in North Wales, narrow-gauge slate wagons were taken to the coast on larger transporter wagons for the same reason. And by the end of the nineteenth century, 'lift vans' were being used by furniture removers and others for the movement of goods around the country by rail without intermediate handling.

But it was not until the days of the Big Four that a nationwide system developed using equipment of a design that was to remain familiar for half a century, and which, at its peak in the 1950s, saw the circulation of over 50,000 containers catering for a wide range of general and specialist traffics. Most numerous were the covered containers of types A and B, especially the latter, which were double the size of the former. C and D were open containers, rather like high-sided open wagons without the underframe, again small and large respectively – although the term 'large' to describe any of these traditional designs is a comparative one: the biggest of the pre-Freightliner boxes loaded no more than five tons.

Within these main classifications there was a number of sub-types, identified by additional code letters. Thus the AF was an insulated container of size A for frozen goods, the BD had double side doors as well as the end doors fitted to the basic B type, the BM was intended for fresh meat, and so on. And there were others: in BR days the FM for frozen meat and the L for bulks like cement and lime were perhaps the most numerous, but the full list is quite a long one, and our understanding of the system is not helped by changes that took place in classification: for some years after their introduction, for example, BK furniture containers were identified simply as K types.

There was considerable variety in materials as well. Early containers were usually of planked construction, though a number of pressed steel designs emerged in the 1930s. Later on, plywood, blockboard and narrow matchboarding came into use, while the more specialised types of the 'fifties and 'sixties were generally fabricated in steel. Aluminium and fibreglass were experimented with as well. Add to this the many detail variations in such things as end bracing, door fastenings and shackle points, and it will be readily understood that the evolution of container design was every bit as complex as that of contemporary wagons. Small wonder, then, that the LNER container diagram book, for instance, had no fewer than forty separate entries – nineteen for B types alone.

Incidentally, the numbering of containers under BR auspices didn't follow quite the same system as for wagons. The initial letter (B, E, M, S or W) denoting the company responsible for construction came *after* the serial number; the letters preceding the number related to the container type – A, BD, L, etc. This led at least one railway periodical to conclude not so long ago that a D type container had been transferred to departmental use, simply because of the first letter of the number. In fact, very few containers of any sort met this fate, although older ones that had been withdrawn from traffic were, like old van bodies, often used as grounded stores.

The potential of the 4mm container market has scarcely been tapped by either ready-to-run or kit manufacturers over the years, and some of the products which have been around in the past are no longer available, such as Triang's L-type. In fact, if you exclude livery variations, there are little more than half-a-dozen on the market at the time of writing, either ready-to-run or in kit form; until recently, the sole representatives of the A-type, for example, were Cambrian's kit of the plywood version and Bachmann's AF insulated container. Speaking of livery variations, this formerly appeared in beautifully-reproduced Birds-Eye colours with some superb lettering; it seems a bit ungrateful to point out that only the rather larger AFP ever bore this livery, or that the only type of wagon to carry it was the specially-built Conflat B. This has only recently become available (from Genesis Kits), together with a suitably-sized AFP container; appropriate transfers can be had from Cambridge Custom Transfers. The same maker also lists L-type containers, with two types of wagon to carry them, and a matchboard A-type among his products. Bill Bedford has also recently added the Conflat L to his range, again with containers to match.

Parkside's kit of the ex-LNER DX-type is the only open container to be produced – although, as we shall see, the design was in fact a standard one that was built by others as well. The same maker has kits for BR-built FM- and BD-types, and Bachmann market ready-to-run versions of the latter both with matchboarded ends and with corrugated steel ones similar to the Parkside kit. And the former Airfix GWR BK furniture container appears in several liveries from more than one manufacturer. This is, I think, the oldest of the prototype designs to be had at the present time: it dates from 1936, around the time when the Railway Clearing House laid down new specifications which all the companies subsequently adhered to, albeit with periodic modifications and developments. Except in size, which conformed to the new rules, the GWR's diagram BK2, of which the model is a sound copy, harked back in appearance to earlier days, and it doesn't look out of place in some of the older liveries in which it appears. Pre-1935 containers were generally smaller, however, and came in a much wider variety of designs. And for all the apparent standardisation which followed, when it comes to any other BKs, for example, or plywood B-types and full-sized insulated containers, or most of the more specialised designs, modellers are still very much left to their own devices.

In the matter of general-purpose container-carrying wagons, we are a little better-served, largely because there are fewer prototypes to choose from. The GWR and the LNER ran dedicated Conflats in some numbers, and British Railways standardised on the former's design for the majority of its needs. The LMS and the Southern were content to put containers on wagons of less specialised configuration: three- and single-plank opens in the case of the first, and vehicles that could also be used for wheeled traffic in the latter case. The LMS also built around a thousand chassis for containerised meat traffic, which were certainly specialised, however; so much so that they were deemed unsuitable for general container carriage.

In any case, as the LMS proved, you didn't have to have particularly sophisticated wagons to carry containers. It was common to see them loaded into standard medium and high-sided opens, and BR frequently resorted to these if Conflats were unavailable – although sometimes the added security of preventing the doors being opened in transit may also have been

Despite the development of purpose-designed wagons for carrying containers, they continued to be loaded into low, medium and high sided vehicles throughout their lifetime whenever Conflats were not available. Here an ex-LMS insulated meat container had been roped onto an unfitted three-plank wagon of similar origin, M474854, and an ex-SR furniture container onto an ex-LNER Lowfit – this was officially against the rules, but E220567 had, rather fortuitously, not yet been branded to this effect. The pictures date from 1949 and 1950 respectively. Interestingly, the photographer had noted that BK1325S, despite having been relettered by its new owners, was still in green livery. A. E. WEST

a motive here. If a Medium was used, the rules stipulated that the container had to be secured by roping; an example can be seen on pp. 6/7 of Part Two. The taller sides of a High obviated this chore.

However, one type of wagon that was *not* – at least, not *officially* – used for containers was the Lowfit, which in BR days was actually branded to this effect (see Volume One). Although there is photographic evidence to show that the rule wasn't always observed – one case is illustrated here – the reason was that Lowfits are generally wider than most ordinary opens, and it was not possible to secure a container sufficiently in one to prevent it moving sideways in transit, when covered containers at least could become out-of-gauge. Similarly, covered containers were not to be carried in Shock wagons because the increased height of the floor could have the same effect.

The fact that some of the wagons used regularly by the LMS and the Southern for container traffic were lettered 'Lowfit' at some time in their lives is a potent source of confusion, therefore, as is the BR rule that open containers should not be loaded onto Conflats because they were not designed to withstand the pull of the securing chains. Instead they were to be carried in low-, medium- or high-sided merchandise wagons; presumably there was no risk of open containers getting out-of-gauge in a Lowfit however much they might move around! Judging by the pictures of D-type containers chained onto Conflats in Peter Tatlow's book, this rule would have been a surprise to the LNER, but although they are sold together, Parkside's DX container shouldn't technically be loaded onto their Conflat S if they have BR markings, it seems. Once again, however, this is a rule that was sometimes honoured in the breach rather than the observance.

Parkside offer a kit for BR's standard Conflat A, which became by far the most numerous type in use after nationalisation. David Geen produces two kits for the GWR's forerunners of this design, together with an early LMS single-plank wagon adapted for container carriage; and he plans to offer a Southern Conflat in due course. If you can lay your hands on one, Cambrian used to make the LMS chassis for meat containers – basically just a wagon underframe, though with a rather daunting 48 separate whitemetal parts: not a kit for the faint-hearted. In addition, there are several ready-to-run offerings of the GWR/BR design.

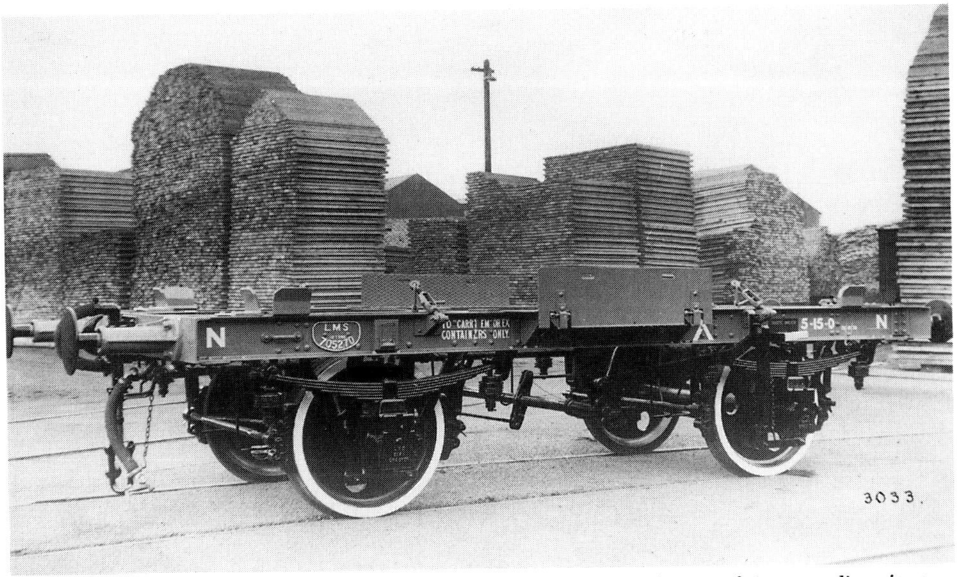

Notwithstanding the use of an ordinary three-plank wagon shown in one of the preceding views, the LMS had a large number of chassis specifically designed to carry meat containers, such as No. 705270, seen when new in the mid-1930s. The chequer-plate flaps could be lowered to assist access to the side doors of a container from a vehicle or platform. HMRS

THREE-BOX COAL WAGONS

Before we consider containers and Conflats from the post-Grouping and post-Nationalisation eras, I would like to look at a type that harks back to the early days of railway containerisation, to the days of local solutions to local problems, but one which against all the odds survived well into the second half of the twentieth century.

The three- (or sometimes four-, five- or even six-) box coal wagon was developed in the mid-nineteenth century as a practical alternative to the time-consuming business of hand-shovelling coal into

Monks Ferry wagons Nos. 16 and 43 photographed at Birkenhead in April 1958. Notice the variations in lettering styles and the piecemeal additions made to the original legends. But can anyone decipher the manuscript inscription on the furthest box on No. 16? According to an article in the February 1947 issue of Model Railway News, *it read 'Forward to Grange Lane Sidings, Birkenhead', but it doesn't look like that to me, although, unlike the empty instructions at this end, it seems improbable that it would have changed dramatically.* JIM PEDEN

Two photographs showing operations at the bunkering jetty at Monks Ferry in earlier years. Full wagons ran down onto the flush-boarded area by gravity, where the elevated travelling crane swung the boxes one at a time over the vessel's bunker hatch, seen immediately forward of the funnel on the larger ship. The two sets of lifting gear show up clearly.

W. A. BROWN

spaces that were too confined to take a full wagonload at one go, such as canal barges, small sailing vessels and steamships' bunkers. A few industrial organisations used them as well. Open-topped containers, each holding three or four tons, were mounted on a four-wheel underframe, which had little more superstructure than some shaped corner-pieces to hold them in place. At the port or canal wharf they were craned off the wagon one at a time, manoeuvred over the hold or bunker hatch of the receiving vessel, and the contents emptied either by simply tipping or by releasing a pair of flap doors which formed the floor.

The majority of these wagons were owned by colliery companies in the North-West and the West Midlands. In the Staffordshire area they tended to be confined to internal rail systems, where narrowboats remained a significant feature of coal distribution until well after World War II. In the North-West, however, they often ran main line to ports around the Mersey and on the Lancashire coast. In fact, two of the constituents of the LMS built variants of their own for supplying bunker coal to their steamer fleets: the Lancashire & Yorkshire at Fleetwood and the Midland at Heysham.

My justification for including such a specialised beast in what is supposed to be a survey of wagon types that might ordinarily be seen in pick-up goods trains is quite simple, though a trifle selfish: just about their last home, at least in main-line use, was the tug-bunkering station at Monks Ferry in Birkenhead, which survived as long as steam vessels lasted in any numbers on the Mersey, closing only in the early 'sixties. Because of their specialised purpose, the wagons owned by the bunkering company escaped pooling during World War II, and must have been some of the very last traditional, grease-lubricated, private-owner vehicles running on BR. They loaded latterly at Ifton Colliery in Shropshire, and could be seen passing through Ruabon and Wrexham in ordinary scheduled goods trains. For my intended layout based in that area I felt I could easily get away with a couple labelled for return to my hypothetical Plas Watkin Colliery.

Although no reliable drawings exist to my knowledge of the Monks Ferry wagons, photographs were fortunately taken near the end of their life by the late Jim Peden, and my models draw heavily on those. Some of the pictures have appeared elsewhere, notably in *Railway Stations of Wirral* published by the Merseyside Railway History Group, and in the book recently brought out by the Historical Model Railway Society on the products of the Ince Waggon Company, which was by far the largest builder of this type of wagon; this contains much useful information, including some basic dimensions. Details of various closely-related, but not identical, vehicles, including drawings, appeared in the March 1987 issue of *Model Railway Constructor*, and in 1982 in the journal of the L&Y Society: I'm grateful to David Goodwin for bringing these articles to my attention, and to Chris Hewitt, who has also researched these wagons for use on his layout 'Regent Road'. Useful pictures can also be found in *London Midland Steam in the North West* (Bradford Barton, 1973: another example of main-line use after nationalisation, this time of former colliery company wagons with the boxes now lettered NCB); in *Celebration of Steam – West Midlands* (Ian Allan, 1995: internal colliery use at Cannock); and finally in the August–September 1997 and April 1999 issues of *Railway Bylines*: the first contains a handy broadside view of a Monks Ferry wagon.

Wagon No. 74 amid the ruins of the original passenger station at Monks Ferry, also in 1958. JIM PEDEN

A five-compartment wagon operated by an industrial user, also in the north-west, photographed in 1934, apparently following refurbishment. Although the wagon had a steel underframe, and the boxes were designed for tipping using the trunnions on each side, the principles were nevertheless similar to those employed on the Monks Ferry wagons. HMRS

The general design of the wagons is hopefully clear from the accompanying photographs, but a word about the operation of discharging the boxes might help to decipher the illustrations. The bottom of each box was divided in two, each leaf or flap being hinged to the lower edge of the longer sides. They weren't fastened in any way, however, so it was necessary to ensure that they stayed shut when the box was hoisted off the wagon and swung over the ship's bunker hatch. To achieve this, the unloading crane had two sets of lifting gear: one set was hooked onto fixed lifting rings at each end of the box, and the second to chains attached to the bottom doors themselves. The chains were held taut until the box was correctly positioned, and then released.

To make sure that the chains remained accessible even when the wagon was loaded, the ring that connected each pair was prevented from falling into the box by a staple bolted on the inside just below the fixed lifting ring. In some photographs of wagons of this type they can be seen dangling over the ends of the boxes, although I suspect that the Monks Ferry company discouraged this practice, which is not generally evident in pictures of their wagons. They also seem to have been keen that the boxes were correctly arranged on the wagons so that the painted legend read 'Monks Ferry Steam Coal'. Although I have seen one or two photographs which give the lie to this, the travelling public was by and large spared the sight of 'Steam Monks Ferry Coal' and the like.

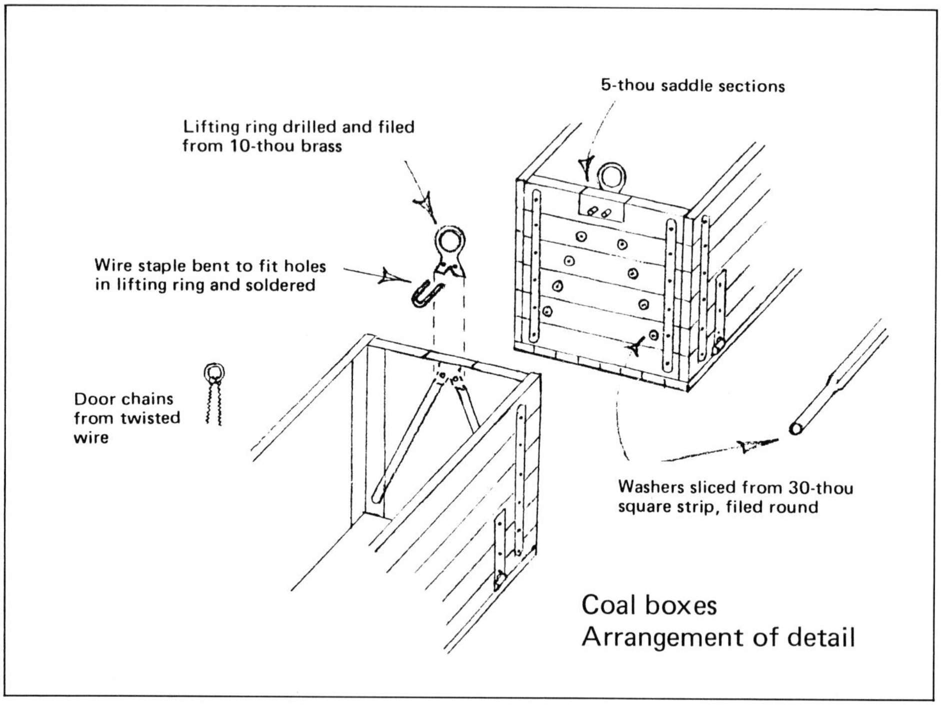

The first model of a three-box wagon described in the text uses the underframe members from a Slater's Charles Roberts mineral kit, albeit with a few embellishments and alterations. The real thing had no floor – the boxes sat directly on the underframe – but this is undetectable with the boxes in place. When the photo was taken, only the left-hand box had had its nuts and bolts added.

For no particular reason I started by making the boxes, for which I used 30-thou styrene, scribed inside and out with my usual tool, a scraperboard knife. Because most of the photographs show them in very much used condition, I distressed some of the pieces by cutting and gouging out slivers here and there to make it look as if the wood had been splintered by rough handling.

Although all the Monks Ferry boxes appeared to be of more or less identical design, those built by and for other concerns, for which I had the evidence of the drawings in *Model Railway Constructor* and the L&Y Society journal, weren't all the same. One area of difference was the way in which the sides and ends of the boxes were joined: some had 4in × 4in wooden posts in the inside, while some had iron corner plates on the outside similar to fixed-end wagons. In the obvious absence of outside corner plates, I had at first assumed that the Monks Ferry boxes would have had the internal posts. Until, that is, I noticed a curious thing: the bolts in the outside washer plates are level with each other in the centre of the planks on both sides of the corner. Though I have no other evidence for it, therefore, I concluded that these boxes must have been held together by *inside* corner plates.

This, at any rate, is how I modelled them. Because there are no corner plates on the outside to disguise the joints, it's quite clear from the photographs that the planks were simply butted up to each other, with the side planks outside the end ones, and not always very tidily. I followed suit, but was puzzled to discover after a few weeks that the sides and ends had almost all pulled in, to the extent that several were quite badly bowed. While this is by no means an unknown phenomenon, I've generally managed to avoid it, and had always reckoned that my habitual use of butt joints, rather than mitred ones, was one reason why my wagons rarely suffer from it. Not so in this case. Perhaps the inside corner plates had something to do with it. Whatever the cause, I only got round the problem by bending the sides and ends out again fairly savagely in my fingers, breaking and remaking several of the corner joints in the process. This seemed to do the trick; no doubt if I'd bowed the parts out first, before sticking them together, which I usually do anyway with wooden-bodied wagons, I might have avoided the problem altogether.

The corner plates, washer plates and hinge straps are all 5-thou strip; the hinges themselves are small noggins of 20-thou square strip, filed round, and set into rebates cut in the bottom edge of the box sides. Note how some of the straps (on No. 16, for instance) are wider at the base (narrow additional slivers of 5-thou on either side), while some are fatter all the way up, as on No. 43. The length is a bit variable as well (No. 16 again). Bearing in mind that the wagons were at least fifty years old when photographed, the boxes in particular were no doubt rather like the old broom that had had five new heads and three new handles.

The fixed lifting rings on the ends of the boxes combined saddles which sat astride the top plank and splayed legs on the inside, evidenced by the upturned vee pattern of the bolt detail on the outside. I'm guessing that the two bolts visible in the saddle plate were the ends of the U-shaped staple that retained the second lifting ring, the one attached to the bottom door chains. As hopefully the diagram shows, I used a mixture of metal and plastic for these fittings, fretting the fixed ring and the top millimetre or two of the splayed legs out of 10-thou brass sheet, and soldering wire for the staple through holes drilled in the legs. Matching holes drilled through the top plank and the 5-thou plastic rectangle that forms the outer saddle plate provide the anchorage for the metal parts: the ends of the wire staple pass through the holes and represent the two upper bolts once they have been trimmed to length. The metal fittings were then epoxied into position, and the rest of the detail built up in plastic: 10-thou strips for the rest of the upturned vee on the inside, except right at the end where the legs overlap the corner plates – at least, I assume they do. For these sections I used 5-thou, and the same for the narrow strip that forms the top of the saddle plate. The circular washers on the outside are discs sliced off the end of a length of 30-thou square strip that has been filed round, and are then smoothed flat once they've dried hard in position. The nuts and bolts are floated on individually by the method described in Parts One and Two (pp.22 and 149 respectively) for what we commonly call 'riveting'.

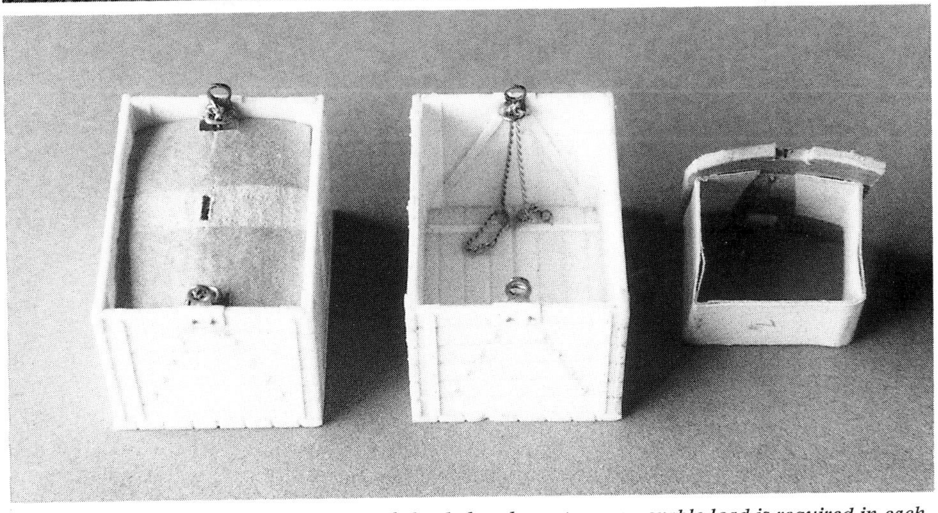

Since the wagon is designed to run both loaded and empty, a removable load is required in each box, to be lifted out by means of a coupling hook engaging in the top – once painted and lettered, the boxes will be glued onto the wagon, making this job easier. With the load removed, the chains that hold the bottom doors shut when the boxes are lifted become visible. The fact that they are just twisted wire may be obvious on close examination, but it's first impressions that count, helped by the 'casual' piles of loose chain on the bottom.

Which leaves only the door chains. Other than the top ring which joins each pair, these can be safely left off if the wagon is to run permanently loaded. However, I want to be able to run mine loaded and empty, so I couldn't get away from some kind of representation of these chains. I know of no source of real chain that comes anywhere close to the seventy or eighty links to the inch they would have in 4mm scale, so I resorted to the method described in Part Two under the heading of gunpowder vans: twisting together two lengths of fine wire. I used 33 swg nickel silver wire, holding the two at one end with pliers or a hand vice and twisting them together progressively, either between finger and thumb nails, or with a second pair of pliers. This produced relatively fine pseudo-chain of about fifty links to the inch – roughly equivalent to 1½ inches per link. I made each length of chain about an inch long, bending the bottom half in a series of whorls that I hoped would look reasonably like loose chain trailing on the floor. At the top I opened the two strands into a loop that wasn't quite a closed one – more a sort of pincer, really. Threading a pair of chains through the staple below the fixed ring, I then closed the pincers over a separate 2mm diameter ring, before epoxying the trailing end of the chains to the box floor. I was as miserly as I could be with the epoxy: I didn't want the chains to be swallowed up in a rusty browny-black blob once they'd been painted. Of course, I could have stapled the ends prototypically to the floor, but I didn't.

I also cheated a bit when I came to build the wagons themselves. Although they had no floor (the containers sat directly on the underframe members), this would not have been apparent when they were in service except when the boxes were craned off to be emptied at Birkenhead. Since I intended to fix the boxes in position once they'd been painted and lettered, therefore, I saved myself the time and trouble of building a complete underframe by attaching the solebars and headstocks around a plain 40-thou floor. For the first wagon I borrowed these from a Slaters Charles Roberts 7-plank mineral kit, which had the same buffers and Attocks grease axleboxes as Monks Ferry No. 16 – except that at least one of the buffers on No. 16 had a step mounted on it (20-thou styrene), and that the axleboxes had to be built up at the top: those on No. 16 were, after all, I realised, a slightly different pattern. Finally, the builder's plates had to be changed, registration plates added, the strap bolts at each end reduced from two to one, and the axleguard bridles altered from straight to curly: all fairly straightforward jobs given the material I was working with.

I also used the brakegear from the kit, although I thought the push rods were a bit thin, and beefed them up with 15-thou strip. And I filed down the bottom of the brake blocks, which are the old single-ended sort on the Monks Ferry wagon. Finally, I filed and bent up my own outer V-hangers, brake levers and guards from 10-thou brass: the absence of quite as much body overhang as on a conventional wagon leaves these rather more exposed to view than usual.

You may be tempted to wonder, given all these alterations, whether it might not have been easier to build the whole lot from scratch in the first place, and you might be right. Certainly when I came to build the second wagon (No. 43) I did just that, using 60-thou styrene for the solebars and headstocks. To some extent I was conditioned by the fact that No. 43 has differ-

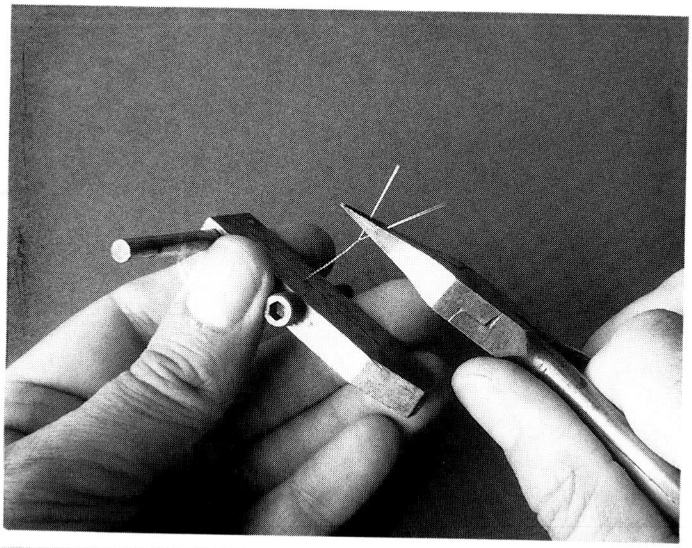

Making fine pseudo-chain using a hand vice and small pliers out of 33 swg / 10 thou / 0.25 mm nickel-silver wire.

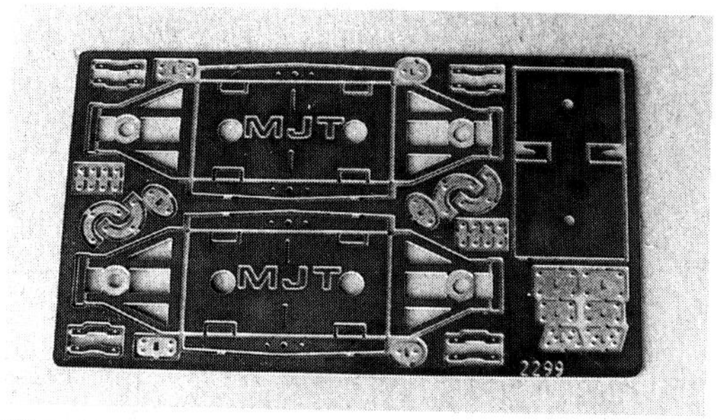

The second three-box wagon employs more extensive scratchbuilding methods, incorporating MJT W-irons. The extra parts included on the etch, such as the curly axleguard bridles and semi-circular crown plates, come in very handy.

ent buffers and axleboxes, which negated the (doubtful) advantage of using the Charles Roberts bits again. Nevertheless, I did pinch the buffers from another Slaters kit, the Gloucester 6-plank, because they were the only ones of the correct pattern I had to hand. Otherwise I relied heavily on MJT (solebar ironwork, axleguards, springs and Ellis axleboxes) and Masokits (brakegear).

As mentioned earlier, the only superstructure on these wagons was the heavy cast-iron corner pieces and timber baulks used to hold the boxes in place, together with a narrow wooden walkway to enable the dockside staff to attach and detach the lifting gear. This catwalk I made from 30-thou strip about 2mm wide, with cosmetic 5-thou bracketwork for the supports attaching it to the solebar. The corner castings were likewise cut and filed from 30-thou, except for the small flange that extends to the outer end of the headstock, for which I used 15-thou. The end buttresses were shaped from 60-thou, again with 5-thou ironwork detail.

The completed model of No. 16 in its final livery of grubby black with white lettering. Of course, it was only to be expected once I had scratchbuilt this wagon and its stablemate that a kit would materialise – from Wizard Models in this case.

LNER CONFLAT S

At the time of nationalisation in 1948, the LNER bequeathed a sizeable fleet of purpose-designed Conflats to the new British Railways. These had been built to several distinct diagrams, but the most numerous, and the longest-lived, was the Conflat S, examples of which remained in traffic at least until the end of steam twenty years later, though probably not for long afterwards.

Both nine- and ten-foot wheelbase examples were inherited by the new regime, but the latter were very much in the majority and are the basis for the Parkside kit. Information on the prototype, including a drawing and several pictures, comes chiefly from Peter Tatlow's *A Pictorial Record of LNER Wagons* (recently re-published); indeed, alternative sources are quite thin on the ground, although a useful photograph can also be found in *Modellers' Backtrack* Vol. I No 2.

The body is a relatively simple affair: a flat floor, a pair of headstocks with buffer guides moulded in, and six pieces representing the low sides and chain pockets, and incorporating container positioning guides and approximations of the fixed cleats for the bottom hooks of the securing chains. These were located inside the chain pockets rather than on the outside of the body, and are therefore almost invisible. In one respect this simplifies things significantly, as we shall see later when we look at the chains themselves. Also provided are the cross-beams or bolsters which locate at the ends of the container. On the real thing these lock into a series of slots in the wagon floor to give a range of positions according to various sizes and combinations of load. The kit includes not only the longer end units, but also the short one

Seen at Cardington in 1940, LNER Conflat S No. 204408 was carrying an early A-type container in grubby blue livery, whose general condition suggests that it would not be long for this world. The position of the board for traders' labels is unusual: these were not originally fitted to containers of this vintage, and had no doubt been added as an afterthought. The securing chains with their tensioners and shock absorbers show up nicely.
A. E. WEST

Two views (above and opposite top) of empty Conflats S. E183557, photographed at Seaton Junction in 1960, was being used for a job for which Conflats were well-suited, namely as a runner beneath an overhanging load. E240959 is seen awaiting its next duty at Nine Elms in 1949; notice the cross-beams used to position and secure the load, and the multiplicity of slots designed to take account of different sizes of container.
A. E. WEST

designed to separate two A-type containers carried together, which dropped into a slot in the floor (also modelled) when not in use.

The chassis represents the standard LNER fitted underframe, with clasp brakes, double V-hangers on one side and a single one on the other. The underside of the floor is recessed to accept the solebars to take account of the fact that the chain pockets are slightly deeper than the floor itself and hide the tops of the solebars as a result. As usual, a measure of tidying up was necessary to remove mould lines from the top edges of the solebars to allow them to sit squarely. Since both solebars are identical, you then need to remove the left-hand moulded V-hanger from one side, and the vacuum cylinder pivot bracket from the other. The cylinder sits close behind the solebar, a little to the right of centre, and on the same side as the single V-hanger, and angled slightly towards it. There is a wedge-shaped pad moulded on the underside of the floor for the cylinder to sit on, but unless I'm missing something very fundamental, it ends up on the wrong side whatever you do.

In any case, I replaced the rather basic vacuum cylinder provided in the kit with a home-made one. A whitemetal cylinder from ABS or Kenline would have been a quicker option, ideally the second one which has the piston and operating arm cast in. The slightly angled mounting can be achieved by filing the top of the cylinder to suit. ABS clasp brake shoes would also have been an improvement on the moulded ones, which are rather plain, but on this occasion I made do with joining the plastic ones with yokes of 30-thou rod set into $\frac{1}{32}$ inch dimples drilled in the backs of the shoes, and added safety loops of 26 swg wire epoxied into 60-thou blocks stuck under the floor. Similarly the moulded brake levers were a touch less three-dimensional than I prefer, so I re-profiled them rather crudely with a 40-thou overlay, chamfering the back of the top edge to reduce the apparent thickness once everything had dried. Lastly, I replaced the plastic buffers provided with cast ones from ABS. The originals are fine from the appearance point of view, but moulded ones with narrow shanks have a habit of breaking off when handled.

Check straps between the bottom of the lever guards and the nearest axleguard are missing from the kit, as are (rather more noticeably) the five body-to-solebar support brackets, and – almost inevitably – the

The Conflat S can be bought complete with the parts for an open container, although for the reasons stated in the preamble to this chapter, D-types were not normally carried on Conflats in BR days.

Another view of the D-type container with its new stretcher bars, chains and additional end bracing.

vacuum hoses. Less obviously, these wagons also had lamp irons on the headstocks at each end. All these details were added in the ways described elsewhere, chiefly in Part One.

Although it's also available separately, the kit includes parts for one of the two principal variants of the full-size open container, the DX-type. Whereas the D-type generally had side doors similar to those fitted to an ordinary high-sided merchandise wagon, together with a single drop-end, the DX had fully demountable (i.e. not hinged) sides, and two drop ends. While the kit nominally represents the LNER version, very similar designs of both types were produced by each of the Big Four and by BR, except that the Southern built no DX containers. Incidentally, not all the companies seem to have recognised the DX as a different breed when it came to lettering: many early photographs show them all classified simply as D-types.

Not surprisingly, the kit is fairly straightforward, although I added a couple of bits of detail. The numbers quoted in the instructions relate to LNER Diagram 32; this shows extra strengthening angle irons on the ends which I applied in 5-thou styrene. And some or all of the DX-types built by the LMS featured a pair of chains strung between the sides, apparently to

An LNER D-type container roped onto an LMS low-sided wagon at Bedford in 1938. In the early days of railway container development, the LMS adapted many such wagons, mainly pre-grouping ones, for the new traffic, usually as here combining fixed ends with dropsides. In this case, however, the unusually high carrying capacity of 15 tons would never have been exploited when the wagon was being used for this purpose. A. E. WEST

A D-type container of LMS parentage being offloaded to road at Beverley in 1960. Unlike the fully-demountable sides and double drop ends of the DX type, the D had only one drop end and a flap door midway along each side. The stretcher bar (usually there were two when the load allowed), designed to brace the sides against the inward force of the lifting gear, had sprung off in this case.
AUTHOR'S COLLECTION

A copy of the LNER diagram for the plywood BD container described in the text, with the addition of a view of the rear; note that its two main horizontal members are channel section. The drawing is reproduced to approximately 4mm scale, but the vertical and horizontal scales are slightly out of proportion to each other. For modelling purposes, therefore, follow the printed dimensions!

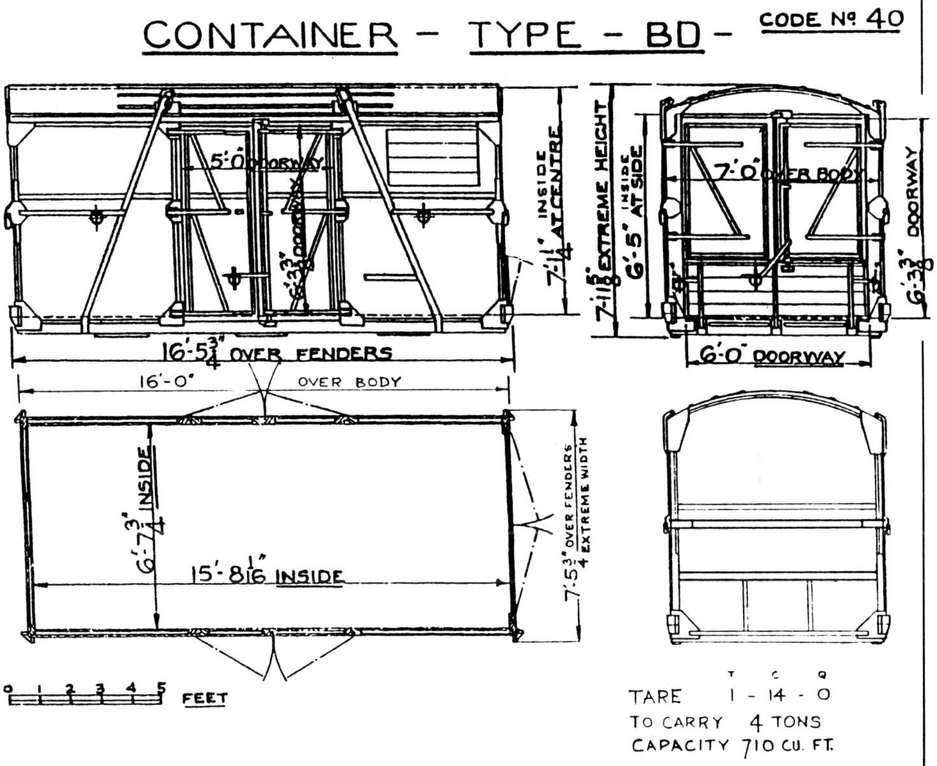

hold them in place while the ends were being raised. I can't say for certain that the LNER fitted these chains, but since the designs are otherwise identical, it seems quite likely, so I decided to err on the safe side. As described elsewhere I made them by twisting together two strands of fine wire (32 swg or thereabouts), and I did the same for the shorter chains securing the ends of the stretcher bars to the sides. The stretcher bars were fitted to all open containers to serve the opposite purpose to the chains: to hold the relatively flimsy sides apart during lifting. They doubled as sheet supports, which explains the hoop across the top. The moulded plastic ones supplied with the kit are very delicately done, but for this reason they struck me as being particularly vulnerable to handling damage. So I replaced the stretchers themselves in 40-thou styrene and the sheet supports in metal: thin strips of nickel-silver for the hoops soldered to 0.5mm wire for the central upright, all epoxied into three holes drilled in the stretcher. The short sections of channel at each end of the stretchers which clip over the tops of the sides were built up in 5-thou on the sides themselves.

Finally, I substituted wire for the moulded chain rings. This was no more than a cosmetic exercise in this case, because, as mentioned in the preamble, open containers were officially barred from Conflats in BR days, and when carried in high-sided merchandise wagons, which it seems they most commonly were, they didn't need securing. In mediums, however, they were required to be roped down, although even then the rings would not always be used.

Instead of the DX, I decided to put an LNER plywood container onto my Conflat S. I chose a fairly late one, BD2299E, of which I happened to have both a photograph (taken when I found it grounded at Goole in 1994) and a copy of the original diagram No. 40, reproduced here. In truth, there was relatively little change in container design after the introduction of the new RCH standard specifications in the mid-'thirties, but I felt that a post-war box was more likely to have lasted into my own modelling period of the second half of the 'fifties than an earlier one: containers had a pretty hard time in use, and didn't generally enjoy extended lives.

Each of the Big Four, and BR, produced containers to the same design as LNER diagram 40, almost 1,600 in total, with the LMS building by far the lion's share. As far as I can tell, they were all virtually identical: the only significant differences I have spotted are (a) the material used for the end flap (the LNER and BR diagrams both show these as planked, but the LMS version says plywood); (b) the design of the fenders or buffers attached to the bottom corners, which went through an evolutionary cycle of their own between the 'thirties and the 'fifties; and (c) the corner brackets to which the securing chains were attached. These last were of two distinct types: older boxes featured a fixed bracket projecting at an angle of 135 degrees, later ones a casting that was able to pivot through a full 270 degrees, which I imagine was better able to withstand the pull of the chain attaching it to the wagon. Exactly when this change took place is difficult to establish, but with the sole exception of the very first L-type container, I have yet to see BR-built containers of any kind with the first type, and have noted very few pre-nationalisation ones fitted with the second.

This typifies the kind of query that faces anyone attempting to study the subject of containers in any detail. Each of the standard texts on the Big Four and BR looks at them, but not always in great depth, and it takes a close reading of David Larkin's data sheet to understand, for example, that the LNER's diagram 40 is the same as the GWR's BD3, the LMSR's 65, the SR's 3026 and BR's 3/51, and that they are all taken from Railway Clearing House diagram No. 2074. (Such generalisations can be dangerous, however: significant variations, especially in the materials used, between containers supposedly built to a single diagram are far from unknown; as always, it pays to work from photographs, if available.) So, with that proviso, it can be very useful to the intending modeller of one of these boxes to know that there are several sources of information to turn to, but less so when he/she realises that none of them says what the back end looks like. They all rely heavily on the original diagrams, but for some reason, official drawings of containers almost always omit the rear and the roof. Thus the rather unusual

A selection of views of grounded containers showing various features of the breed, including a comparison of earlier and later designs of corner bracket on two otherwise similar BD types, and the cruciform end bracing found on a number of LMS-built containers, in this case B2142M. 2142's corrugated iron roof is a provision shared by an unidentified RCH diagram 2074 container similar to BD2299E, the one modelled in this section. Finally, there are two shots of a standard BR matchboarded box, BD6534B. Interestingly, the diagrams for this and the LMS B type call for boarded flap doors and complete matchboarded construction respectively, but the substitution of other materials – plywood in both cases – was not uncommon in practice. AUTHOR cruciform bracing I have seen on the back of various grounded ex-LMS containers has, until now, apparently escaped documentation. But since only one of these could be positively identified by number, I'm still in darkness as to how extensively this style was employed.

Anyone contemplating a foray into container building, especially from scratch, would be well advised to read Roger Marsh's article in *Model Railway Journal* No. 43, backed up by Gerry Beale's experiences related in *MRJ* Nos. 89 and 121. Both explore this little-known subject in some detail, and with a degree of insight which, as far as I know, is matched nowhere else in print. But the scope of each article is understandably limited to the handful of prototypes studied, and an in-depth treatise on the subject in general is still to be written.

However, armed with my photograph of BD2299E and the LNER drawing, I felt I had enough information to model this particular design. Finding another (albeit unidentified) container to RCH diagram 2074 in a field in Shropshire was a bonus, and helped to confirm the detailed layout of the back. Together with rough sketches of 2299, this enabled me to add an impression of this elevation to the diagram reproduced here.

When scratchbuilding containers the obvious method is to construct the basic shape as you would the body of a box van: 40-thou for the sides and ends, 20-thou for the roof reinforced with a second skin of the same underneath to fix the arc of the curve, and 40-thou for a floor or similar internal partition to obviate any risk of the sides bowing in. An alternative that I've used on several occasions is to take a ready-to-run example and to file off all the surface detail before re-detailing the plain shell in plastic strip. This could be applied directly to the smoothed surface of the original, but I've found it preferable to add an outer skin of 10- or 15-thou first.

Which ready-to-run product you choose is up to you, but the Airfix/Dapol ex GWR BK has less surface detail to remove than, say, the Bachmann BD, and the planking is less heavily incised. This is significant because unless you file back to a smooth surface, removing every trace of boarding, a thin overlay can sink into the grooves through the softening effect of the solvent. In any case, we don't want the addition of the overlay to result in a container that is oversize; this is especially important if it's being made to fit the Conflat S, where the thickness of the plastic used for the guide plates makes even Parkside's own BD a tight fit at best. With No. 2299 I found I had to omit some of the detail along the bottom edges of the sides to get it to slot in between the guides. This fudge is invisible once the container is in position, however, and since the wagon was to run loaded all the time, I was none too concerned at having to do it.

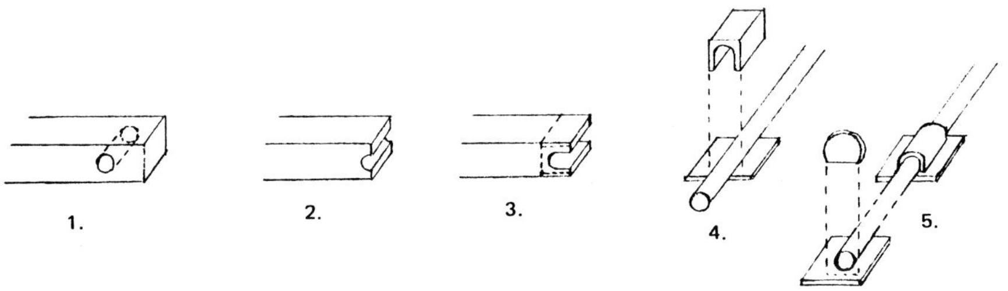

Door bar collars and dogs

You may also wish to consider before you go any further whether the roof line matches that of the container you're building. If it does, you probably don't need to do anything with it: after the mid-'thirties the roof detail didn't vary much from one design to another, and in any case you'll be quite lucky if you can get specific information on your particular prototype. For the record, the combination of four lifting shackles, a series of treads to improve the foothold of the staff who attached or detached the lifting gear, and a central plate to protect the roof covering from damage when the gear was lowered or released, was pretty much universal. Choosing a prototype with a significantly different roof line, such as the more arched profile of many BC (cycle) containers, does rather negate the advantage of using a ready-to-run product as the starting point. Nevertheless, it is possible to alter the outline by using overlays of different thickness and filing them to the new shape when set, and on this occasion I raised the rather flat arc of the Bachmann BD by three-quarters of a millimetre using a central strip of 30-thou flanked by rather narrower strips of 20- and 10-thou, each gently curved before fitting as described elsewhere.

Talking about lifting gear, don't forget that the gross weight of a loaded B-type container could be five and a half tons – or even more once both standard A- and B-types had been uprated by BR to four and five tons capacity respectively, after which even an A could turn the scales at around five tons laden. This was beyond the capacity of the yard cranes at many country stations, and whilst they could usually be loaded or emptied at an end- or side-loading dock without being removed from a Conflat, this cancelled out the benefit of the door-to-door concept they were designed for. So container traffic might not often be seen at wayside goods yards.

Back with 2299, the first job was to scribe the outline of the doors and the planking of the end flap. Don't be in too much of a hurry to do this, though: a thin overlay might well be softened by the solvent used to glue it to the box, and should be left for some time to harden off: two to three days, or even longer if possible. Otherwise you risk tearing it with the scriber.

From now on the job starts to get more complicated. The average container, especially one with side doors, has a lot more detail on it than, say, a standard box van, most of which in 4mm scale consists of 5- and 10-thou strip: I counted about four hundred pieces on 2299, and that's without the nuts and bolts. Having said that, most of the work is fairly straightforward, if a mite tedious: a large proportion of it is flat strip, and only a few of the more elaborate features call for explanation. The door locking bars, for example, are lengths of 20-thou plastic rod mounted slightly clear of the surface on rectangles of 5-thou. These are placed wherever the bar passes through a collar, and also at the top and bottom where the dogs are located that hold the doors firmly closed. The collars themselves can be made as described under the heading of gunpowder vans in Part Two; an alternative, and perhaps slightly simpler, method is to cut a strip of 40-thou styrene about 1.0mm wide, drill it 0.5mm close to one end, and then chop the end away up to half the width of the hole. Use the drill bit to enlarge the remainder of the hole into a U-shape, and narrow the width of the strip as far as you dare by cutting or filing. Now cut across the strip as close as possible to the edge of the hole, and clip the collar over the rod, securing it with a dab of solvent. The square corners can be rounded off with knife and file when everything has dried.

The dogs are simpler: a disc of 10- or 15-thou with a flat across about a quarter of the circumference, stuck, flat edge on, to the 5-thou baseplate, over each end of the door bar. You will understand that the real thing is considerably more complicated than this, but even in twelve-inch to the foot scale it requires pretty close inspection to fathom out how it works.

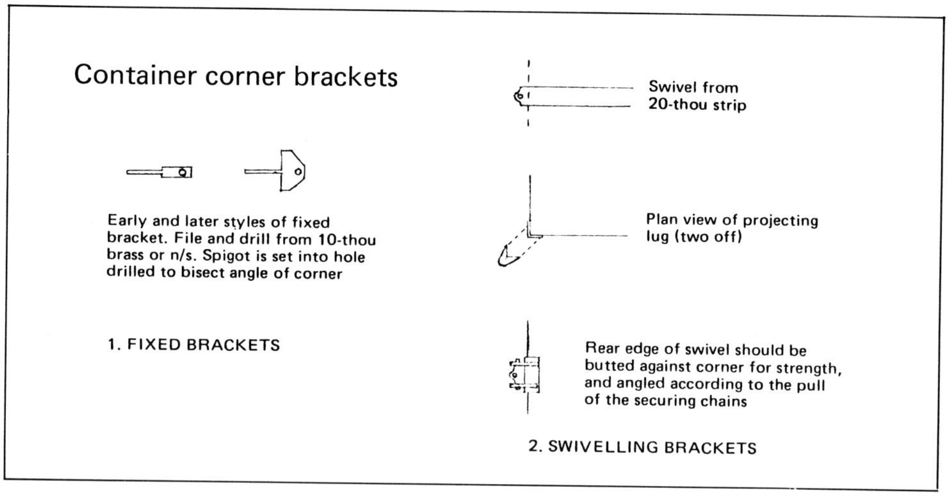

Each of the door bars incorporates a hasp that closes over a staple mounted either on the adjoining side door or on the bottom flap on the end. The latter requires the hasp to be curved into a gentle S-shape; this can either be formed by cutting to shape from flat sheet, or by bending straight strip carefully with a pair of smooth-jawed pliers: 5- or 10-thou styrene strip can be curved across the flat into surprisingly tight radii before it breaks. The hasps are secured to the staples by conventional pin and chain fastenings: the chains I made from twisted wire, as described elsewhere, and although I could have incorporated into each one the ring attaching it to the styrene pin, on this occasion I formed these and the two rings half-way up each side by drilling a $\frac{1}{32}$ inch hole in 10-thou sheet and chopping round it in a series of tangents to the circumference.

I did, however, use metal for the elongated rings in the corner brackets that hold the securing chains by which the container is fastened to the wagon. In fact, because of its vulnerability, I also used metal for the protruding part of each bracket: this was fashioned from 10-thou nickel-silver sheet with a narrow tongue epoxied into a hole drilled into the corner at the appropriate angle. The flat sections of bracketwork attached to the sides of the box were made in the usual way from 5-thou plastic.

The later design of corner bracket, the one with the swivelling casting, is rather less straightforward to make, even if, like me, you shy away from any attempt to make it actually swivel, which means it can be made in plastic. Each assembly consists of a pair of flat steel lugs, shaped rather like arrowheads with a rounded point, projecting from a piece of angle-iron attached to the corner of the container. The swivelling casting pivots between them, and incorporates an eye for the ring onto which the securing chain is hooked. The shape of the casting is quite subtle, but not too challenging to file up from a 2mm-wide length of 20-thou strip.

The securing chains are a feature that isn't often modelled, at least in 4mm scale; they are omitted from almost all the kits* and ready-to-run offerings I've seen, but to my mind a loaded Conflat looks naked without them, and even a piece of plain chain makes a significant difference. The real things were rather more complex than this, however, as the various accompanying illustrations prove. Typically they consisted of a hook top and bottom, a tensioning device in the form of a turnbuckle or miniature screw coupling, a cylindrical shock absorber, and a handful of plain oblong links to hold them all together.

Some help is available from the trade: Roxey Mouldings produce frets of etched tensioners, eyes and hooks, and at the time of writing Exactoscale are trying out some fittings in lost-wax brass, combined with the ingenious use of some fine elastic yarn. And some very nice little hooks are incorporated in PC coupling etchings for the ends of safety chains fitted to early locos and coaches. Ambis is another source of similar hooks. However, if you can't lay your hands on any of these, it is possible to make your own from fine soft wire (32 or 33 swg is about right), and this is in any case the most appropriate material for the plain

The Parkside Conflat S with its remodelled Bachmann BD container, awaiting only its securing chains for completion. It hardly needs saying that there's an awful lot of detail on the average container. The end view opposite shows how easily a thin overlay can sink into the moulded planking if this isn't properly filed back to start with.

* To my knowledge, only Bill Bedford's recently-introduced Conflat L includes etchings for these fastenings; unfortunately, the turnbuckles are of a type largely restricted to these particular wagons.

The finished combination with chains attached, and duly painted in maroon with yellow lettering for the box and bauxite with white markings for the wagon.

links. With practice, and a good pair of tweezers or needle-nosed pliers, loops down to a scale four inches or so are quite practicable, and circular eyes about half this size can be fashioned by wrapping the wire tightly round a piece of the same stuck into a block of balsa, cutting it where it overlaps, and gently clenching it flat. (The neatest way to cut wire I have found is to score it with an old blade, and to break it by bending it to and fro; this avoids the distortion you tend to get with most types of cutter, especially in confined spaces like this.)

Tensioners, or at least a representation of them, can be made by incorporating squared ends in two rather larger links, and simply soldering a piece of straight wire between them. The tommy-bar, if you want one, can be included by doubling over the end of the straight piece and turning the tail out at ninety degrees. Shock absorbers are merely short lengths of 40-thou square plastic strip, filed round, drilled $1/64$ inch up the middle, and threaded onto a piece of wire with an eye at each end. For the Conflat S, however, you don't need an eye at the bottom, nor even a hook: because of the way the anchorage points are concealed in the channels edging the wagon floor, it's enough to drill a hole through the plastic corresponding with the angle of the chain and epoxy the plain end of the wire into it.

However, by itself this dodge isn't enough to solve the problem of fitting the chains once you've made them. Until you've tried to attach four half-inch-long loose chains to eight separate points and

Holding a chain in tension with the right-hand hook round a length of wire pushed into a block of balsa, so that it can be soldered solid. This makes fitting much easier, and it also looks better if the chains appear taut rather than slack once attached. Swift work with the iron is needed if the home-made tensioner and plastic shock-absorber are to survive unscathed. Etched tensioners are, however, available from suppliers such as Roxey and Ambis.

keep each one on while you tackle the next, you won't believe what a pain it can be. And besides, they tend to look rather slack when and if you ever do get them on. I came to the conclusion that they'd be a lot easier to fit if they were rigid, so by the simple expedient of hooking one end round a pin stuck into a bit of balsa, and holding the other end taut, I soldered the whole thing up solid. All the same, a dab of glue is useful to stop the hooks becoming disengaged when you finally assemble everything after painting.

Finally, the lifting shackles: you only need to make these, of course, if you're building completely from scratch or if you've found it necessary to alter the roof profile of your r-t-r original. Although simple enough in principle, the real things are angled slightly to the surface of the roof in order to minimise the stresses imposed when the box is being lifted. Thus the top of the side bracing is twisted slightly where it bends over the edge of the roof, and one end of the shackle pin, and one side of the shackle itself are therefore higher than the other. Furthermore, there is clear air between these and the roof surface. Assuming, however, that we can accept a bit of visual deception on the model, this gap can be disguised, and the angled parts reproduced, by building them up directly onto the roof using over-thick strip, and then judiciously filing and scraping the upper surfaces to a semblance of the correct profile. A cheat, admittedly, but a none-too-obvious one under a coat of matt grey paint.

GWR/BR CONFLATS

As I mentioned in the introduction to this section, the standard design of Conflat built by British Railways, the Conflat A, was inherited directly from the Great Western, which had built many hundreds to the same basic pattern, starting in 1931 with Diagram H6. Indeed, the changeover was virtually seamless, and apart from a batch of 200 built at Wolverton with LMS-style underframes – but with GW-pattern bodies – Swindon went on to produce several hundred more up to 1952 that were practically indistinguishable from their company-built predecessors.

Even after that, the only significant changes to the superstructure that crept in up to the end of construction in 1958 were the appearance of a three-foot-long central gap in the hitherto continuous low body-side, and the replacement of the GWR's four chain hooks on each side with a battery of ten or twelve loose rings. Below the

Already twenty or so years old when photographed doing duty as a runner at Dorchester in 1952, W39035 was one of the GWR's earliest purpose-built Conflats. Built to Diagram H6 with 9ft wheelbase, it retained the twin chain pockets below the headstocks, although it had lost the hooks originally fitted at each end. W39740, on the other hand, represents H7, the largest single diagram in terms of numbers built (913 out of a total of just over 2,000). Seen at Cardington in 1939 carrying a container built to Diagram BD2 in the previous year, the principal changes from H6 were the loss of the end chain pockets and hooks, the longer side pockets, and the increased wheelbase of 10ft. A. E. WEST solebar, eight-shoe brakegear in due course took the place of four-shoe Morton brakes, and later batches sported Oleo buffers instead of eighteen-inch spindle ones. (The GWR had used 20½-inch fitted stock buffers for their wagons, and although BR followed suit for their first Conflat diagram, D1/061, they then reverted to the shorter ones for subsequent diagrams, and for some other first-generation, vacuum-braked designs.) Official records also apparently say that the last BR diagram, 1/069, had roller bearings rather than oil boxes, but a quick survey of over a dozen photographs hasn't revealed a single one with roller bearings. Still, there were almost 12,000 built to this diagram, so it's not impossible that some were so fitted.

David Geen produces whitemetal-cum-etched brass kits for the first two GWR diagrams to this pattern. The H6 vehicles had a nine-foot wheelbase and chain hooks on both sides and ends, together with prominent chain stowage lockers in both positions. The hooks and lockers on the ends were dispensed with for H7, which also saw the wheelbase extended to ten feet, changes which were to fix the appearance of all subsequent new buildings until the early 'fifties. Except for diagrams H8 and H9, which were for slightly longer conversions from four-wheel milk tanks, and a batch of unfitted vehicles respectively, I believe that, minor details apart, all the later GWR and early BR Conflats were visually identical, varying chiefly in 'invisible' things like underframe layout and journal size.

Having said that, there is a suggestion in an article in the June 1979 issue of *Model Railway Constructor* that the overall width was narrowed from H10 onwards, but this isn't borne out by *Great Western Wagons Plan Book*, nor is it mentioned in *GWR Goods Wagons*. Where there does seem to be an element of uncertainty is over the length of the side chain lockers, or pockets. These were six feet long on H6, and the drawing in *GWR Goods Wagons* (reproduced in the kit instructions) suggests that this also applied to H7. However, the photographic evidence is that they were lengthened by about nine inches, and the H7 kit confirms this by having the longer version. All authorities agree that the later diagrams have longer pockets, as do the BR-built wagons according to the drawing in *British Railways Wagons*.

If there remains a grey area, it relates to the superstructure modifications mentioned earlier. Published photographs of late GWR and early BR vehicles are rare,

B735826, built in 1952 to BR Diagram 1/062, is virtually indistinguishable from all the later GWR construction; only the axleguards betray its later origins. Photographed in original condition in 1953, it is seen here with an early (1929-built) B-type container in, I would guess, BR crimson. B735233 was turned out two years before B735826, and should, therefore, have had the same continuous low side raves, but when seen at Millerhill in 1962 loaded with a grimy and much-patched AF-type container, it had clearly acquired the 3ft gap that had become standard on new construction from the mid-1950s. So, too, had W36958, built around the time of nationalisation to GWR Diagram H11 and seen carrying a ventilated meat container (also, no doubt, in red livery) at Bude in 1961. The modifications to this wagon had gone a stage further by exchanging the four upturned hooks for the later twelve (or sometimes ten) chain rings with which all the later BR-built vehicles were equipped from new. A. E. WEST, D. ROWLAND, A. E. WEST

David Geen's kit for the GWR Diagram H7 Conflat is almost equally at home being used as the basis for a large proportion of early BR production, which perpetuated such Swindon features as the continuous low bodysides, the chain hooks and the ratchet-type brake lever guards (not included in the kit but reproduced here using a Masokits etching). The only really significant early change introduced after nationalisation was the use of BR-type axleguards. The rather crude conversion seen here should become much less obvious under a coat of underframe grime.

and the only specific reference I can find to either feature is the note in the appendix to *British Railways Wagons* listing diagrams and lot numbers which states that the gap in the sides came in with diagram 1/065 in 1954. This seems to be borne out by the continuous sides on B735999, built in 1952 to the previous diagram, 1/062, and pictured in a BR publicity leaflet of the time. Other photos, however, including some reproduced here, show earlier-built wagons, pre-nationalisation ones among them, with cut-outs, and even with rings instead of hooks. Now to the best of my knowledge, no GWR Conflats were built with a gap in the sides, so I'm driven to the conclusion that these features were fairly routinely applied as in-service modifications from the mid-'fifties onwards.

All of which rather begs the question of the purpose of these cut-outs. My instincts tell me that it might have been to facilitate the barrowing of goods into and out of a container on a Conflat at a side-loading dock, but I'm open to other ideas.

As for the change from hooks to rings, the youngest wagon numerically that I've seen with the earlier fitting is B737220, and the oldest with the later one B737371. Both were built in 1953 on lot 2500, again to diagram 1/062 (and both, when photographed, had a gap in the sides).

Something that all these Swindon-built wagons have in common is the GWR style of saw-toothed brake lever rack. It seems that the works went on fitting this well into the 'fifties to Conflats and many other designs. Again, a quick trawl through available photographs suggests that this continued up to and including diagram 1/067 in 1956. Even an early 1/069 wagon built in the following year has been noted with this fitting, but this appears to have been its last gasp.

The net result of all this is that I can see no good reason why David Geen's H7 kit should not be used for any of the later GWR diagrams except H8, or for any of the first two thousand or so of the wagons built for BR at Swindon – but not, of course, B735000–735199, the ones turned out by Wolverton with LMS-style underframes, and with the caveat that modifications may have to be made by anyone modelling these vehicles in their later years. Photographic evidence should, of course, be sought but on the face of it any wagon in the range B735200 to at least B737220 can be produced from the H7 kit. Thereafter, the Parkside kit for the BR Conflat A probably becomes more appropriate.

These, at least, were my conclusions from the evidence I could unearth. In reality, of course, things might have been more complicated, but I felt confident in choosing B735999 as the subject of my model in this case, applying the adage that photographs can't lie – even if they can sometimes be economical with the truth.

According to the instructions, the first job is to attach the axleguards to the solebars, having drilled out the holes for the bearings. Choosing a post-nationalisation wagon immediately adds an extra step here: all the BR vehicles I've seen had axleguards with capstan/horse-hook holes, rather than the open W pattern. So rather crudely I filled in the open vees below the springs with triangles of 20-thou styrene. If you use copious amounts of solvent to soften the edges of the fill-in pieces, they will tend to mould themselves to fit the openings. Solvent is not a good long-term adhesive between plastic and whitemetal, however, so I added a smear of Evostik across the back, and when all was dry, drilled a 1/32nd hole at the point of one vee in each axleguard: two to the left of the axlebox and two to the right. The axleguards were then fixed to the solebars with epoxy.

Having horse-hook holes in the axleguards meant that the BR wagons had no need of hooks on the solebar, so these were chiselled off, together with the cast number plates, which BR generally fitted close up to the back of the headstock. They were replaced in 10-thou styrene, and label clips (omitted from the castings) added above the left-hand spring stop on each side.

The instructions suggest assembling the underframe sections first and slotting the etched floor in afterwards, but because I was using epoxy as my main adhesive, I had reservations about getting the corners square and rigid with the limited mating surfaces on offer. So I attached the solebars to the edges of the floor first, suiting my choice of bearings to the spacing of the axleguards as I did so. As I've remarked elsewhere, it's useful to have a selection of bearings on hand with varying cone depth in situations where it's less easy to adjust the axleguard spacing than it would be, for instance, with etched brass W-irons.

The headstocks were added when I was satisfied that everything was square and parallel from all angles. I swapped the buffers supplied with the kit for 18-inch RCH ones from ABS. In fact, the buffers provided are of the same length, although to the different pattern adopted by the

GWR. Strictly speaking, however, for a pre-1948 wagon, they should be fitted stock buffers which were 2½ inches longer.

Although I had built the underframe round the floor, which meant that the cast centre plate was superfluous as a structural item, the brake shoe/push rod castings and vacuum cylinder are designed to sit on it, so I fitted it anyway. Nevertheless, I found it necessary to file about ½ mm off the carrier block of the brake shoe castings before the holes in the central tumblers would line up with those in the V-hangers. I also felt that the vacuum cylinder would benefit from being a touch lower, and mounted it accordingly on a pad of 40-thou plastic.

Incidentally, the instructions don't make it clear that the cylinder should be closest to, and on the left of, the V-hanger on the side without the Morton clutch; it's quite possible to fit the central plate with its locating hole, and to assemble the brakes, differently to this if you're not careful. And make sure that the upper push rod acts on the same wheelset on each side. (It's also possible, as I discovered, to put the etched chain pocket overlays on upside-down – the line of horizontal rivets goes at the top.)

I also discarded the chunky cast brake lever and guard in favour of Masokits etchings, the only source I know of the characteristic pattern of GW toothed brake rack.

Finally, I fitted the etched chain hooks to the sides. These are lovely little things in, I believe, beryllium copper, and, at the risk of stating the obvious, they fit upside-down. It remains to be seen how they will stand up to normal operation or regular handling: it's very easy to snag them accidentally, and, although it wouldn't be prototypical, I'm tempted to wonder whether circular eyes might not have been safer and stronger in this particular application. Time will tell.

As a change from the much more common B-type container, I wanted to put the smaller A-type on B735999. I could have chosen the Cambrian kit of the plywood version, but I fancied a matchboarded one, which at the time meant scratchbuilding. By far the most numerous variant of BR's non-insulated A-type containers (3,800 out of around 5,000) was diagram 3/001, which married matchboarded sides and end doors to a corrugated steel back. Good photographs, fortuitously showing both ends, can be found in *British Railways Wagons* and in David Larkin's *BR Standard Freight Wagons*,

Reproducing the characteristic ridge-and-furrow layout of a corrugated van or container end is described in detail in the text. Here we see the scratchbuilt A-type destined for the David Geen Conflat A: the upper half of the end has been shaped to the final profile, while the lower part more obviously shows the crudely chamfered strips of 60-thou awaiting treatment. So far they have only been filed across the tops to ensure that none stands out more than any other.

and a drawing appears in the April 2002 edition of *British Railway Modelling*. Furthermore, the BR containers were virtually identical in appearance and dimensions to the 150 produced by the LMS to their diagram No. 20, a drawing of which appears in *An Illustrated History of LMS Wagons, Vol. II*. The only visible difference I can see between the BR boxes and their LMS predecessors (which only emerged from Earlestown after nationalisation), is the shape of the corner fenders. The A-type illustrated (but not identified) in *British Railways Wagons* also shows the common variant of a plywood end flap, whereas both diagrams officially say planked, but whether this was an original fitting or resulted from a later repair isn't clear.

Neither of the published drawings shows the layout of the corrugated rear, but this was in fact identical to the larger BD, as was the front, and scratchbuilders can save themselves a good deal of time and effort by using the equivalent parts from Parkside's BD kit. If you decide to do it the hard way, the only feature we haven't so far met is the simulation of the corrugated steel end. One way of doing this – similar to the method apparently adopted by Parkside's pattern-maker – is to take a sheet of 40-thou plastic and file the edge to a rounded profile. Using a sharp blade you then carefully slice the rounded edge away from the sheet, cut the resulting strip into the appropriate lengths, chamfer and round off the ends, and stick them to the plain, flat surface of the van or container end at 1.5mm centres.

This is moderately convincing from normal viewing distances, and I'd used the same method myself on other occasions. But it fails to satisfy on close inspection because on the real thing the concave furrows are dished to match the convex ridges. So more recently I have used 60-thou rather than 40-thou, and instead of filing it half-round along the edge, have bevelled it at about 45 degrees on each side and then rounded the peak slightly between these bevels. Sliced off the sheet to produce what in section now becomes a flattish triangle with a curved apex, this strip is cut into 26mm lengths (except for the two at the top and one at the bottom, which are shorter), again chamfered and rounded at the ends, and each length attached to the flat end of the container so that it butts up to its neighbour. This automatically achieves the 1.5mm wavelength between each of the ridges. A gap equivalent to slightly less than one corrugation is left in the centre, where the joint between the two separate sections of the pressing is simulated by a scribed line surmounted by a course of horizontal rivets.

Once everything has set hard, the V between each pair of strips can be turned into a U. I find the most useful tool for this operation is a rat-tailed file with the tip broken off. You may need to run a coarse flat file across the top of the ridges first to ensure that none of them stands proud of its neighbours. It's quite a long job to work each furrow down so that the bottom of the troughs is just about back to the original flat surface of the end panel, but the result repays the effort required.

Incidentally, it was quite acceptable to load two A-types onto one Conflat. Unless they were to be loaded/unloaded without being taken off the wagon, the rules stated that the doors should face inwards for security if they were non-insulated boxes. AFs and AFUs were to face outwards, however, perhaps because the more prominent door locking gear left insufficient room to load them the other way round. If there weren't enough chains available for both containers, ropes were to be used in the middle to tie them to each other and to the wagon. Use of GW-pattern hooks was not permissible, however: in this case the rope was to be fastened 'to some other appropriate wagon fitting'. I quote.

As I said earlier, the Parkside kit is more suitable for the bulk of the BR-built fleet of Conflat As, chiefly because of the changeover from hooks to rings for the side-mounted chain anchorages. With some modifications to the buffing and brakegear it could be used for any of the later 17,000-odd vehicles, although strictly speaking it represents only the 4,500 built in the mid-'fifties to diagram 1/067. In fact, if you want to be picky, we should exclude the 1,500 built at Swindon with the Great Western style of brake lever guard, leaving only those produced by Derby and Ashford, namely B700500 to B703499.

Actually, the choice can be narrowed even further: a minor peculiarity of some, though not all D1/067 wagons was that they had only ten, instead of the more usual twelve, chain rings on each side, the next-to-the-outermost fitting at both ends being a single ring rather than a pair. The kit as moulded has ten; whether this was the more common variant, I can't say: of the eight photographs I've traced of wagons built to this diagram, four have ten and four have twelve. It's possible that extra rings could have been fitted to some vehicles during their lifetime, of course. For the record, the numbers of those with ten rings are B700352, 701283, 702326 and 703843.

I chose the second of these, which is illustrated in *British Railways Wagons*. Now when I had first looked at the underframe parts supplied with the kit, I had been slightly disappointed with the axleboxes, which struck me as a rather poor representation of the RCH split pattern, and with the fact that the axleguards were standard W-irons instead of the BR style with horse-hook holes, with which I believe all BR-built Conflat As were fitted. Now my kit had been languishing in a drawer for some time, and I've noticed that more recent examples now have square platefront axleboxes. But they still have RCH W-irons. The BR underframe parts that come with Parkside's PA16 kit, however, not only have the right axleguards, they also have the large platefront boxes worn by B701283 when it was photographed in 1968. So I substituted the solebars from the underframe kit for those supplied with the Conflat kit, packing each end with a sliver of 10-thou styrene to compensate for the fact that they were about half a millimetre too short.

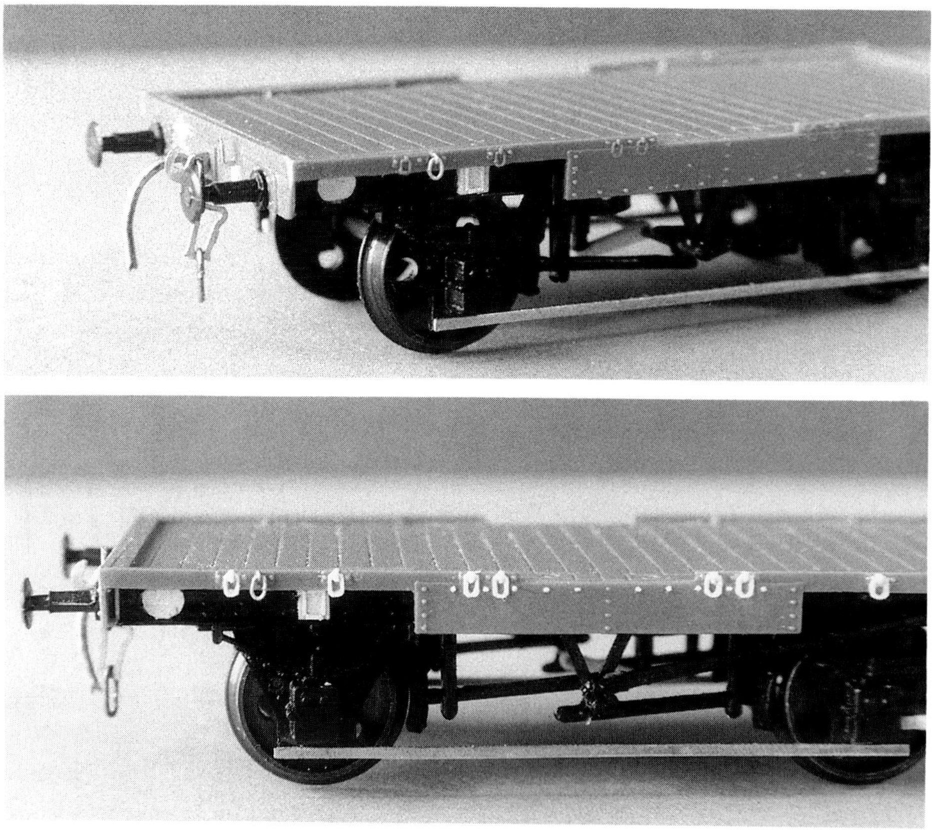

Although the main reason for replacing the moulded chain rings on the side of the Parkside Conflat A is to ensure that the working ones don't stand out too much, the originals are a bit understated if you compare them with the real thing. Also shown is the repositioned horizontal rivet detail on the chain pockets.

The PA16 parts incorporate eight-shoe clasp brakegear, and would in this respect be ideal for later batches of Conflat As, but D1/067 had four-shoe brakes, so I retained the components provided with the original kit. Nonetheless, there was some scope for improving these: I lengthened the brake shoe mouldings by about a millimetre (as described in Part One, page 30), and profiled the brake levers by a combination of judicious bending and chamfering, adding check straps to secure the bottom ends of the lever guards. And I mounted the brake cylinder (the one in the PA16 kit, which was nicer, but too shallow) on a 2½mm-thick pad to make it more visible, adding a pivot bracket and an actuating lever connecting the piston to the 30-thou cross-shaft.

The use of the PA16 parts for a wagon with four-shoe vacuum brakes meant that I also had to fabricate tie-bars to fit between the axleguards; these were conventionally used on such vehicles, where they were required to counteract the outward forces exerted by the push-rods when the power brakes were applied; with eight-shoe brakegear these forces were rather better equalised. I used 1mm-wide brass strip Evo-stuck over the moulded bridles at the bottom of the axleguards, which I had first filed flat.

The buffers supplied with the kit are nice little mouldings, but they're rather short. I could have replaced them with cast ones, but I made do with packing them out with rather crude Plastikard washers to achieve the required 6mm. I also carved the top and bottom ribs off the buffer guides: slightly unusually, B701283 looks to have been fitted with two-rib ones. Also a little out of the ordinary was the fact that the lamp irons (or at least the visible one) were to the right of the drawhook rather than the left. So I sliced off the moulded one and made a new one – L-shaped brass strip epoxied into a hole drilled in the headstock, with a rectangle of 5-thou below it to simulate the flat leg bolted to the face. Finally, I fitted Instanter couplings, which many of the earlier Conflats seem to have received. This may have been a mistake; on reflection, it occurs to me that wagons not built at Swindon (and 701283 was a Derby product) were more likely to have had screw couplings. However, at least one Ashford-built vehicle (B702386) did have Instanters, so I may be over-complicating things here.

Parkside's own BD container seemed an appropriate load for their Conflat. It went together exactly as per the instructions, and the only modification I made was to replace the rather vestigial corner brackets with something to which I could attach securing chains. These were made just as described previously. However, the addition of chains meant a further modification to the wagon itself: a couple of the rings on each side needed to be proper usable ones instead of the moulded representations. On the real thing these rings are quite hefty pieces of kit, and replacing some of them with working ones (a link of 33 swg n/s wire hung from an eye fashioned on the end of a length of the same, epoxied into a hole drilled in the bodyside as close to the top edge as I dared) only served to highlight the fact that the moulded ones aren't really prominent enough and are actually slightly on the small side: you should be able to see daylight below the bodyside at the bottom of each ring. So I carved off the remaining rings (but not the brackets by which they are in reality riveted to the body), and replaced each one in 10-thou plastic: two small holes drilled in a piece of sheet or strip, joined together by working the drill bit carefully in and out, and the resulting elongated hole chopped round with a sharp blade to produce an oblong link. Don't worry if the result is a bit angular: solvent will help to soften the edges, and they can always be tidied up a bit once they've set hard. The fixed eye is half a circular ring formed in the same way. They're still non-working, of course, but a bit more satisfyingly chunky than the originals.

While I was doing this job I noticed an odd aberration in the rivet detail on the outside of the chain pockets: as moulded, the line of horizontal rivets is along the bottom edge, whereas on all the photographs I've studied, they are along the top. So I corrected this as part of the process.

Three views of a remodelled Airfix B-type rehashed into a standard matchboarded BD. Only the roof remains untouched.

The Parkside BD requires no modifications except those necessary to enable securing chains to be attached. Each corner bracket consists of five main bits of styrene. A simplified swivelling casting (non-working on the model, of course) is shown having been shaped on the end of a 20-thou strip sized to be an interference fit between the two projecting prongs above it.

SOUTHERN RAILWAY CONFLATS

Four photographs taken at Huntingdon in 1953 of S39049, the subject of the model whose construction is described in this section. Originally unfitted and coded Conflat A, it was subsequently vacuum-fitted by the Southern and recoded Conflat B accordingly. Later, however, the designation was changed again, this time to Conflat S, also carried by the most common version of ex-LNER container wagons. And for a while, at least, some of the fleet bore Lowfit markings as well.
A. E. WEST

In Part One, under the heading of 'Low-Sided Wagons', I referred to the marking of a batch of ex-Southern Railway long-wheelbase car-carrying wagons as Conflats, stating that this involved a change of use. This I now realise was rather misleading since they were, in fact, orginally built as vehicles that could carry both containers and wheeled traffic, and were officially described as Conflats from the start. The same applied to the much more numerous short-wheelbased versions, although in many cases these did have their code name changed to Carfit in due course when they came to be regarded as dedicated car-carriers. Others are known to have been branded Lowfit at some stage in their lives, reflecting the fact that they could be used for a wider variety of wheeled cargo than just motor vehicles.

Although the Southern generally classed them all as Conflats, and the diagrams involved use this description, they were indeed more like a conventional Lowfit in appearance, with shallow drop sides and end flaps. Three diagrams were issued: No. 1382 covered 250 wagons with 9ft wheelbase numbered 39001 to 39250 built in the early 'thirties. All but 25 were vacuum-fitted with the Southern's eight-shoe, centre-pull, double V-hanger style of power brake, and were coded Conflat B; the unfitted wagons (39026–50, coded Conflat A) were converted to vacuum a few years later, but using four-shoe brakes with the alternative offset V-hanger layout. The same fitted brakegear was used on the first hundred wagons to Diagram 1399, Nos. 39251 to 39350, built in 1935 with the wheelbase increased to ten feet. Further batches produced up to nationalisation (39351–450 and 39651–955) had Morton brakes, again vacuum-fitted, but without any change in diagram number. Finally, Diagram 1383 related to 150 vehicles with 18ft 7in wheelbase, 29 feet over headstocks, numbered 39501 to 39650, and coded Conflat C or D according to whether they were unfitted or vacuum-braked. All vehicles that had vacuum brakes also had through steam-heating pipes whatever their diagram number.

By WWII some at least of the nine- and ten-foot wheelbase wagons were being re-coded Conflat S – the same designation accorded to the LNER design we've already looked at. And in BR days many came to be branded Carfit S. Although they continued to be used for containers to some extent for quite a while after nationalisation, I suspect they were less favoured in that role by the authorities, possibly on the grounds that the lashing points set into the floor weren't ideal for normal container shackles: photographs show that containers were always roped onto these wagons. In any case, no chain pockets were fitted.

That said, until the recent publication of Volume Four of *An Illustrated History of Southern Wagons*, good photos of these wagons with or without containers were hard to find, although examples of both short and long vehicles appear in *Pre-Nationalisation Freight Wagons on British Railways*, and there is a nice, slightly elevated view of an unidentifiable 10ft wheelbase, Morton-braked example loaded with farm machinery in the July 2000 issue of *British Railways Illustrated*. Two of the best pictures can be found rather surprisingly in *Freight Wagons and Loads in Service on the Great Western Railway and British Rail, Western Region* and Volume Two of *An Illustrated History of LMS Wagons*; the latter has a photo of No. 39154 taken in 1944, at which time it was coded Lowfit. This second view also appears in *Modellers' Backtrack* Vol 1 No 2, and both can now be found in *Southern Wagons*, Volume Four, together with appropriate drawings. The latter were unavailable, however, when I was building the model described here.

Drawings showing the long wagons and each of the principal variants of the short wagons are also available in Mike King's range, and a further drawing, of an early 9ft wheelbase wagon, is obtainable from Edwards Bros. of Cardiff. This shows some useful detail, but the wrong brakegear for the number quoted.

No kit exists for these vehicles, although at the time of writing one is promised from David Geen. In the meantime scratchbuilding is the only option. I decided to model one of the wagons illustrated here, S39049, simply because it has the offset V-hanger style of brakegear, and, having sketched this in Part One, I thought it only right and proper that at least one of the wagons studied in these pages should feature this layout. 39049 was one of the twenty-five wagons originally built unfitted that acquired vacuum brakegear a few years later.

The first decision to make in this case is the choice of materials. This arises because of the form of construction of the wagon sides, which were steel angle in the shape of an upturned L, surmounted by a flat bar in which was drilled a series of holes to take pins for securing a pair of movable wheelbars. For once Plastikard seemed an inappropriate material, and I came to the conclusion that metal would be preferable, for these parts at least. In the end I limited the use of styrene to the floor planking and the end flaps; even these were no more than plastic overlays on a metal base.

Checking my stock of brass and nickel-silver sheet and profiles, it struck me that 3mm × 1.5mm brass angle would come in very handy in several places, albeit with a degree of filing down here and there. In particular, it would serve very well for the L-shaped drop sides, and for the curb rail along the edges of the floor below them. In the event I also used it for the solebars, and for strengthening the headstocks.

I began by soldering a length of the angle to each long edge of a rectangle of 10-thou nickel silver measuring 69.5mm × 28.5mm, in such a way that the shorter leg of the angle formed the upstanding curb rail, and that the overall width was a gnat's whisker over 33mm. This meant that the overlap of the sheet beneath the longer leg

of the angle was barely half a millimetre on each side, which wasn't ideal, but I wanted the edges of the sheet to represent the top flange of the solebars, so I couldn't afford to make it any wider.

I then filed down the curb rail to a millimetre. The overall height of the sides, minus the perforated bar on the top, is a touch under nine inches. Of this, the curb rail accounts for three inches, the drop side for another five, and there's a narrow gap between them, allowing you to see daylight from a low angle – although this is partly because the drop side is also set slightly outside the line of the curb rail.

I made the headstocks from the same 10-thou nickel-silver sheet, deep enough to include the curb rail on the ends and a lower flange which was turned inwards using a hand-vice as an anvil. Before attaching them, I soldered a 25mm-long section of the 3 × 1.5mm angle to the underside of the floor at each end, partly to reinforce the headstocks, and partly also to locate the ends of the solebars at the right spacing. With a millimetre or so of the flange filed away at each end, the solebars slotted into place behind the headstocks and butted up to these spacing/strengthening angles to give a rigid framework on which to start building up the surface detail.

First, however, I made the four corner posts from 1.5mm × 1.5mm brass angle. They fitted outside the headstock and curb rail on the ends, but flush with the curb rail along the sides, to which they were attached by small gusset plates over the joint. The ends of these curb rails therefore needed to be filed back to accommodate them. I made the plates from brass shim, impressing the four rivet heads from the back with a small punch, using hand pressure only, before tinning them and sweating them into place. The three rivets round the corner that secure the post to the headstock couldn't be made this way because of the gauge of the material, so before fitting the posts, I drilled them from the back until the bit was on the point of breaking through. The resulting pimples aren't very strong, so care needs to be taken when working near them, but I did the same for all the thicker bits of metal used for hinges, door springs, etc. Fortunately there aren't too many of them on these wagons, unless you feel obliged to rivet the solebars as well. I didn't.

To give me something to hold onto while I was soldering the corner posts into place, I left each one attached to the main stem of the length of angle they came from, but filed part way through this first so that it could just be snapped off when I was satisfied that each post was in the right place. And I was in no hurry to clean up the ragged end that this caused, leaving the posts overlength at the top until I'd made the side flaps. In the raised position these were attached to the corner posts in the conventional way: stout pins or lugs in the posts mated with holes in the ends of the sides, which were held there by a cotter and chain. It seems that the end flaps were originally secured in the same way, but post-nationalisation photos generally show them held up by a pair of rather basic chocks that slotted into brackets on the headstocks.

The first job to do on the drop sides was to file down the width of the longer web of the brass angle to rather less than 2mm, and to remove the ends of the shorter web to fit between the corner posts. The perforated bar was made from 10-thou nickel silver: close to the edge of the sheet I scribed a guide line on which I initially marked a series of five points at intervals of 16mm-and-a-bit for the studs that fixed each bar to the top angle of the sides. These I drilled 0.52mm to take ½mm brass wire. Between these holes I then marked and drilled the pin holes used for securing the wheelbars. I wasn't certain how many of these there should be: they're not shown on the Edwards Bros. drawing, and Mike King's drawing isn't consistent in the number shown in each section, and none of the photographs I had helped very much. In the end I put eleven between each of the studs, which works out at about one every scale four inches, and was gratified to find when David Geen subsequently produced a copy of the General Arrangement drawing of the early vehicles that my guesstimate was correct.

I didn't drill these holes all the way through: I reckoned that a dimple would be fairly convincing on all but the closest of inspections, and I didn't want to weaken still further what I felt would be an already rather flimsy and vulnerable detail. Nor did I make any attempt to reproduce the corresponding holes in the top angle of the sides, except, of course, for the five needed to take the fixing studs.

When it came to cutting out the perforated strips from the main part of the sheet, I was anxious not to distort them, which ruled out my usual cutting tool, a pair of scissors. So I pretended that the nickel-silver was styrene sheet and used a blade, one that was already close to being discarded as too blunt. Between ten and twenty strokes against a steel straight-edge were enough to part the strips from the sheet; they came away perfectly straight needing only the smallest amount of gentle tidying with a file to clean up the edge. Needless to say, the blade went straight to the bin.

Having used the five holes in each strip to mark and drill the corresponding holes in the top flange of the sides, I soldered each pair together, threading a washer or spacer cut and filed from a strip of 20-thou nickel-silver onto each stud as I did so.

I used the same ½mm wire for the securing pins in the corner posts, although for no very good reason that I can think of, I attached them to the sides rather than to the posts. On the outside I decorated them with rings and chains twisted up from fine wire as illustrated under the heading of three box coal wagons.

The four drop side hinges are a composite of three different pieces of metal. The vertical straps are again strips of 10-thou nickel-silver, part-drilled as before to represent the rivet heads, and doubled-over at the bottom to give the extra thickness required: being mounted outside the corner posts, the flap stands proud of the curb rail by the thickness of the material. I used the hinge straps as the only soldered joints securing the sides: I didn't dare try to put the iron on the end pins for fear of melting everything.

The hinges proper, and the bottom straps, were made by crimping strips of brass shim around 0.7mm wire, which was cut off so that it extended slightly outside the shim at each side. These projections were reduced by careful filing to represent the ends of the hinge pins, and the assembly soldered to the underside of the curb rail.

10-thou n/s strip was also used for the body-to-solebar support brackets and the door springs. While there were always two springs, mounted on the outer brackets, the number of brackets varied according to the design of the wagons: the 9ft wheelbase vehicles that were built with fitted brakegear had four, while the later 10ft wagons had three. So, too, did the 9ft ones that were originally unfitted, like 39049. On those with three brackets, the middle one seems to have been slightly offset, and it appears that the offset was towards the same end on both sides, namely on the same side of the centre line as the vacuum cylinder. This was certainly true of 39049.

I'd fitted the first drop side, and completed this detailing, when it occurred to me that it would be easier to make the plastic floorboarding before attaching the other side: because the planks extend right up to the curb rail, they're actually slightly longer than the gap between the flanges of the drop sides. I'd come to the conclusion that the wooden floor would be made up of two thicknesses of 20-thou plastic laminated together, with the lower layer sized to fit between the horizontal legs of the brass angle used for the curb rails. Before I could mark out the planking, however, I had to decide the spacing of the C-hooks set into the edges of the floor at intervals for lashing purposes. On Mike King's drawings there are ten of these on each side, but the only photographic evidence I had (the HMRS picture of No. 39082 reproduced here) shows seven, with the hooks being spaced in the ends of every fourth plank. This was also the layout on S39524, one of the longer vehicles I had myself observed late in its life when it was in use as a match wagon with Mersey electric stock at Birkenhead in 1985. So I stuck with the evidence of the photograph, which was again confirmed by the G.A. drawing kindly supplied by David Geen. He also revealed that all or most of the later 10ft wheelbase wagons had rings rather than hooks, though these were still not used for container shackles, and photographs of these vehicles carrying the longer containers introduced in the mid-'thirties usually show them roped to the buffer guides. The booklet produced by BR to help its staff in such matters confirms that this was officially authorised, as the accompanying sketch proves.

I scribed 29 equal planks in the floor, and, starting three planks in from each end, cut triangular slots out of every fourth one, using these as a template to mark the hook positions on the horizontal flanges of the curb rails. In reality both hooks and rings were bolted to the lower edge of these flanges with nothing but fresh air beneath them. Having made the floor solid on the model, however, I didn't have enough depth to reproduce the hooks in entirety, so I drilled a 1/64th inch hole in each position and soldered into them lengths of 30swg nickel-silver wire with the ends curled over to represent the tops of the hooks.

Here the G.A. drawing proved me wrong, in that there should be thirty planks in the floor. This slightly upsets the pattern of the cut-outs, which therefore don't coincide exactly with the width of a single plank in every case, but I didn't feel constrained to alter the model at this stage. Incidentally, the later style of lashing ring required a longer cut-out spanning the equivalent of two plank widths.

Because of the soldering I still had to do, I didn't fit the plastic floor at this stage. In fact, I went on to fit and detail the second drop side (which meant that I had to trim ½mm off the floor to slot it between the sides when I came to fit it), and then turned my attention to the ends. These are far more cluttered than the sides, and I'd already come to the conclusion that I wanted to reproduce as much of the

Southern Railway insulated container No. F684 roped onto Conflat B No. 39082. Although published elsewhere, few other photographs I have seen illustrate so clearly the design of the dropsides or the SR's individual approach to securing containers in transit, using C-hooks set into the floor. The standard of roping would rarely have been matched in day-to-day practice, however. HMRS

Overall length apart, the wagons built to SR Diagram 1383 were very similar to their shorter counterparts. One survives on the Bluebell Line, but S39524 was photographed in 1985 at Birkenhead when in use as a match wagon for Mersey electric stock, unaltered except for the addition of an air brake pipe. AUTHOR

As related in the text, most SR Conflats came to be used exclusively for wheeled traffic in later life, being then once again recoded, this time to Carfit S. Another Diagram 1382 vehicle, S39177 is seen in this guise at Axminster in 1960. Notice that the pin and cotter fastenings were still in use for securing the end flap on this wagon, and that it had not received the wedges that were often fitted in place of, or in addition to them. (But the flap did have the cut-outs needed to clear the non-existent brackets when it was lowered!) A. E. WEST

detail as possible in plastic rather than metal. So I cut and filed the profile of the drop flaps from thin n/s sheet, and soldered them to the corner posts, trying to reproduce the not-quite-upright slant that the real things always seemed to adopt, especially after the fastenings were changed from pin and cotter to the stout wedges that usually replaced them.

I supported the centre of the flaps rather unprototypically by soldering them to the tops of the hinge-straps on the headstocks, which I made in metal as I had done on the sides. However, most of the fittings on the end flaps themselves are built up in plastic on a 30-thou rectangular overlay Evo-stuck to the thin n/s profile. This leaves exposed the shaped ends which originally slotted over the pins in the corner posts; in reality these were steel plates set into the back of the timber flap, secured by nuts and bolts whose washer plates can be seen on the outside at each end. The inner pair doubled as the means of holding the lamp-irons: originally there often seem to have been two of these, one on each side, but most post-1948 shots show only one. On 39049 it was the right-hand one that remained, though this wasn't always so. Where the other had been removed, separate washers were used behind the nuts. As usual, I made the lamp-irons themselves of metal strip, bent into an L and epoxied into a hole in the 30-thou overlay; the bottom half is a strip of 5-thou plastic.

Inside these fittings are the blocks that supported the end flaps in the lowered position by resting on the buffer guides. They were mainly of two patterns: the plain rectangular sort fitted to 39049 and the shaped ones borne by 39524, which straddled the buffer. Finally came the chocks or wedges which latterly held the flap upright, or nearly so. These were set into U-shaped brackets mounted on the headstocks, and held in place with pin and chain fastenings. Cut-outs in the timber behind the chocks prevented the flap from fouling the bracket when lowered. Except for the pins and chains (two strands of 5-amp fuse wire twisted together), these were all worked up in situ from noggins of plastic. The backing plates for the brackets were Evo-stuck to the headstocks; the brackets proper are solid rectangles of 40-thou on edge, while the wedges are 30-thou square strip filed to shape with a slight taper.

I used cast whitemetal SR unfitted buffers from ABS, packed-out from the headstocks with pads of 40-thou plastic to lengthen them as per the prototype when it was converted to automatic brake. Vacuum and steam heating hoses were bent up from paper-clip wire (a little light on surface detail, but so much stronger than plastic, whitemetal or even cast brass ones), and the rather prominent dummy coupling for the vacuum pipe soldered and fettled out of brass strip. PC screw couplings completed this part of the job.

The main challenge with the running gear is the fiendishly complex vacuum brake rigging, especially when crammed into a 9ft wheelbase. Even with the aid of a Masokits etch for this so-called Monarch gear, getting the geometry of the various layers right in relation to each other is something of a trial, and I made things no easier for myself by having to cut a 10ft wheelbase etch down by a scale foot. In fact, this resolved itself fairly simply into knocking 2mm off the outer ends of each set of push-rods.

Nevertheless, when doing surgery of this kind, I tend to play it safe by fabricating the brakegear first, and adjusting the wheelbase a bit to suit if necessary. (This is of limited benefit, however, when one set of brakeshoes ends up rather more than half a millimetre longer than the other, as it did here.) As described elsewhere, I use a sketch glued to a block of balsa as a makeshift jig for this job, pinning the components through the paper with wire pivots before soldering everything up solid. The hardest bit to get right, I found, was the relationship of the assymetric V-hanger, brake lever, lifting link and operating crank – the one with the strange curly bit on the end that the Masokits etch no doubt wisely simplifies into a flat piece. Again, I made the job more difficult for myself by filing and bending these up from L-shaped bits cut from the corners of the etch.

For the vacuum brake cylinder I used an ABS casting married to a home-made piston and crank assembly – I found the etched crank provided by Masokits to be marginally too short to allow the cylinder to fit into the very restricted space left for it by the shortened brakegear. Also home-made was the safety loop surrounding the crank and bolted to the bottom face of the cylinder – although in my case the two legs of the brass strip I used were epoxied into holes drilled in the casting.

MJT provided the etched W-iron assemblies, together with the cast RCH axleboxes and springs. I packed the W-iron units off the floor with rectangles of 10-thou plastic to achieve the correct ride height. In common with almost all wagons fitted with four-shoe vacuum brakegear, 39049 acquired tie-rods between the axleguards as part of the exercise – I'm pretty sure it wouldn't have had them in its original hand-braked condition. On this vehicle the Southern favoured round bar for the ties, and not knowing the exact thickness to use, I opted for 24 swg n/s wire as looking about right.

When I've fitted round tie-bars before, I've generally clenched or hammered the ends flat, trimmed the edges, and stuck or soldered them across the bottom of the axleguards to double as the bridles. Looking closely at the photos of 39049, however, it seems that they were fitted in line with the axleguards, and since the MJT etchings already had the bridles included, I set the ends of the bars into holes drilled in small L-shaped brackets bent up from n/s strip, and soldered the longer legs of the brackets behind the axleguards. Since I was building a solid chassis I wasn't worried about using a bit too much solder here, but if you can contrive to let the ends of the rods float in their holes, or alternatively pivot the longer leg of the brackets in the axleguards, no doubt the system could be adapted to compensated underframes as well.

Finally, the wheelbars. I'm not certain whether these would have been carried all the time, and I've seen no positive photographic evidence of them except on wagons that were in use for wheeled traffic. However, since it was my intention to provide 39049 with an appropriate Lowfit-type load in due course, I went ahead and made them anyway. Basically they consisted of a length of round bar or tube with a forked projection at each end that slotted over and under the perforated strip along the top of the sides, to which they were then pinned through holes in the projections. These forked brackets were offset from the centre line of the bar, allowing a measure of adjustment to match the wheel size or wheelbase of the load by placing the bars slightly above or slightly below the level of the perforated strip. Once in posi-

The underside of the SR Conflat prior to fitting the brakegear. Here again I've used MJT axleguard units. The small L-shaped brackets on the ends of the tie-bars can be seen soldered behind the inner leg of the W-irons; with care, these could be pivoted to allow for compensation.

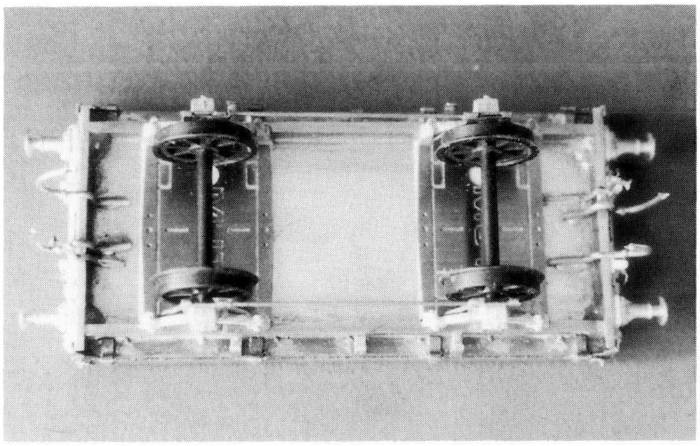

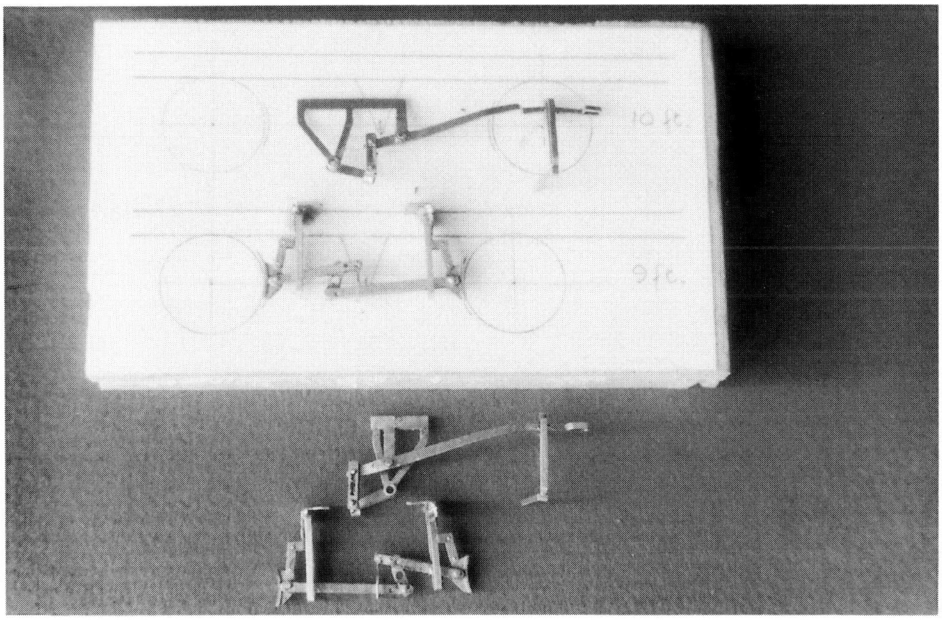

The Masokits brakegear units soldered up ready for fitting. For this job I find it easiest to pin the components using various gauges of wire to a lump of balsa onto which has been pasted an outline of the appropriate wheelbase. This ensures that the geometry of the brakegear is correct before you commit yourself to soldering it up solid. For clarity's sake, a new drawing is shown here, one that isn't specific to this rather unusual brakegear; in use the paper soon gets dirty and damaged.

One side of the wagon with the brakegear now in place. The shape of the ends of the wheelbars enables them to be located at two different heights to cope with varying wheel diameters.

In later years as longer containers were introduced, use of the C-hooks (and the later rings) declined, and other lashing points were adopted – quite officially, as the accompanying diagram, culled from a BR instruction booklet, clearly shows. The same guidance also applied when containers were roped onto Medfits, but in practice was no doubt simplified in much the same way as is evident in the case of this ex-SR meat container on one of the later (1942-built) 10ft wheelbase Conflats to Diagram 1399, photographed at Crewkerne in 1952. A. E. WEST

(c) **Ex S.R. conflat wagons (painted numbers prefixed S).**

These vehicles are not fitted with facilities for chaining and containers must be secured by roping at each end, from corner securing rings to buffers, in accordance with the method illustrated below:-

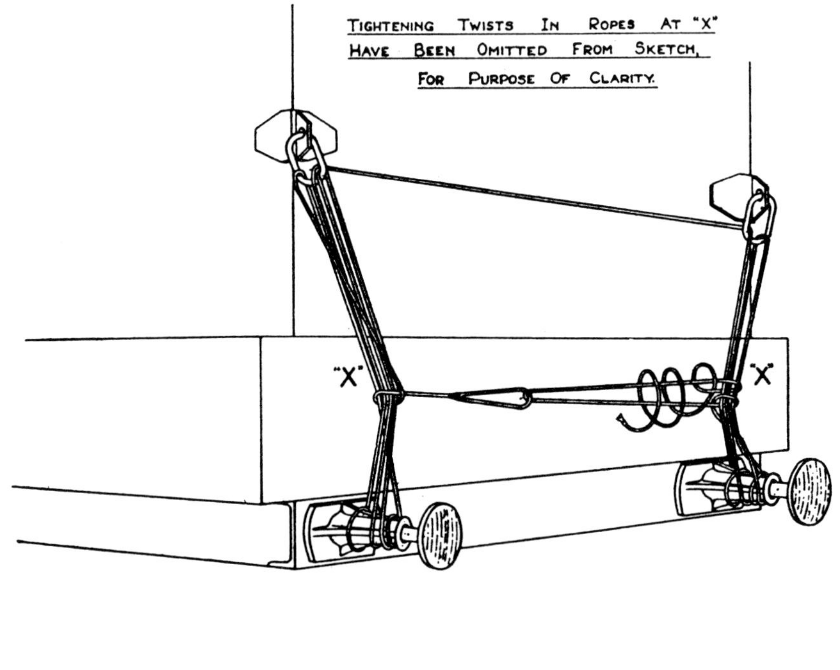

tion, the load was tied to the bars and also, no doubt, to the hooks in the floor as well. At least one photograph shows the bars equipped with webbing straps for this purpose, but in other cases ropes were used.

As far as I could tell, the bars were about four inches in diameter, so I used the thinnest brass tube I could find, and made up the end brackets from two pieces of n/s strip, one bent into an L and drilled to accept a tongue filed on the end of the other, which then located in the tube. If you can size the hole in the L to match the bore of the tube, and the tongue to make an interference fit in both, you stand a chance of being able to solder all three bits together in the right position first time. All that's left is to drill through both projections to match the dimples in the perforated strip; when the time finally comes to secure the load, I shall drill through the appropriate dimples and solder the bars to them with wire pins.

As I mentioned earlier, the use of these wagons for carrying containers seems to have been gradually phased out after nationalisation. Up to the early 'fifties, however, such a load would have been quite normal. Although the Railway Clearing House had agreed to rather larger dimensions for containers in the mid-'thirties, after which the products of the individual railway companies, and, later, of BR, all looked pretty similar, the Southern persisted for some years with its smaller designs of covered container, in which much use was made of plywood and sheet-metal cladding. This, together with the long, swivelling door-bars and the transverse braces across the roof, made many of them noticeably different. However, as with other pre-war designs, few survived the first ten years of public ownership.

Above: *The opposite side to that shown at the foot of page 29.* Right: *The end of the finished vehicle. No less complex than the rest of it, I decided to represent the bulk of the detail on the end flaps as a plastic overlay glued to a plain outline of thin nickel-silver sheet.*

A Southern K-type (later BK) furniture container being used for a house removal, probably some time before World War Two. According to the HMRS Livery Register, the colours were two shades of green, with the main lettering in either stone or yellow. The box was securely roped onto its solid-tyred lorry, but it is to be hoped that the distribution of the weight took account of the position of the rear axle, forward of centre. At one time it was quite common to see the lifting tackle left on the roof during the road transport leg of the journey. HMRS

The roof braces have always been for me a slightly puzzling feature of these containers. Where they are shown on official diagrams, they generally appear to be curved in both planes. On the face of it, this would seem to reduce their strength, however. Most photographs are unhelpful, having been taken from a low angle, but close examination of a surviving Diagram 3021 BD (improbably resting on the site of Llandrinio Road Station on the Criggion branch of the Shropshire & Montgomeryshire Railway) might help to explain the mystery. BD1156 S has two lengths of I-section measuring 3in by 1½in running across the roof between each pair of lifting shackles. While these beams are only curved in a single plane to match the arc of the roof, they are set at a slight (10-degree?) angle to the vertical, leaning towards the centre of the container, presumably to balance the strain exerted on the door uprights and the angled side-braces when the box is lifted. This means that they are actually closer to each other at the mid-point of their arc than they are at each end. On containers with a more arched roof than 1156 this effect would be more pronounced, although whether it was ever as extreme as some of the official diagrams suggest is open to question.

Hopefully the accompanying photos, together with the illustrated article by Roger Marsh in *MRJ* 43, which coincidentally deals with sister container BD1153 S, will help the enterprising scratchbuilder to interpret the drawing of a Diagram 3021 container reproduced in Volume Four of *Southern Wagons*. Contemporary insulated containers from the same stable shared many of the features of the BD. Apart from the sources quoted already, it's worth mentioning in conclusion that a pair of nice photographs from different angles of two Diagram 3002 insulated containers can be found in Brian Haresnape's *Railway Liveries: Southern Railway* (Ian Allan, 1982) and in *Railway-Owned Commercial Vehicles* (also Ian Allan, originally published 1987 and reprinted in 1999).

Photographs of a pair of grounded ex-SR containers taken in the 1990s. The one with the corrugated iron 'roof' is 1942-built BD1156S, seen in Montgomeryshire, still with traces of its BR crimson livery. The other box is even further afield in a garden near Edinburgh. Though it has many features in common with the BD, it seems to be a Diagram 3002 insulated container. It has suffered serious structural failure, but is remarkably complete; the inward lean of the transverse roof braces is quite apparent. AUTHOR

CONFLAT L

The Conflat L brings our brief survey of Conflats and containers full circle, since the concept very clearly harks back to the three-box coal wagon with which we began. A BR development of a late-GWR approach to the carriage of bulk materials, particularly powders such as cement and lime, each wagon carried three four-ton capacity, top-loading, bottom-emptying, metal boxes. These were designed to be removed from the wagon for emptying into a lorry or hopper, and could be taken to a remote location, if necessary, for either loading or discharging.

Although a fairly specialised design, more than two thousand of the wagons, and well over six thousand of the containers, were built in the ten years from 1951, and they ran into the 1980s, chiefly between limestone-quarrying areas and industrial centres such as steel works or major construction sites. Photographic evidence suggests that they often ran singly or in twos and threes, in mixed goods trains, and when being used for their intended purpose the wagons were hardly ever seen without the containers, except of course at terminals. Latterly, however, a number were adapted to run empty as match wagons with Class 03 shunters, reputedly because the engines alone were too short to operate track circuit indicators reliably when being used for carriage shunting duties at main line stations.

Two designs of wagon were produced. Diagrams 1/064 and 1/066 accounted for 873 with low drop sides and ends after the style of the contemporary steel Lowfit. Since the containers were located in position by steel corner guides attached to the wagon bed, the upstanding sides and ends were clearly deemed to be superfluous, and later batches built to D1/068 dispensed with them. Nevertheless, examples of both types lasted as long as the breed as a whole.

Although a number of photographs have been printed over the years, especially in David Larkin's albums published by Bradford Barton and Santona, and most recently in *British Goods Wagons in Colour* from Midland Publishing, these vehicles are generally quite poorly documented. Until the recent advent of kits, complete with containers, from Genesis and Bill Bedford, modellers were left pretty much to their own devices, at least as far as the wagons were concerned. However, reason-

Diagram 1/068 Conflat L No. B734491 having suffered a bit of a mishap with two of the containers punctured, and the brake lever lying in the chain pocket. Note the slightly lower corner brackets on the furthest container. The style of turnbuckle used to secure L-type containers is well shown.

New L-type containers prior to delivery in the 1950s.
AUTHOR'S COLLECTION

Left: *A publicity shot of the very first L-type container built at Eastleigh in 1951, clearly showing the bottom doors in the open position. It is thought that the very low, fixed corner brackets were unique to this one box.* Right: *For a while in the 1950s, L-type containers were used to carry alumina from Burntisland to Ballachulish for onward movement by road to the British Aluminium Company's works at Kinlochleven. Here containers were being transferred to lorry from two of the older pattern of Conflat L wagons built to Diagrams 1/063 and 1/066.*
AUTHORS' COLLECTION

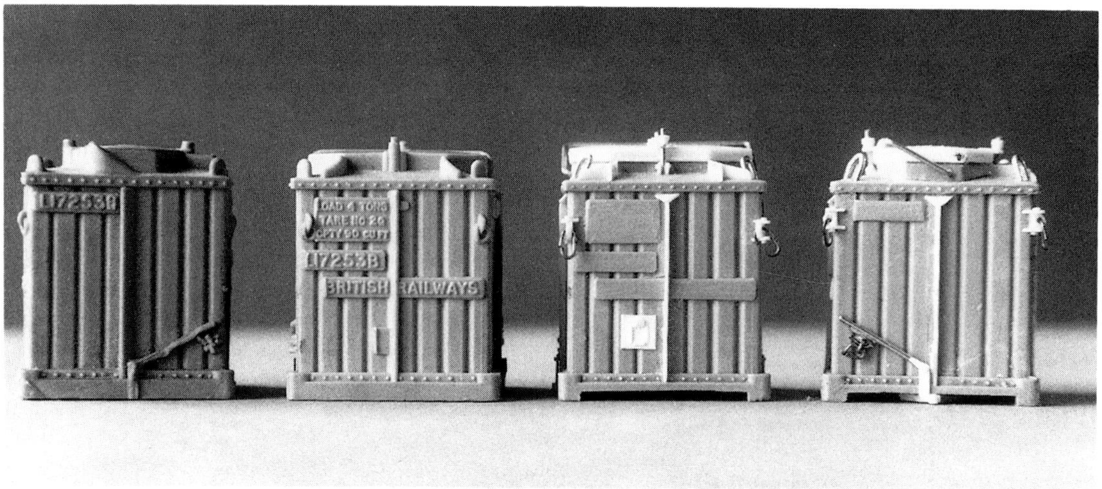

The two faces of Triang L-type containers: on the left as originally moulded, and on the right as re-detailed. The only significant difference between any of the production runs of the real thing seems to have been the height of the corner brackets to which the securing chains were attached. The container on the right has them in the higher position used for the earlier batches, while the one next to it shows the later, slightly lower mounting.

able – and improvable – models of the containers might have been found by diligently scouring sources of second-hand bits and pieces at exhibitions and swap-meets.

For back beyond the dawn of time, Triang produced what they called a Three Container Wagon. This was actually Rovex-speak for a Conflat L, and while the wagon itself was less than breathtaking, the containers (often mistaken for transformers) were in fact pretty good. A drawing of one appears in *British Railways Wagons*, and close comparison with it shows that the Triang version is a tad underscale: 4ft 6in square instead of 4ft 10in. But if you can live with this, they are well worth re-detailing.

Ten minutes with a sharp blade and a file removes moulded handles, rings, brackets and raised lettering, and produces the cut-outs in the bottom framing that were created by the deeper angle-iron 'feet' attached to each corner. The shape of these cut-outs was later modified, it seems, by additional gusset-plates inside the angle-irons, which were themselves also beefed-up in many cases. Realising that on the real thing the lid overlapped the sides of the loading hatch, I also filed the top flat, then added a slightly oversize cap of 40-thou, which, once set, was shaped to restore the shallow hipped profile of the original. This, however, reduced the apparent depth of the rim of the lid, so I deepened this all round with 15-thou strip, and faired it in once it had set hard.

Like most containers, the L-type bristled with surface detail like lifting eyes, lashing points, top door opening bar and fasteners, and bottom door release levers. Most of these were reproduced in wire of various gauges and bits of styrene. It's to be hoped that the accompanying photographs will illustrate their design and layout, but a word or two about the operation of the top and bottom doors may help. In the closed position the top door was secured by a screw clamp on each long side, a knurled (or sometimes winged) locking nut being tightened over a lug welded to the lid. With the clamps undone, the long bar, which pivots at each end and also on the lid itself, is raised, causing the lid to rise at one side and to slide back on the other, the bottom edge of the rim bearing on the rather crude runners that carry the lid over the two lifting eyes on that side.

The bottom doors are released by a pair of levers, one at each side, which are held shut by rings, or loops, that are slipped over U-shaped bars welded to the levers themselves. Note that both levers point the same way, which is towards the same side as the top door bar when the lid is closed: the Triang moulding has the two levers facing in opposite directions.

All the containers seem to have been identical except in the position of the corner securing brackets to which the fastening chains were attached. Apart from L17250B, the only one built on lot 2433 in 1951, which I assume was the prototype, and which had fixed corner brackets about a third of the way up, all the production examples had swivelling ones of the style fitted to contemporary A- and B-type containers. However, while the early batches had them about 3in below the top flange, they were lowered slightly, to about 7½in down, on later examples. The change seems to have occurred in 1955 during the production of the L19xxxB series. It would be logical to suppose that it actually happened at the start of lot 2832 with L19750B, but I can't confirm this with certainty.

Incidentally, there were clear instructions that the containers should be positioned on the wagons with the door bars running fore-and-aft, although it was permissible for them to face either side. Even so, odd examples have been noted with the bar athwartships.

Some time ago, with no prospect of a kit then in view, I scratchbuilt one of the later wagons, based largely on my observations of a group lying condemned at Worksop in 1984. Although I had taken no dimensions, I was able to use various known measurements (overall length 17ft 6in, buffer centres 5ft 7½in, depth of headstock and solebar 9in, wheelbase 10ft, and so on) to work out from my less-than-brilliant slides the size and spacing of the principal features of the design, which, as with most Conflats, was a fairly basic one. The sheet steel bed, barely wide enough to span the solebars, had twelve right-angled corner guides welded to it, forming three square frames for the containers to sit in. With the aid of the drawing in *British Railways Wagons* I calculated that each of these should be a touch under 20mm square, with virtually equal gaps between each set, and at each end, of slightly less than 3mm. Allowing for the marginally underscale Triang containers, and the thickness of the 10-thou plastic I intended to use for the corner brackets, I adjusted these measurements to just under 19mm and 3mm dead respectively.

I used 10-thou for the floor as well, reinforced underneath with 40-thou over the whole area between the solebars and headstocks, which I made as described elsewhere (see particularly the section in Part One dealing with the BR Medfit). The 40-thou strengthening automatically gave the correct ride height for the EM Gauge Society W-iron assemblies I was using, bearing in mind that I was building a rigid chassis. Compensation would have required some modification to the reinforcement at one end to give a rebate for the rocking unit to sit in. In that case I would have explored the possibility of laminating two thicknesses of plastic, or perhaps a plastic/metal sandwich, to give the necessary support beneath the thin floor.

Modelling the wagon as a runner would also complicate things. Most Conflat Ls had holes in the floor beneath the containers: two small circular ones in each pocket in the case of the earlier wagons, and a single, larger, hexagonal one in the case of D1/068. I'm not clear as to the purpose of these holes; certainly not to enable the containers to be emptied on the wagon, since the bottom doors could only be opened with the boxes suspended. Weight reduction, perhaps, or easy disposal of spillage? Whatever the reason for them, the larger holes in particular exposed parts of the underframe and running gear, which would be incompatible with standard methods of compensation. Something else would have to be devised here, perhaps along the lines of the lash-up developed for the anchor-mounted tank wagon in Part Two.

Since these vehicles usually ran in service with the containers on board, either loaded or empty, however, I felt safe in omitting the holes entirely. The corner guides were each fashioned from two pieces of 10-thou about 3mm square, with

The first Conflat L I built, a model of a D1/068 wagon without either suspension or compensation. The most tedious part of the job was soldering up the twelve chains, but they are very prominent on photos of the real thing and, as I hope this picture proves, it looks naked without them.

the outer top corners chamfered diagonally, and the top edge gently bent outwards with a pair of pliers before assembly. These flares, which were no doubt intended to assist in locating the containers as they were lowered into position, leave a small vee-shaped gap in the angle of each guide. I later realised that the floor is reinforced inside each angle with a triangular plate, and I added these bases accordingly, also in 10-thou.

The chain pockets project about 3.5mm outside the face of the solebars (actually, it's about a foot on the real thing, but the thicker material used for the plastic solebars on the model reduces this a bit). They extend between the centre lines of the two outer containers and over the full depth of the solebars, except for the last couple of feet or so at the right-hand end, where the bottom slopes up to clear the brake lever. At each end, and in the centre, is a shackle point for the chains that secure each corner of every container.

To begin with, I believe the pockets had lids like other Conflats, but it seems these were quite quickly dispensed with in service, leaving the bottom of the pockets open to view. The wagons I examined at Worksop had a mixture of plate and mesh bottoms, and I am guessing that the latter were a modification: without lids, the original solid ones probably rotted out owing to a build-up of damp sludge, which the mesh would discourage. Mesh obviously presents problems with plastic construction, and a measure of ingenuity would be necessary to incorporate etched brass mesh into such a model. Working on the basis that this modification wouldn't have been needed as early as my modelling period of the late 'fifties, however, I decided to sidestep the issue, and settled for solid bottoms.

I used 10-thou for these, 15-thou for the ends and for the intermediate divider in which the shackles are mounted (10-thou would have been nearer to scale, but I wanted a bit of extra strength to take the strain of the shackles and chains), and 30-thou for the faces; this is visually acceptable because the top edge of the face is reinforced all the way along on the inside with angle-iron, which significantly increases its apparent thickness.

The D-shackles took a bit of thinking about. Wire was the obvious material to use, but how to represent the shackle pin that passes conspicuously through eyes on the ends of the shackle itself, and then fasten it so that it pivots in a piece of flimsy plastic? I used 32 swg brass wire for the shackles, forming an eye on each end of a piece about 8 or 9mm long, large enough to accept a 26 swg pin. Threading the shackle onto the end of a length of this wire, I soldered just one of the eyes to it, then cut the wire so that it protruded 10-thou or so outside the eyes at each side. I then opened out the shackle by slipping the unsoldered eye off the pin, which was passed through a 0.5mm hole drilled in the pivot plate. The unsoldered eye was then clenched back over the pin to keep it there; I left it unsoldered for fear of melting the plastic.

The securing chains, all twelve of them, were made much as previously described, except that the standard adjusting mechanism seems to have been a proper turnbuckle on the Conflat L rather than a miniature screw coupling. I bent these up from thin brass strip cut from a sheet with a pair of scissors, each one laboriously drilled after bending with four 1/64 inch holes, one at each end for an eye to be soldered in, and a pair in the centre for the tommy bar. It occurred to me afterwards that using etched signal ladder sides might have made this job easier.

A NOTE ON SUSPENSION SYSTEMS

Some time after I'd completed my scratch-built Conflat L, I obtained, courtesy of John Brighton, a test etch for a kit of the same vehicle by Bill Bedford. This incorporates his wagon springing system. Now sprung suspension for wagons is something that has been developed by several manufacturers since I started this series of books, and as someone who doesn't normally build even compensation into his models, I'd been mulling over for some time whether to include the subject of suspension in Part Three, and, if so, how I should tackle it. So this seemed too good an opportunity to miss.

In reading my comments, however, bear in mind that these are the subjective reactions of someone for whom the whole business of springing wagons was a new concept, one that I approached in a spirit of experimentation, and with not a little trepidation.

In summary, Bill Bedford's system consists of an etched bearing carrier that slides up and down behind the W-iron. The W-iron is normal in appearance, except that the hole for the pinpoint bearing is elongated to enable this movement to take place. A moment's thought will tell you that the hole in the back of the axlebox needs to be correspondingly enlarged as well; however the use of waisted bearings significantly reduces the amount of metal or plastic you have to remove.

The bearing carrier is sprung by being clipped to a length of wire whose ends locate in holes in small brackets or wings set about 20mm apart on each side of the axleguard behind the solebar. Spring steel or phosphor-bronze wire between 9- and 12-thou is recommended, depending on the weight of the wagon. After a bit of trial and error, I settled on 10-thou as about the right gauge of p-b wire for the etched brass Conflat L. This equates to 33 swg; 30 swg would be the equivalent, more or less, of 12-thou.

Although the instructions say that the wire can be straight and just clipped between the prongs at the top of the bearing carrier, I found that in the case of the Conflat L this allowed insufficient upward movement before the assembly contacted the underside of the wagon floor. In any case, the ride height was slightly too low. To remedy this, I bent the spring wire into a gentle curve; this gave the correct ride height, but I couldn't nip the prongs tightly enough to prevent the wire from turning. With straight wire, of course, this wouldn't have been a problem (there seemed to be no danger of its becoming detached from the carrier), but the curved wire had to be held in the same attitude to remain effective, so in the end I soldered it in place. I also soldered the bearing in, which the instructions say is unnecessary, but I found it rather tiresome keeping both bearings, particularly waisted ones, in the carriers, and at the same time holding the carriers themselves upright and central, while I tried to insert the wheelset against the springiness of the axleguards. I suppose that the more rigid soldering work you build in, the less flexible the system potentially becomes, but if you find this to be a problem (I didn't), you could always tinker with the gauge of wire you use.

This ability to adjust the tension of the springs by altering the thickness of the wire is a major advantage of the system, allowing it to be applied to any model almost irrespective of its final weight. Once you've got the ride height correct, you only need to make sure that you have about ½mm of free up and down movement of each wheel to enable a wagon to cope with track irregularities, which I'm pleased to say the Conflat L does admirably. At the same time it's wonderfully free-running. Although it's hardly a fair test, I can scoot it time and again from the middle of Retford's fiddle yard right round through the station (about a scale mile and a half) without a hint of uncertainty at point-and-crossing work, or at track and baseboard joints. I suspect that the real thing would very quickly come to grief at a fraction of this velocity.

While this is by no means intended to be an exhaustive study of wagon suspension systems, I felt that for comparison purposes I should look at at least one other, and as a very satisfied user of Mike Clark's brakegear kits, I chose the Masokits version. Since I also wanted a model of the first style of Conflat L, the one with low dropsides, it seemed appropriate to scratchbuild one of these as a test bed. Apart from the sides, the main visible difference between the early diagrams and the later one was that the floor around the containers and the chain pockets was sheathed in timber. The reason for this feature eludes me, and, like the dropsides, it was abandoned for diagram 1/068. On the model, I represented the timber with strips of 20-thou plastic. The same thickness was used for the sides and ends, which were cut integrally with the chain pocket sides and headstocks respectively. The ribs were cut from 10-thou sheet: strips rather more than a millimetre wide for the upper flanges, which were stuck on top of the sides and ends, and slightly less than a millimetre for the lower ones and the verticals, which of course were attached on edge to the face of the material.

Otherwise, except in one regard, construction mirrored the later version already described. Because of the design of the Masokits system, it wasn't possible to reinforce the 10-thou floor underneath as I had with the D/1068 wagon: the full 3mm depth of the solebars is required to accommodate the completed suspension unit, in which both pairs of axleguards are joined by a central spine that doubles as a spacing jig. However, because this is fairly rigid in itself, I found it did no harm to sacrifice a degree of stiffness in the body. In any case, the sides and floor timbering went a long way to compensate for the absence of the 40-thou underfloor reinforcement I'd put in before.

In principle, the Masokits suspension system is similar to the Bill Bedford one,

Two views of the prototype of Bill Bedford's kit for the D1/068 wagons, compared with an elevated shot of the scratchbuilt body for one of the earlier pattern. These mostly had a pair of circular holes in the floor beneath each container, which, of course, were only visible with the containers removed. So I ignored them.

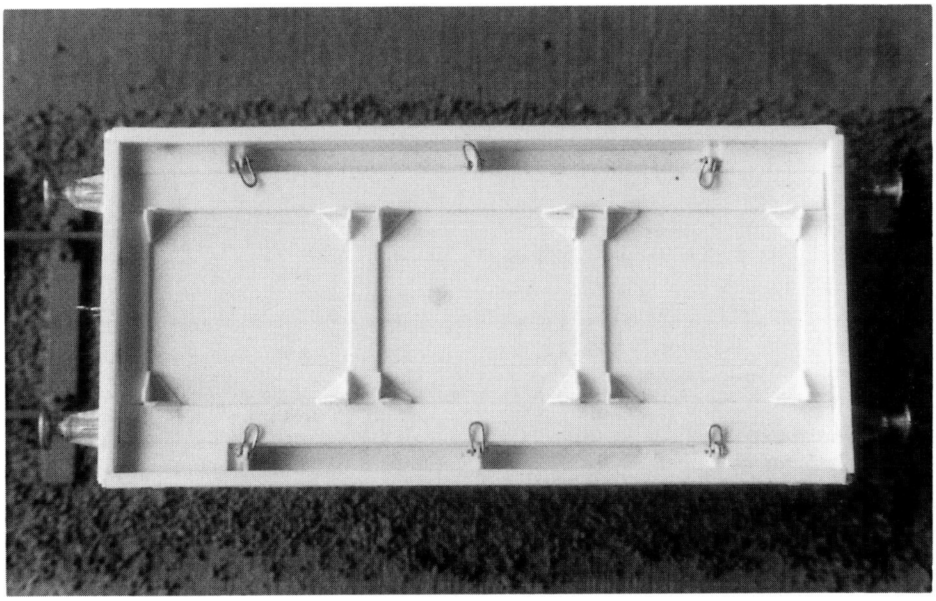

although the sliding bearing carrier and the spring are etched in one piece from stainless steel, and the bits come complete with the jig for accurately spacing the W-iron assemblies, together with facilities for inside-bearing conversions of ready-to-run stock, and a very detailed set of instructions incorporating copious diagrams. The system has been described in print in *Model Railway Journal* No. 72 (by Bob How), and in issues 1 and 4 of *Rail Model Digest* (by John Chambers and Simon de Souza respectively). Simon's article also describes the pioneering Exactoscale system, although I believe there have been some modifications to this since it was introduced. Finally, both the Masokits and Exactoscale systems are examined in detail in John Hayes' book in this series *The 4mm Coal Wagon, A Step-by-Step Guide*.

The Masokits parts also include a jig for filing down top-hat bearings, in order to minimise the extent to which the holes in the back of the axleboxes need to be elongated. Using waisted bearings eliminates this operation, however, and, as with Bill Bedford's method, very much reduces the amount of material that needs to be removed from the axlebox hole: a few twiddles with a 2mm drill bit or the end of a craft knife will do the job nicely.

Since the spring and bearing carrier are etched in one piece, the spring needs to be bent over through ninety degrees. The instructions are careful to point out that stainless steel is brittle, and that this operation must be done quickly and cleanly in one go. The bend then requires a fillet of solder to stiffen it up: Carr's Brown Label Flux is the stuff to use with stainless steel, both for this job and to secure the bearing in the carrier. Use as little as possible, and clean all the surplus off afterwards: I discovered that any residue quickly creates corrosion, which significantly impairs the free action of the moving parts.

Unlike Bill Bedford's parts, where if the wheelset is removed the bearing carrier and its spring wire can slide out of position when the bearing becomes disengaged from the slot in the axleguard, the etched Masokits spring includes small tabs that slot between the fold-up sides of the base of the axleguard unit to prevent side-to-side movement. The base also incorporates a strip that is folded down to retain each pair of bearing carrier-cum-spring units, once you've satisfied yourself that everything works as it is intended to do. I didn't have a problem with the rather simpler Bill Bedford version, however: once the axle is in place the assembly is in effect locked into position and can't fall apart when the wagon is lifted.

One other refinement of the Masokits system is a set of etched washers designed to cope with the effects of varying cone depths found in turned brass bearings from different sources. The parts include a gauge to help you determine the depth of the cone and so tell you whether the bearings need to be packed out from the carrier by the insertion of a washer. I must have mis-measured, however, because I calculated that I didn't need to do this, but found on assembling the parts that there was an

As described in the text, I fitted Masokits suspension units to the second scratch-built wagon to compare it with Bill Bedford's system, fitted as standard to his kit. Hopefully these photographs illustrate the essential features of the two.

Not the Bill Bedford version, but the scratchbuilt D 1/068 wagon described earlier, now painted and lettered along with its containers, and quite heavily weathered to simulate generous deposits of lime dust and sludge.

unacceptable amount of slop in the axles. Fortunately, the washers can also be put on the outside of the carrier (i.e. between the carrier and the axleguard), and the result is equally effective, though perhaps slightly less satisfying to the critical eye.

To my mind, the only area where one system scores over the other is that of spring tension: whereas Bill Bedford's is adjustable by the use of different gauges of wire, the effectiveness of the Masokits version depends on getting the weight of the wagon right. The instructions suggest that 1 oz/28 grams per axle is the ideal, which unaugmented is rarely achieved by anything other than a whitemetal kit. How demanding a requirement this is depends on a number of factors: how long your goods trains are, how powerful your locos, how steep your gradients, etc. However, I have to say that, whitemetal kits apart, virtually none of my wagons from any source exceeds an ounce in total, and many are substantially less than this, even after a bit of extra weight has been added. In my experience, even compensated vehicles will perform perfectly well at no more than half an ounce per axle – as does the Bill Bedford Conflat L with an unladen weight of barely ¾oz in total.

Of course, I would have been pushed to find a wagon with less space to hide extra weight – or more need for it – than a Conflat L scratchbuilt in plastic. Even laden, and equipped with a full range of whitemetal fittings, it turned the scale at only about an ounce, and a chunk of lead flashing 100mm long, 15mm wide and 1.5mm thick was needed to bring it up to the required weight. Fortunately, I can just about get this in the three containers, but you might struggle with an unladen Lowfit or Single, for example – though the ever-helpful Masokits instructions do offer some tips on how this might be done.

Once weighted, the scratchbuilt wagon with Masokits suspension performs just as well as the Bill Bedford kit. There's no doubt that they glide impressively, and cope with track joints with a satisfying click. So why do I still have reservations about the need for suspension in principle? Well, for a start, in OO or EM neither suspension nor compensation is necessary to keep wagons from derailing, as long as both stock and track are properly built. So is the better performance of stock with suspension not reason enough in itself to embrace it wholeheartedly? Yes, perhaps so, especially if you have the scope to display trains moving at a steady speed over a fair distance. But it's at slower speeds, particularly shunting, that you tend to become aware of unsprung models lurching and bumping as they negotiate track joints and pointwork, and at these speeds the impression of smooth momentum that suspension can conjure up is rather less marked. And significantly, it's at these slower speeds that the real thing more noticeably thuds, clanks and judders its way over what is often, in any case, substandard trackwork. In other words, on smaller layouts with a predominance of slow-speed movements, wagon springing gets less opportunity to display its effectiveness. In fact at shunting speed I can detect no very significant difference in performance between rigid, compensated and sprung wagons.

However, if you're working in S4/EM18.83 and are routinely fitting wagons with compensation, I suggest that it's certainly worth considering suspension as an alternative. Moreover, there are certain wagon types – hoppers and tank wagons, for instance – where the exposed nature of the underframe makes it quite difficult to fit conventional methods of compensation unobtrusively, but where you would have a much better chance of concealing the plumbing of a suspension system quite effectively behind the solebar.

This trio of Diagram 1798 wagons, photographed more than twenty years apart, illustrates most of the changes that affected them over their lifetime: physical ones like the addition of clips over the capping irons and the replacement of the original single-plank sides and ends with two planks; and others such as the substitution of Plate for Long Low, and the uprating of the capacity from 20 to 22 tons. Nos. 45461 and 43160 were pictured in 1939 and M43140 in 1961.
A. E. WEST

CHAPTER TWO

WAGONS FOR LONG LOADS AND STEEL

In this chapter we shall look at bolster wagons of various kinds, together with a few of the other, less specialised vehicles used for steel products. It's not my intention to delve deeply into the area of wagons used exclusively in connection with the iron and steel industry, such as trestle wagons and those designed for wire rod or strip coil, for example, which wouldn't often be seen moving in the pick-up goods trains we are supposed to be concentrating on. But any rural branchline might see the occasional load of constructional steelwork, and a small fishing port could well have a modest ship repair yard demanding a consignment of steel plate now and then. And many market towns used to have foundries specialising in agricultural machinery which would need periodic supplies of raw materials such as pig iron.

Any of these could arrive in four-wheeled plate wagons, which were more versatile than their name would suggest: stone, vehicles, and even woodpulp in bales, are known to have been carried in them as well. Longer sections of steel, such as piling, beams or reinforcing bar for construction work, would more often be loaded onto bolsters, which would also be used to move logs, telegraph poles or long lengths of sawn timber. In the context of the pick-up goods, bogie vehicles would probably be seen less often than single or double bolsters, but it would be wrong to ignore them completely, so a glance at one or two of these would be appropriate.

Finally, we shall conclude with pipe and tube wagons. As with plate wagons, they were designed for a specific purpose, but quite often seen in more general use outside areas of heavy industry, so they deserve inclusion in this survey as well.

FROM LONG LOW TO PLATE WAGON

Diagram 1924 covers the next development of LMS Long Low/Plate wagon design, namely the adoption of double dropsides. Once again, the original single plank had been replaced with two narrower ones. Seen in 1962, M497534 also illustrates the change from Morton to standard 20-ton brakegear. A. E. WEST

The four-wheel, low-sided, long-wheelbase stock familiar to students of the British Railways scene for well over thirty years as Plate Wagons owed its design and its name to the LNER, who had moved from wooden- to steel-bodied vehicles of that same basic pattern at least as early as 1930. Initially of twelve tons capacity, later production was uprated to twenty, and then twenty-two, tons, which became the standard for all four-wheel Plates built by BR up to 1961.

The LMS persisted with wooden-bodied wagons for rather longer, but after building, in the fifteen years up to 1942, well over two thousand of this style, which they christened Long Low, they then adopted the LNER steel design towards the end of World War II, together with its code name. Early LMS production had fixed wooden sides, dropsides following from 1933 onwards. Whilst the LNER designation aptly described the main traffic carried by this type of wagon, the LMS name related more to their appearance: the longest were getting on for twice as long as a contemporary low-sided open, up to 31 feet over headstocks on a wheelbase of 17ft 6in. However, once the name Plate had been accorded to new steel-bodied construction from 1944, the older wagons were re-coded, and their carrying capacity of twenty tons was also increased to match the payload of the new vehicles.

In deciding which of the LMS wooden designs to model, it would have been logical to have chosen one of the much more numerous drop-sided versions, examples of which certainly lasted in traffic into the 'sixties: David Larkin in *Working Wagons Vol. I* has a picture of one in use as late as 1969. The youngest of the fixed-sided vehicles, on the other hand, were built as early as 1930, and I had doubts as to how many would have lasted into my own modelling period of the mid-to-late 'fifties, partly by reason of their age, and partly because I suspect the lack of drop-sides might have made them less favoured for their main traffic. The accompanying photograph of M43140 is in fact the only one I have seen of this design in BR colours.

The fact that this one, at least, did survive, however, conditioned my thinking, as did, more significantly, the presence in my stock cupboard of a Blacksmith Models etched kit for the Diagram 1798 version, of which 43140 was an example, one of four hundred built. Information on the prototype came from Volume One of *An Illustrated History of LMS Wagons* and from *The LMS Wagon*. An article in the February 1964 issue of *Railway Modeller* is also useful. Drawings can be found in all three sources, but that in the first shows no detail below the solebar, while those in the other two show the wrong brakegear – at least, it's at variance with both the accompanying texts and with all but one of the available photographs. Finally, at least one preserved example exists on the Peakrail line in Derbyshire.

The kit is designed to be built as two separate units, with the body and underframe being assembled individually and only united towards the end of construction. The body is simplicity itself, with the sides, ends and floor being folded up from a single sheet of brass. Something approximating to the scale thickness of the sides and ends is achieved by incorporating an extra layer of metal which is doubled over and soldered inside the outer skin. Before doing this, however, I scribed an extra horizontal line around the outside and inside folds: although as built the sides and ends consisted of a single wide plank, in-service repairs often resulted in two narrower timbers being substituted, and 43140 was no exception, at least as far as the two visible elevations are concerned.

The insert of 20-thou styrene, with its added battens, was kept separate until construction was otherwise finished; plastic and soldering irons don't go together, I've found.

I made two other additions to the body. 43140 had at some time received the common modification of small, U-shaped clips or straps over the capping irons along the top of the sides and ends. These were bent up from brass shim and soldered into place – all twenty-four of them. Fortunately, you don't have to be too precise about this job: photographs suggest that the number and position of them varied quite a lot, and they weren't always square to the edges of the body.

The second modification concerned the floor: the method of construction means that inadequate account is taken of the thickness of the floor planking, so that on the inside the wagon appears deeper than it should. I made an insert of 20-thou styrene to make up for this, and incorporated 4mm-wide battens of 30-thou at the appropriate intervals: there were eight of these altogether, all at 16mm centres except the two end ones, where the centre-to-centre gap was reduced to 14mm. Their purpose was to hold the load clear of the floor to facilitate the attachment of lifting gear (slings, dogs, chains and the like), and all plate wagons had them in one form or another. As it happens, they are shown quite well in a photograph in one of the earlier books of this series (pp. 4/5 of Part One), although the wagon concerned is an example of the later drop-sided version.

The underframe is designed for compensation, and while I believe this is generally something of a luxury in OO and EM, where it tends to be a substitute for smoothly laid, accurate pointwork and all-round squareness of chassis construction, I have to admit that it assumes greater importance with long-wheelbase non-bogie stock, and I felt that I would not be doing justice to the kit if I avoided it. However, I didn't anticipate the difficulties I met in incorporating it. To begin with, if you fold the rocking unit up squarely, it ends up a full 2mm narrower than the (just about scale) distance between the backs of the solebars. This rather generous clearance means that the W-irons are a bit too close together to accept easily standard 26mm pinpoint axles and bearings.

Fortunately, on the real thing the axle-guards (which should, in fact, be a touch wider than the etched ones) are reinforced with riveted plate hornguides, which are clearly visible on each side of the axleboxes. The kit makes no provision for these, but I found that by fabricating them out of sheet brass and enlarging the holes in the etched W-irons to a slightly greater diameter than the flanges on the bearings, I could get just enough extra clearance to take the axle with next to no end float. An alternative might have been to use flangeless bearings, but I'm always a little wary of drilling out the holes in the axleboxes just the right amount to get the spacing correct first time. Because if you don't, unless you drill the holes oversize, it's almost impossible to get the little beggars out again tidily, and I dislike the resultant waste of a perfectly good cast axlebox. (Plastic axleboxes are easier to repair: it's usually possible to plug the dent in the face left by a strategically-positioned punch with a noggin of styrene – see the section on SR brakevans in Chapter 3.)

The second problem I found was that when I had folded down the etched bracket that includes the tabs which locate and hold the rocking unit, the compensated end of the wagon sat a good millimetre too high off the track. The presence of the tabs, coupled with the filing angle imposed by the solebars, made it easier to cut the bracket away from the floor in order to remove the excess from the top, before resoldering it in position.

Right and overleaf: ***The underside of the completed Long Low, with and without the rocking unit. The slots filed in the unit to clear the brakeshoe hangers and safety loops are clearly visible.***

Finally, the length and width of the slots in the rocking unit through which the tabs fitted were enough to give what seemed a bit too much fore-and-aft movement in the axleboxes, so I reduced both with an overlay of brass strip cut from the spare material around the etch.

Turning to the brakegear, I felt that the rather brief instructions presupposed too close an acquaintance in the modeller with both the prototype wagons and the working of the brakes with which they were fitted. Two sorts of brakegear, Morton and 20-ton slotted link, appear on the etch. Now all the references I consulted, and the instructions for the kit, state that these wagons were equipped with Morton brakes; however, the instructions include sketches of both types, but they only show one side of each, and they don't explain that slotted link brakes were, in the main, only fitted to the later drop-sided diagrams. Confusingly, the D1798 drawings that accompany both the *Railway Modeller* article and the description in *The LMS Wagon* show slotted link, rather than Morton, brakes, although the texts refer only to the latter. But apart from one, not very clear, photograph in *An Illustrated History of LMS Wagons*, which appears to show one of these vehicles, 324599, fitted with the later style, I could find no firm published evidence that slotted-link brakes were an option for D1798 wagons. In any case, M43140 certainly had plain Morton brakes, so I put the slotted-link parts to one side.

But, crucially, at this point I realised that I couldn't find on the etch a number of brakegear parts: for a start, there were no pushrods; nor were there any safety loops, nor a Morton clutch, nor any mention in the instructions of either these or the cross-shaft between the V-irons. Fortunately, it wasn't especially difficult to fabricate them all from brass strip and wire. (In fairness I understand that some or all of the missing parts are on a separate etch, which seems to have been left out of my kit.)

A further difficulty presented itself when I read how the brakegear was supposed to fit together: the brakeshoe hangers at the compensated end appear to be designed to be soldered to the rocking unit (which is extended towards the centre of the wagon in order to incorporate the additional bracing strut that was a feature of the axleguards of all these vehicles). But unless they are made to pivot in both the brakeshoes and the tumbler behind the V-irons, which the instructions don't suggest, the pushrods would surely work against the rocking unit performing its proper function.

Pivoting the pushrods smacked to me of over-engineering, so I cut slots at each side of the rocking unit large enough to clear both the brakeshoe hangers and the safety loops, which I soldered directly to the underside of the floor. The pushrods were then fabricated of three pieces of strip, with each of the outer members extended to fit round the shoes at one end and the tumbler at the other. These ends were drilled 0.45mm to match the holes etched in the shoes and the tumbler, pinned to them with 26swg n/s wire, and soldered up in situ, rather after the fashion of Masokits brakegear. Incidentally, the Morton brake sketch in the instructions shows the tumbler angled the wrong way: the upper end should point to eleven o'clock rather than one o'clock, which has an obvious effect on the length of the pushrods.

The difficulty with mounting the brake hangers and safety loops clearly doesn't apply at the fixed end, where an etched support bracket is provided to aid their location. However, I did find this slightly too wide to fit comfortably between the solebars, and bent a pronounced vee into the middle of it to overcome this.

The instructions are unhelpful in judging the accurate position of the brake lever guards. Furthermore, none of the published drawings is of any assistance, either: as mentioned, the two that have any brakegear detail show the lifting link sort, which features shorter levers, and guards mounted on the inside of the axles, rather than on the headstock side as with Morton brakes. In fact, the correct position is about 5mm to the right of the centreline of the axle. The etched guards can, with care, be bent up to include a short spigot that can be soldered into a hole drilled in the solebar, but to make an assured fitting doubly sure, I left the extreme outer end of the handbrake lever, which is turned inwards to form the end of the handle itself, long enough to fit into another hole drilled in the solebar, where a second, fairly unobtrusive, soldered joint can be made.

The underframe was finished off with spring stops and label clips of styrene, and horse/capstan hooks of 33swg wire soldered to the underside of the lower solebar flange. A series of etched holes is provided in the floor section of the underframe to assist in making a sound soldered joint when the time comes to unite body to chassis. But they don't help to position the two parts accurately, and I found that the best way to do this was to solder the flats of the four end stanchions in position first, which locates the body correctly lengthways, and enables you to concentrate on getting it central laterally in relation to the headstocks and solebars. A touch of the iron then secures the downward projection of the flats to the headstocks, leaving just the webs of the stanchions, plus the eight side brackets, to finish the job. However, only by scaling from the outline drawing on the cover of the box the kit came in – or by reference to a published drawing elsewhere – can the spacing of the side brackets be determined. For the record, they are set at 26mm centres, with the centre line of the two outer ones 23mm in from the corners of the body.

With the wagon now in one piece, I added top and bottom flanges in 1mm wide brass to the outer ends of the headstocks (which look a bit weedy without them), and fitted buffers and drawhooks. The buffers provided have nice turned heads and rams force-fitted into cast whitemetal guides. However, standard 13in heads have been used, whereas all the drawings, corroborated by photographic evidence, show larger ones, generally of 16in diameter. With some care, so as not to damage the castings, I pulled out the heads supplied and substituted a set of old PC coach buffers which I found in my stock, and which happened to have both 16in heads and rams of the right bore. An alternative would have been to use MJT heads of this size, and to have sprung them as described in the next section.

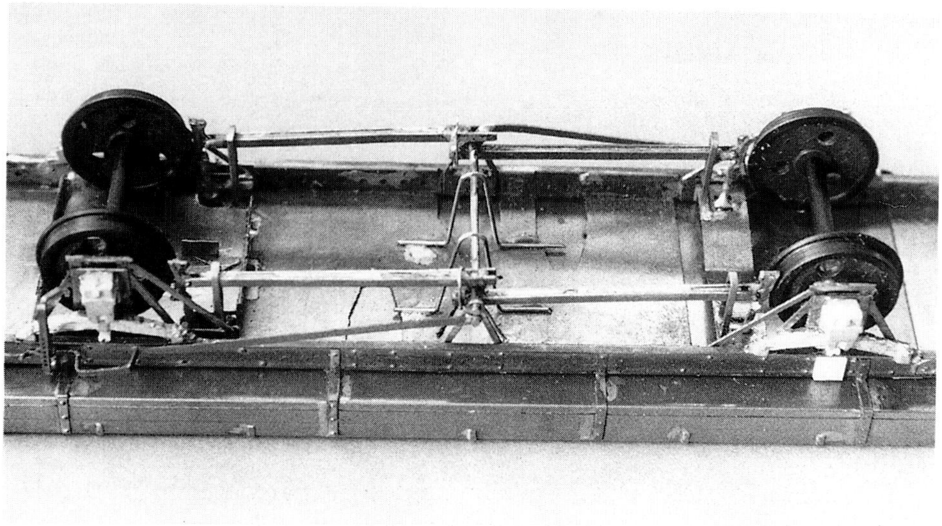

I made the mistake of painting the Long Low without reference to the photograph of the real M43140, so the patches and lettering don't quite match. But maybe it was different on the other side.

Although outwardly similar, there are some significant differences between these two LNER plate wagons. The older one (seen in 1960) was of riveted construction and had Morton two-shoe brakegear, with a capacity of only 12 tons. The newer wagon was welded, had four-shoe brakes, and a capacity of 22 tons, with deeper solebars and heavier springs to suit. Its stronger construction was reflected in a much higher tare weight. From 1944 similar steel-bodied wagons were also turned out by the LMS.
DON ROWLAND and ROGER CARPENTER

It was noted earlier that by the end of World War II the LMS had adopted the LNER pattern of steel plate wagon, and the two companies continued to build both riveted and welded examples until nationalisation. Parkside offer a kit for the LNER welded version, which can without much modification be used for the LMS vehicles as well. In fact, if you care to float on the rivets (see pages 22 of Part One and 149 of Part Two), both construction methods can be reproduced. The same goes for the wagons built by BR, who perpetuated the design for several more years without major changes. By this time all-welded sides had become the norm, but both riveted and welded ends were applied for the first decade of public ownership.

Up to the mid-'fifties the bulk of production had been fitted with hand brakes only, a single batch of LNER vehicles (Nos. 292095 to 292344, built in 1947) having been turned out with vacuum brakegear to that company's standard pattern. Rather surprisingly, a full seven years after nationalisation, BR chose the same style of brakegear for its first fitted vehicles, the 1,200 produced to Diagram 1/432 between 1955 and 1958.

Pocket Money Kits produce an etched brass-cum-whitemetal kit for the vacuum-braked LNER wagons which can, without too much extra work, be used for the BR version as well. In fact, in one small way, it's more suited to the later wagons than to the company-built ones, because each of the drop door castings has four hinges, rather than three. Now as far as I can tell, all the LNER wagons, and the early BR ones, only had three hinges per door, but all the Diagram 1/432 vehicles seem to have had four. In one or two other respects, however, building the BR version from the kit requires a bit of ingenuity: in particular, the plate axleguards fitted by BR are totally different and the ends of all the BR wagons were riveted, whereas the kit provides welded ones – although the drawings in the instructions are inclined to dispute this.

Information on the BR vehicles was culled chiefly from *An Illustrated History of BR Wagons, Volume One* and from an article by two of the authors of that book in *Model Railway Constructor Annual 1983*. The same drawing is reproduced in both, but each contains a different photograph of an example of D1/432; a third useful photograph appears in *Working Wagons Volume I*, and it was this vehicle, B933389, that I opted to model. Incidentally, if you choose to build the LNER version, I know of only two photographs of vacuum-braked wagons that can be studied: one is, not surprisingly, in *A Pictorial Record of LNER Wagons*, and the other is in *Pre-Nationalisation Freight Wagons on British Railways*. However, notwithstanding the few differences, information from all these sources is valuable whichever prototype you are building. Lastly, I discovered after I'd finished the model that a 1958-built example, B933947, has been preserved on the Keighley and Worth Valley Railway. Although it has received new buffers and roller bearings at some time, it retains its original vacuum brakegear.

The main etched parts of the underframe assembly went together quickly and cleanly at the first time of asking. The solebar rivet detail is half-etched from the rear, and needs to be pushed out with a not-too-pointed tool on a slightly springy surface like a sheet of cardboard: I used the worn end of an old set of school compasses and firm hand pressure. I failed to heed the note in the instructions that the solebars only fit one way round: the one with a single set of vee-hanger rivets goes on the same side of the floor pan as the slot for the inboard vacuum cylinder support. The mistake is not irredeemable, but I was left without locating slots for the safety loops and for one of the vee-hanger tabs, and with the need to create a new way of mounting the inner vac cylinder bracket –

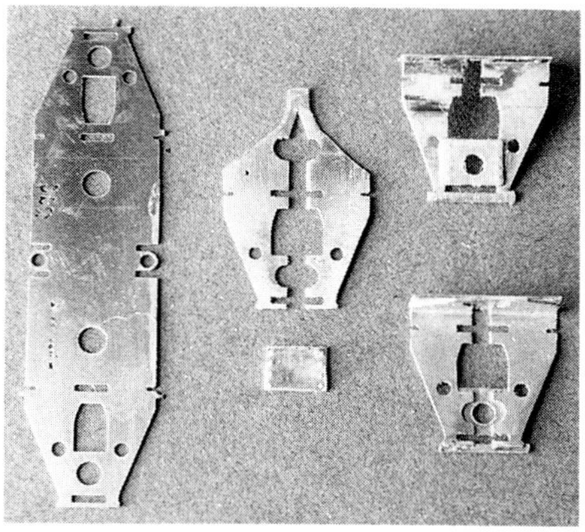

The principal stages in widening the EM Gauge Society BR roller-bearing axleguards to make heavy-duty ones suitable for the plate wagon. The surgery is fairly drastic, but the result is reasonably effective once the spring and axlebox have been added.

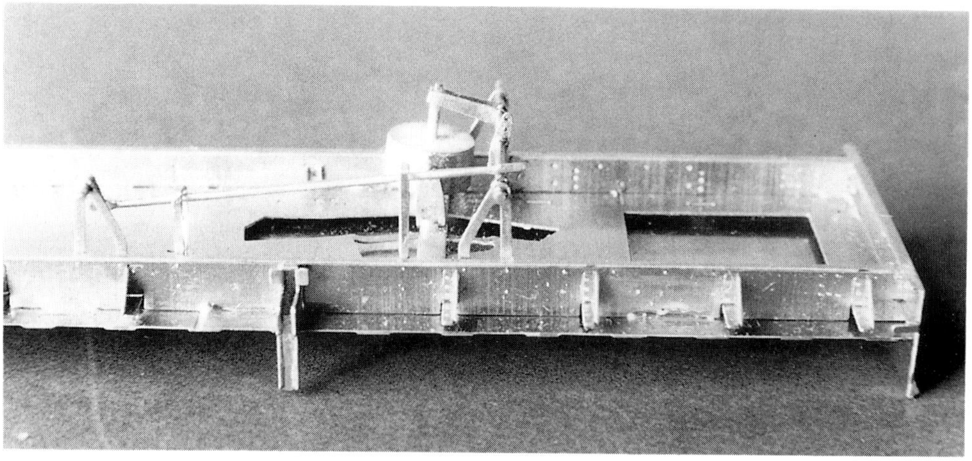

Views from each side of the partially-completed underframe of the LNER/BR plate wagon. As mentioned in the text, I complicated things for myself by getting the solebars, which are handed, on the wrong sides. As a result, to ensure that the impressed rivets corresponded with the various fittings, I had to cobble up the mounting of the inner vacuum cylinder support bracket because of the holes in the floor.

not straightforward, because it coincides with etched gaps in the floor pan where other components have been removed. Eventually I soldered in a bridging piece cut from scrap brass, and drilled it 1/32 inch to take the filed-down tab of the bracket.

The brakegear fits together nicely, although here again the written instructions are terse to the point of reticence, and tend to assume an intimate knowledge of how LNER fitted brakes work. But there is a drawing to help, even if the pull rod, attached as shown, would actually lift the brakes off rather than apply them. (This isn't a major criticism: the area concerned is hidden behind the wheels, and even if the complex linkage that equalises the force of the clasp brakes were modelled in full, it would be virtually invisible. But if you want to see how it should look, study the isometric drawing and photograph on pp. 2/3 of *A Pictorial Record of LNER Wagons*.)

Two more minor points about the brakegear: according to the photographs that show it, the long, inclined link that reverses the action of the brake lever on the side with two vee-hangers is actually round rod rather than flat bar. The kit allows for a stiffening overlay to the etched link, and it's a simple matter to narrow down the width of the thickened link and to file it half-round on the visible side. And, although they're shown on the scale drawing in the instructions, there is no other mention of the safety loops around the brake yokes. But there's ample 0.5mm wire supplied with the kit to make these up and fit them as described elsewhere.

The kit makes provision for an axlebox tie-bar, with which most, if not all, of the LNER-built wagons, fitted and unfitted, were originally equipped. Diagram 1/432 vehicles seem, by and large, not to have received them, although at least two, including B933145, have been noted with them. And the photograph of E292144 in *Pre-Nationalisation Freight Wagons on British Railways* shows that by 1969 it had lost its tie-bars (assuming it had had any), and had received BR plate axleguards into the bargain.

As I've already mentioned, the axleguards are one of the more significant differences between D1/432 wagons and their LNER predecessors. They were noticeably wider than the standard fitting and, as with the LMS vehicles we have already looked at, they were reinforced with riveted hornguides behind the axleboxes. Suitable etchings are available to members of the Scalefour Society, and there is a version from Exactoscale designed to accommodate the maker's springing system, but at the time the nearest approximation I could find in my stock were those supplied through the EM Gauge Society as BR roller bearing axleguards, which lack any form of the triangular holes that characterise traditional W-irons. They are still too narrow, however. Well, nothing ventured ... Using a pair of household scissors, I cut one up the centre line, and then cut away most of the metal on either side above the axleguard proper, leaving in effect a 2mm-wide tongue that was a couple of millimetres longer than my initial cut. With a combination of fingers and pliers, I then bent the two halves apart by about 1.5mm. Being metal, of course, they stayed in their correct relative positions while I soldered a bridle across the bottom (cut from one of the redundant tie-bars), and then added a 6mm × 4mm reinforcing plate above it. This had had the eight rivets impressed from the rear before fitting, but I left drilling the bearing hole until afterwards to make sure it was central. Finally, I bent what remained above the axleguard at 90 degrees (a) to give a more secure fitting and (b) to try to ensure that the centre of the bearing/axle would be at the required 5.5/6mm below the solebar in each one.

Lateral positioning of the axleguards is assisted by register marks thoughtfully etched into the underfloor, but nonetheless it pays to attach one side first and then to check the position of the opposite side with bearings and wheelsets in place, to make sure that both axles are parallel and at right-angles to the longitudinal axis of the wagon. If, to begin with, you carefully size the holes in the hornguide overlays to make the bearings a decent interference fit, you can pop one out more easily in order to enlarge the hole one way or the other to compensate for any minor discrepancy you may discover after the axleguards have been finally attached. A touch of solder will then secure this bearing in the corrected position; the others can remain a push fit until they are fixed by the addition of the axleboxes.

Some of the BR-built plate wagons received LNER axleboxes from new, but B933389 apparently wasn't one of them. Instead it had large, rectangular, platefront ones, which I fabricated in styrene as described elsewhere. I married them to MJT seven-leaf springs (the five-leaf ones supplied with the kit are, in any case, strictly speaking, only suitable for the LNER's early twelve-ton plate wagons), and these parts, together with the addition of a styrene spring stop Evo-stuck beneath the bottom solebar flange, help to disguise the slightly wide gap in the centre of the axleguard resulting from the surgery carried out earlier.

The second main difference between the LNER and the BR wagons concerned the ends, which were welded on the former and riveted on the latter. Had the rivets been confined to the four vertical T-iron stanchions on each end, I might have contented myself with impressing them into the whitemetal castings supplied with a needle in a pin chuck: from normal viewing distances, it's surprising how effectively a pock mark can deputise for a pimple. But there are two horizontal and two vertical rows of rivets on the end plating as well, and having already fitted the ends without planning ahead as to how I was going to tackle the problem, the only solution I could now come up with was to add an overlay of 10-thou styrene, to which the rivets could be applied individually by the 'floating-on' method. Brass

B933947 is a 1958-built wagon to BR Diagram 1/432 similar to the one modelled here. Seen as preserved on the Keighley & Worth Valley Railway, it has LNER-style fitted brake gear, but has been converted to roller bearings, and the butterfly sheet string cleat on the end of the headstock has been replaced with a step. AUTHOR

Detail shots of No. B931520, a diagram 1/431 plate wagon built in 1951. As with B933947, it combined riveted ends with welded sides, but was originally built with only hand brakes. Subsequently it had received 8-shoe fitted brakegear, modern axleboxes and long Oleo buffers, for which the drawhook had to be bracketed off the headstock. However, it retained three-hinge doors and the older style of sheet string cleat. Photographed at Immingham in 1991. AUTHOR

shim, with the rivets embossed from behind, would have been an alternative, but I felt less confident of doing this as neatly as with plastic, which gave me the opportunity as well of making up styrene T-stanchions which are rather less chunky than the castings that came with the kit.

As it happened, there was a further, unlooked-for benefit of applying an overlay: the buffers provided are 20½-inch fitted stock buffers as used by the LNER, but the BR diagram calls for 18-inch ones. Almost a third of the difference can be accounted for by cutting a hole in the overlay that matches the shape of the cast base plate of the buffer guide. Rebating the buffer in this way would have been enough for me in most cases, but with these wagons, as with the Long Low, larger diameter heads were often fitted, and this seems to have been the case with 933389. So I broke off the cast heads and substituted turned 16-inch ones from MJT. These are designed for springing, which is not something I normally do with goods stock, but the extra labour involved was minimal, so I drilled through the casting 0.52mm, and then opened up about two-thirds of the hole to a diameter of 3/64-inch to take the spring and the wider end of the ram just behind the head. When I was satisfied that the spring would compress sufficiently to bring the head into contact with the guide, I bent the tail through ninety degrees and cut off enough of the surplus to prevent it binding on the back of the solebar. By judging where to make the bend, I was able to shorten the buffers' apparent overall length (coupled with the rebating) to the requisite 6mm.

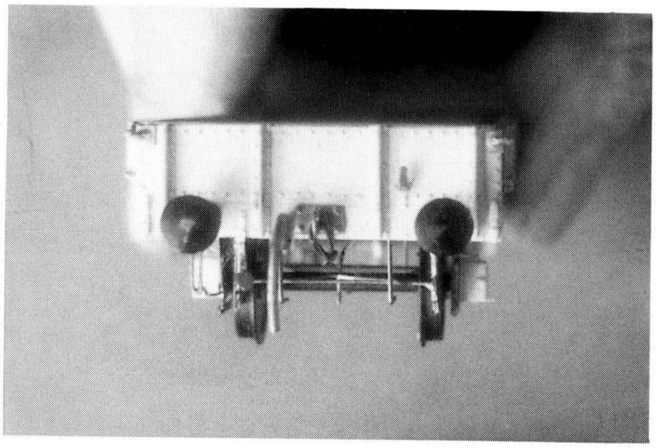

Side and end views of the completed wagon. The riveted end detail is built up on an overlay of 10-thou plastic stuck to the plain etched end that comes with the kit.

The most substantial of the cast parts in the kit are the sides. These were a perfect fit between the etched ends and the central door pillar (which is removable on the real thing when the doors are dropped) but the vertical and horizontal webs or flanges are a bit on the meaty side. Whether for this reason or not, the overall top-to-bottom dimension of 6.5mm is around ¾mm more than the consensus of the various drawings of steel plate wagons. Not a huge amount, I accept, but even after filing as much as I dared off the top and bottom edges, the difference in height compared with vehicles from other sources is noticeable.

One final Plastikard addition was the twelve prominent rope cleats attached horizontally below the side doors and vertically to the ends of the headstocks. Earlier vehicles from all sources had had rather less obtrusive hooks for sheet strings on the solebars, but D1/432 followed the pattern of some other contemporary wagons in having much larger cleats of a double-winged design. These were filed up from 20-thou styrene strip as illustrated in Part One under the heading of Palbrick wagons.

BOLSTER WAGONS

SINGLE BOLSTERS

The later history of the single bolster was a distinctly chequered one, especially under BR auspices. Prior to the Grouping many companies had favoured the type, sometimes in the form of permanently-coupled pairs or twins; the GWR was particularly fond of this arrangement, building many hundreds of twins, which they coded Mite. After 1923, however, only the LMS and LNER saw fit to build new ones, turning out between them over 6,500 up to the time of nationalisation. Echoing the dependence of the North Eastern Railway on singles for carrying steel products, almost four out of every five of these were built by the LNER.

Initially both companies concentrated on traditional all-timber construction, and this accounted for almost 4,000 of the total. Both followed this with small batches with timber bodies and steel underframes, before the LNER adopted an all-steel design which was to be perpetuated by BR. Not that the new authority seemed very keen on singles: after completing a thousand of them in 1949/50 (probably to an outstanding LNER order), it was apparently felt that there were enough relatively modern examples to cope with what was already perhaps seen as a declining demand, and no more were initially planned. But possibly because of entrenched attitudes in the steel industry, coupled with the rapidly dwindling number of pre-grouping survivors, BR was forced into a dramatic volte-face, building an astonishing 7,000 more in barely two years from 1956.

Nonetheless, the writing was already on the wall. The second half of a final batch of a thousand in 1958 was cancelled, and within a decade the single bolster was almost extinct. They weren't all scrapped immediately: some lingered on in departmental use, and there were a few attempts at conversion into something more useful. In particular, several hundred singles, together with redundant Lowfits and Conflat As, were adapted to run as permanently-coupled twins. This was mainly to replace a varied fleet of makeshift wartime conver-

Photographed new in 1937, No. 205175 represents the all-wooden style of LNER-built single bolster. Although slightly newer, E240198 below was in very used condition by the time it was pictured in 1960. The layout of the swivelling bolster and its associated tackle are well shown.
HMRS and A. E. WEST

sions of wooden mineral wagons; for details of one version of these, see especially Pete Jary's article in *Model Railway Journal* No. 132. Almost all of the last (curtailed) batch of singles, which were vacuum-fitted, were involved in what must have seemed a fairly logical move: singles had nearly always run in pairs or multiple, except when being used as runners beneath overhanging loads. But double bolsters (which the twins effectively were) were soon on the wane as well, so this was a fairly short-lived conversion. For over half of BR's production, and all the earlier wagons, the 8ft wheelbase told against them, and there was no reprieve.

Although over the years there has been a sprinkling of kits for pre-grouping singles of various origins, the LMS, LNER and BR designs have been largely overlooked. Currently, as far as I am aware, only the Connoisseur Models' (Pocket Money Kits) etched brass pair of LNER steel-bodied wagons occupies this niche, although since the first 4,000 BR-built vehicles turned out before the wheelbase was lengthened to 10ft in 1957 were very

By way of comparison we see a pair of LMS all-wooden singles, also built in the late 'thirties. No. 722736 and M722042 were photographed in 1938 and 1952 respectively. Once again, the bolster swivelling arrangement can be clearly seen. A. E. WEST

similar, the kit does cover a fair proportion of the total. It should be noted, however, that after the first 1,000 wagons had been built with the two-shoe Morton brakes favoured by the LNER, BR began to fit four-shoe brakes; the kit doesn't provide for this change.

Nevertheless, with a bit of work, it could probably be used as the basis for all the later wagons as well: the overall length remained unchanged, and the cast whitemetal axleguards lend themselves to being spaced at wider centres, although, strictly speaking, since they are of RCH pattern with LNER axleboxes, they're not suitable as they stand for the majority of BR production. Longer brakegear would be needed as well, of course. More sophisticated buffing gear came in with the longer wheelbase of diagram 1/402, which had an early form of Dowty hydraulic buffer with unusual flat-topped and flat-sided guides – not available in model form as far as I know. And one or two small changes were made to the body in the course of production, including the substitution of box section for the vertical end stanchions instead of the T-irons used previously, and the addition of small riveted gusset plates halfway along the sides.

Furthermore, there is one modification to the superstructure which any builder of the kit will need to consider. According to the main source of information on the wagons built by BR, *An Illustrated History of BR Wagons, Volume I*, all post-nationalisation production had fixed bolsters, which can be read to mean that they weren't designed to swivel. The drawing of a D1/402 vehicle featured in the book conforms with this interpretation, and although no other source that I've come across is specific on the point, the kit appears to confirm that the LNER-built wagons were the same by omitting some of the fittings needed for the bolsters to swivel. However, many earlier designs of single had had bolsters that were able to pivot with the movement of the load – to which, of course, they were usually attached – when the wagons negotiated a curve. Such bolsters were 'fixed' solely to the extent that there was only one position for them (i.e. in the centre of the wagon), and that they may not always have been readily removable for day-to-day traffic purposes. Even so, some certainly were removable, and the NER for one had developed a design where the bolster, when not required, could be dropped into a longitudinal slot in the wagon bed.

By postwar years the LNER had progressed to all-steel wagons to a design later taken up by BR. In other respects, however, they were unchanged from the earlier pattern, with a length over the body of 15ft 6in, wheelbase of 8ft, and Morton two-shoe brakes. LNER 292886 and B910866, seen in 1947 and 1952 respectively, illustrate the similarity of pre- and post-nationalisation construction, although BR would introduce several changes in due course (see text). The view of the interior of one of the later wagons, B916135, built in 1957, is included to show the central pivot and radiused end pathways made visible by the removal of the bolster, required by its conversion to a crane match wagon. Seen at Shrewsbury in 1992.
ROGER CARPENTER, A. E. WEST and AUTHOR

Two more photographs showing bolster detail on ex-LNER singles. In the upper picture, taken at Chippenham in 1958, the subject is E205360, a Diagram 118 all-wooden wagon dating from the late 'thirties. The bolster in the lower view, at Huntingdon in 1952, belonged to ex-NER single E62665, a broadside view of which appears in A Pictorial Record of LNER Wagons.

Now it may be that some of the steel-bodied singles built by the LNER and BR didn't have swivelling bolsters, but there's ample photographic evidence to prove that many did have them, as did all the ones that I've seen in the flesh. The design and position of the curved steel pathways or rubbing plates that supported the ends of the bolster should be evident from the pictures reproduced here. To incorporate this feature in building the kit, I would be inclined to create the shallow well in the centre of the wagon by raising the floor on either side with overlays of 20-thou plastic, scribed to represent the planking. The rubbing plates and the raised central pivot could be cut from thin metal sheet and soldered to the floor; the etched plank grooves that remained visible could either be filled with solder and then ground smooth, or covered with an overlay of shim before the raised detail is applied.

The LMS singles certainly had swivelling bolsters, as did, I believe, all of the LNER's diagrams covering their wooden-bodied wagons. In the absence of a kit, the LMS version would have to be scratch-built; the two standard publications on LMS wagons provide considerable information, and general arrangement drawings of both the steel and wooden underframed vehicles appear in *Official Drawings of LMS Wagons* No. 1 and No. 2 respectively. Finally, the May 1969 issue of *Railway Modeller* has an illustrated article on the subject, complete with drawing.

Some years ago I built a model of the principal LNER design of timber-framed single bolster using a cut-down Mainline Lowfit body and shortened 3H wooden solebars and brakegear. A more direct route would now be found in the Parkside LNER Lowfit kit, similarly cut down and married to their PA05 bolster set – although this isn't a perfect match, and doesn't represent the swivelling type. The swivelling arrangement on the wooden stock was rather different from that on the steel-bodied wagons, being derived from NER practice, but the photographs here, and a drawing in *A Pictorial Record of LNER Wagons* should provide sufficient information.

These two single bolsters were built some time ago when no kits were available for any of the post-1923 designs. Accordingly the LNER wooden-bodied and framed wagon uses a cut-down Mainline lowfit body teamed with a similarly shortened 3H underframe. The BR example is completely scratchbuilt except for the brakegear (reduced 3H again), but could nowadays be produced from the Connoisseur etched kit for the later LNER version.

These three photographs of wooden-bodied LMS double bolsters illustrate the main phases of development of these vehicles prior to the move to all-steel construction. No. 315583, seen in 1938, was built to Diagram 1674, the design represented by the Colin Ashby kit, with Morton brakes and low bolsters. As narrated in the text, however, I chose to build the kit to the next diagram, D1949, with higher bolsters and 20-ton brakegear; M725436, photographed in 1960, represents this version, and I also used its load of steel beams as the original for the load carried by the model. A. E. WEST

Finally, M725809 foreshadowed the steelbodied wagons built by the LMS, the LNER and BR by having double dropsides and removable bolsters, enabling it to be readily converted to a plate wagon whenever necessary. It was built to D2067 and photographed in 1950. A. E. WEST

LMS DOUBLE BOLSTER

As with its early plate wagons, the LNER's wooden-bodied double bolsters were of lighter carrying capacity than the LMS equivalents. Seen in 1963 and 1962 respectively, E184751 and E137020 exemplify these. The auxiliary pins or stanchions could be mounted either inside or outside the bodyside. A. E. WEST and DON ROWLAND

Between 1923 and 1948, as with plate wagons, only the LMS and LNER built double bolsters in any quantity, and, as with plate wagons, they progressed from wooden- to steel-bodied vehicles, adopting a design that was perpetuated after 1948 by BR. Indeed, their later wagons were essentially plate wagons with bolsters, and as the need for doubles declined in the 'fifties and 'sixties, many had the bolsters removed in order to augment the plate wagon fleet.

As a variation of their steel-bodied LNER plate wagon kit, Parkside offer one for the same company's later double bolster, which can, without too much work, be used for the LMS and BR versions as well. As far as I know, however, there is no current kit for the LNER's wooden-bodied wagons, which were somewhat shorter than the corresponding LMS design rated at 20 tons (later raised to 22 tons in line with the LMS wooden plate wagons), and had a carrying capacity of only twelve tons. Colin Ashby's kit for the LMS version (originally marketed by Ian Kirk) nominally represents the 1,411 vehicles built to diagram 1674 between 1925 and 1930. A further 800 were turned out to a slightly modified design, D1949, in the late 'thirties; officially the earlier wagons all had Morton brakes whereas the later ones had 20-ton lifting-link gear. In practice, many of the D1674 wagons had this as well, together with the higher bolsters supposedly featured only by the later diagram, so it clearly pays to work to a photograph.

As with the LMS plate wagon, the best sources of information are *The LMS Wagon* and Volume One of *An Illustrated History of LMS Wagons*, augmented in this case by *Official Drawings of LMS Wagons*, No. 1, which contains both photographs and General Arrangement drawings of D1949. A 1965 picture of M725782 in this book persuaded me to adapt the kit to produce an example of the later diagram. Finally, a drawing also appears in the March 1963 issue of *Railway Modeller.*

Excluding the bolsters, of which more anon, the body assembly is straightforward. As usual, I put together each side/end pair first, and then joined these before inserting the floor. Although on this occasion the floor needed very little trimming to fit snugly, I would rather alter the floor as necessary than risk the poorly-mating corner joints that so frequently result from attaching the ends and sides to the floor one after the other. The only alterations I made to the body were to fit RCH buffers from MJT (13in heads this time, as per the diagram), and to extend the headstocks by a millimetre or so at each end. The kit already has the square-ended headstocks featured by D1949, rather than the angled ones of D1674; however, the fact that they are a bit short gives you the chance to lengthen them with the appearance of channel section using 10-thou strip. A full-length bottom flange is optional, but I felt that the headstocks actually needed to be a little deeper as well, and took the opportunity to kill two birds with one stone.

The underframe, on the other hand, did call for something more in the way of remodelling, and not just because I was fitting different brakegear. To begin with, the downward extensions of the vertical bodyside ironwork are missing from the solebars, though it was a simple matter to add these in 10-thou strip. Rather more complex were the axleguard modifications. In describing the Blacksmith kit for the Long Low, I remarked that the axleguards weren't wide enough, although I didn't trouble to do anything about it. Whilst it was shorter in overall length than most of the Long Lows, the double bolster shared the same wheelbase and underframe fittings, and the kit's moulded axleguards share the same shortcoming, even though in this case they do have the heavy-duty hornguides that the etched kit lacked. And being plastic, they lend themselves to a bit of cosmetic bodging designed to make them look somewhat wider.

First, however, I filed off the plastic springs, which have only three leaves, intending to replace them in due course with cast whitemetal seven-leaf ones, again from MJT. This enabled me to pare away with a craft knife some of the meat on the inner edge of the vertical legs of the W-irons in the aperture above the axleboxes, reducing them to about half their original width. I then did the same with the inner edge of the inclined legs, although the scope for reduction is not so great here; nevertheless it needs to be done to maximise the width of the V-shaped opening, because the next step is to glue strips of 20-thou to the outer edges of the vertical legs, increasing the measurement across these to around the necessary 7mm. The relief surface of the bridle was then filed flush, and replaced with a strip of 10-thou long enough to span the widened W-iron.

By 1965 M725782 had received large rectangular platefront axleboxes. Rather than completely replace the kit's moulded RCH ones, I filed the detail off the front and added an overlay of 15-thou, to which a further, slightly smaller one of 5-thou was applied. Finally, after the new springs had been epoxied into place, spring stops, fashioned as described on page 70 of Part One, were glued to the underside of the bottom solebar flange. With luck, all these modifications will be evident from the photographs.

As moulded, the brakegear is very much too short, the shoes ending up more than a millimetre from the tyres of scale wheels (one pair of three-hole discs, and one pair of spoked, if I read the photograph of 725782 correctly). The mouldings can be lengthened by cutting them in two centrally, and grafting extra material, cut from 40-thou sheet, into place. Although the result is a bit representational, the rather plain, sort of Z-shaped bit incorporating the ends of the push-rods and the tumbler is at least partly hidden behind the V-hanger and brake lever, and once painted a nondescript grey-brown, merges happily with the background. The joints are made stronger by adding flitch plates, or splints, behind them; once again, the principles are set out in Part One, this time on page 30.

One set of mouldings also needs to be reversed. Both sets should not be the same: wherever there is a cross-shaft between the V-hangers (excluded from the kit, but easily represented by wire or 30/40-thou plastic rod), each pair of push-rods acting on the same wheelset should be inclined the same way. This is true of both Morton and lifting-link brakegear. You could simply fit one set back-to-front (after it's been lengthened, of course), remembering that the push-rods behind the direct-acting lever are the upper ones and those behind the lifting-link or Morton clutch side lever

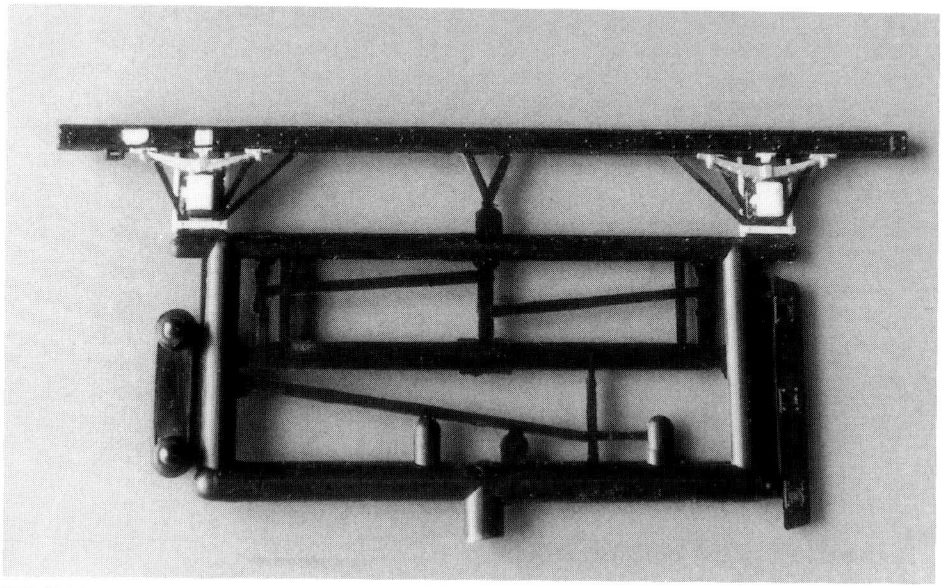

For some reason, I chose to make the alterations to axleguard, spring and axlebox assemblies of the LMS double bolster before separating the parts from the sprue. However, this shot does serve to illustrate the rather basic nature of the brakegear parts. As may hopefully be seen from the views of the finished wagon, these benefit from some remodelling in the area of the V-irons, and from the additional relief work required to the brakeshoe/pushrod assembly that needs to be reversed on the lifting-link side. The levers, guards and other parts made necessary by the change to 20-ton brakegear are a mixture of Masokits and home-made metal components.

are on the bottom. But it's nice to add a bit of relief detail on the otherwise plain surface; again, the photographs should illustrate what's required.

The brake levers supplied with the kit are very two-dimensional, and don't include the lifting-link option for 20-ton gear; (if it comes to that, the alternative Morton clutch arrangement isn't reproduced either). While some cosmetic improvements would be possible if Morton brakes were being fitted (Part One again, page 29, and also the pipe wagon section of this chapter), the lifting-link variation, coupled with the shorter levers used with this gear, made complete replacement with the metal parts the better choice. Except for the lever guards, which I made up myself in brass strip incorporating a spigot to slot through a hole drilled in the solebar, I used Masokits bits. The geometry of the lifting-link side is not entirely straightforward (the lower link, for example, needs to be kinked to fit behind the foot of the V-hanger), but by pinning the parts to a slab of balsa while soldering them, I was able to tweak the assembly bit-by-bit until it fitted.

Turning to the bolsters, the kit makes provision for both the lower ones fitted originally to D1674 and the higher ones adopted later. In checking the sources of information for confirmation of the exact dimensions, I found that, whilst the width of the baulks was constant at ten inches, it seems there were in fact three height variations. The drawing of D1674 in Volume One of *An Illustrated History of LMS Wagons* has been amended to read 13¾ inches; the original figure seems to have been 8¾ inches, and comparison with the drawing of the contemporary D2029 confirms this. However, the G.A. drawing of D1949 reproduced in *Official Drawings of LMS Wagons No. 1*, backed up by the line drawing in *An Illustrated History of LMS Wagons*, indicated that the height was later raised again to 1ft 3in. 1¼ inches is fairly academic, I suppose, in the smaller scales, and the difference isn't very obvious in photographs; however, I laminated three strips of 60-thou and one of 20-thou together in order to achieve the higher figure.

I had decided to make my own bolsters after taking advice on how I could best arrange to run the wagon both loaded and empty. The problem centred on the fact that any load should properly be chained down, which seemed to rule out having it sitting loosely on the bolsters: the chains would be difficult or impossible to maintain in the correct attitude when the load was being removed and replaced. I have Peter Smith to thank for the answer: removable bolsters, one set permanently attached to the load, with a second pair to take their place when the load is taken off. The drawback was having to make two full sets of chains as well, but there seemed to be no way round this.

There also had to be some form of positive location for the bolsters, particularly the empty ones. However, making my own bolsters enabled me to crack this by extending each of the 1/32 inch wire stanchions right through the bolsters and plugging them into corresponding holes drilled in the wagon floor. Actually, the holes are a touch oversize, partly to accommodate my slightly approximate production methods, which resulted in the spacing of the pins varying by a few thou from one bolster to the next, and partly to make sure that the bolsters could all be taken out and refitted fairly easily. Register marks scratched into the floor and the underside of the bolsters ensure that they are always put in the right holes and the right way round. Incidentally, the pips moulded on the inside of the wagon sides to show the position of the bolsters are about 2mm too close together: the bolsters were at 15ft centres.

Going back to the chains, these are helpfully shown in some detail on the drawings reproduced in *Official Drawings of LMS Wagons*. It seems that each bolster had a pair of chains permanently attached to the large shackles on the ends: at one side was a binding chain, long enough to pass round or over the load being carried, and at the other a shorter tensioning chain incorporating a bottle screw that resembled a standard screw coupling. Several hooks were provided to take up slack and give additional purchase. The exact length of chain involved is not clear: most photographs of empties either show the chains neatly stowed across the bolsters on new wagons, or piled haphazardly on the floor of wagons in traffic. In pictures of loaded vehicles, the load itself usually gets in the way.

Fine chain suitable for this purpose is available from a number of suppliers, including the kit manufacturer, Colin Ashby. Langley Models and Backwoods Miniatures are two more current sources. What you're looking for is chain with a link size of about 2mm, or a bit less – say 15–20 links to the inch. Some of the chain I've seen has links which are rather too rounded; it pays in this case to clench them gently with a pair of pliers in order to straighten the sides. Or you could make your own chain out of 30 swg wire, or similar. I've resorted to this cheap but tedious solution on occasions, and did so here where just a handful of links was required at each end of the tensioner, for instance. Home-made ones are a bit easier to close up, I've found, over hooks, shackles and the like than ready-made links that have to be cut and opened out to begin with.

As with container chains, etched hooks with eyes are available from such as Roxey and PC; tensioners are also to be had from Roxey, but be warned – they're very delicate and liable to distort however gently

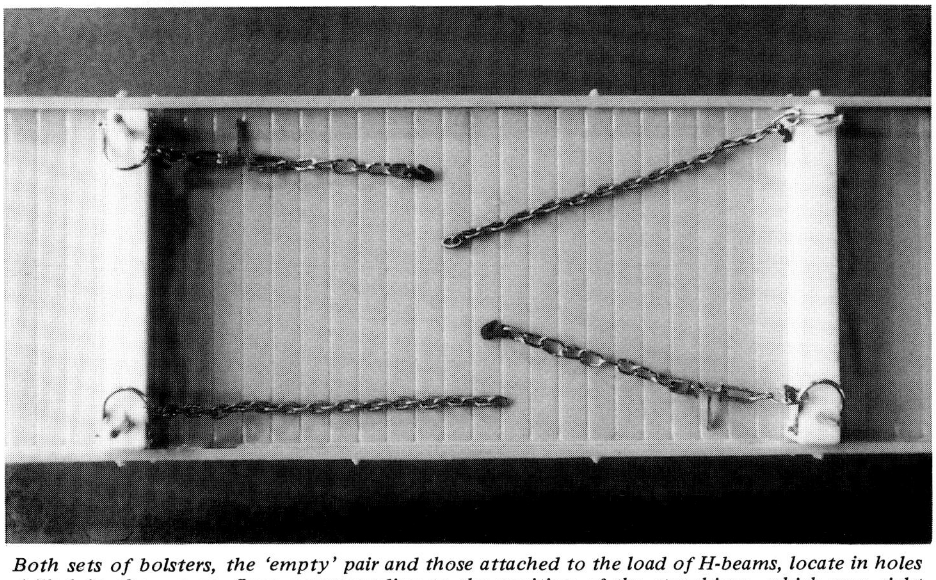

Both sets of bolsters, the 'empty' pair and those attached to the load of H-beams, locate in holes drilled in the wagon floor corresponding to the position of the stanchions, which pass right through the bolsters. As described in the text, the chains are partly commercial items and partly home-made, both with PC hooks and Roxey tensioners.

you handle them. I ended up soldering two together, but even then the tommy bar was still susceptible to damage.

I made the shackles from 26 swg nickel-silver wire with the ends clenched flat and drilled 0.5mm to accept a pin of the same gauge, touch-soldered at each end. The load of steel beams was made up from 10-thou plastic to match one of the photographs reproduced here; (ready-made alternatives are available from manufacturers such as Ratio, Plastruct and Evergreen). For solidity and ease of handling they were all stuck together in a single lump, and then stuck to one of the sets of bolsters. The binding chains were passed right round the load and spot soldered on top to keep them taut. The hooks on the end of the tensioning chains were then engaged in the furthest link they would reach, and secured with a dab of epoxy. So were the loose ends of the binding chains, although on reflection this probably wasn't necessary, and I left the chains on the 'empty' bolsters unsecured to find their own resting place on the wagon bed.

A. E. WEST

Two loaded LMS doubles, one full size and one in model form. No. 289658 was pictured at Cardington in 1939 and typifies the difficulty of working out from a photograph exactly how the securing chains should be rigged. Notice that although built to the same diagram 1674 as No. 315583 pictured earlier, it had the brakegear and higher bolsters associated with the D1949 wagons represented by the model.

BOGIE BOLSTERS

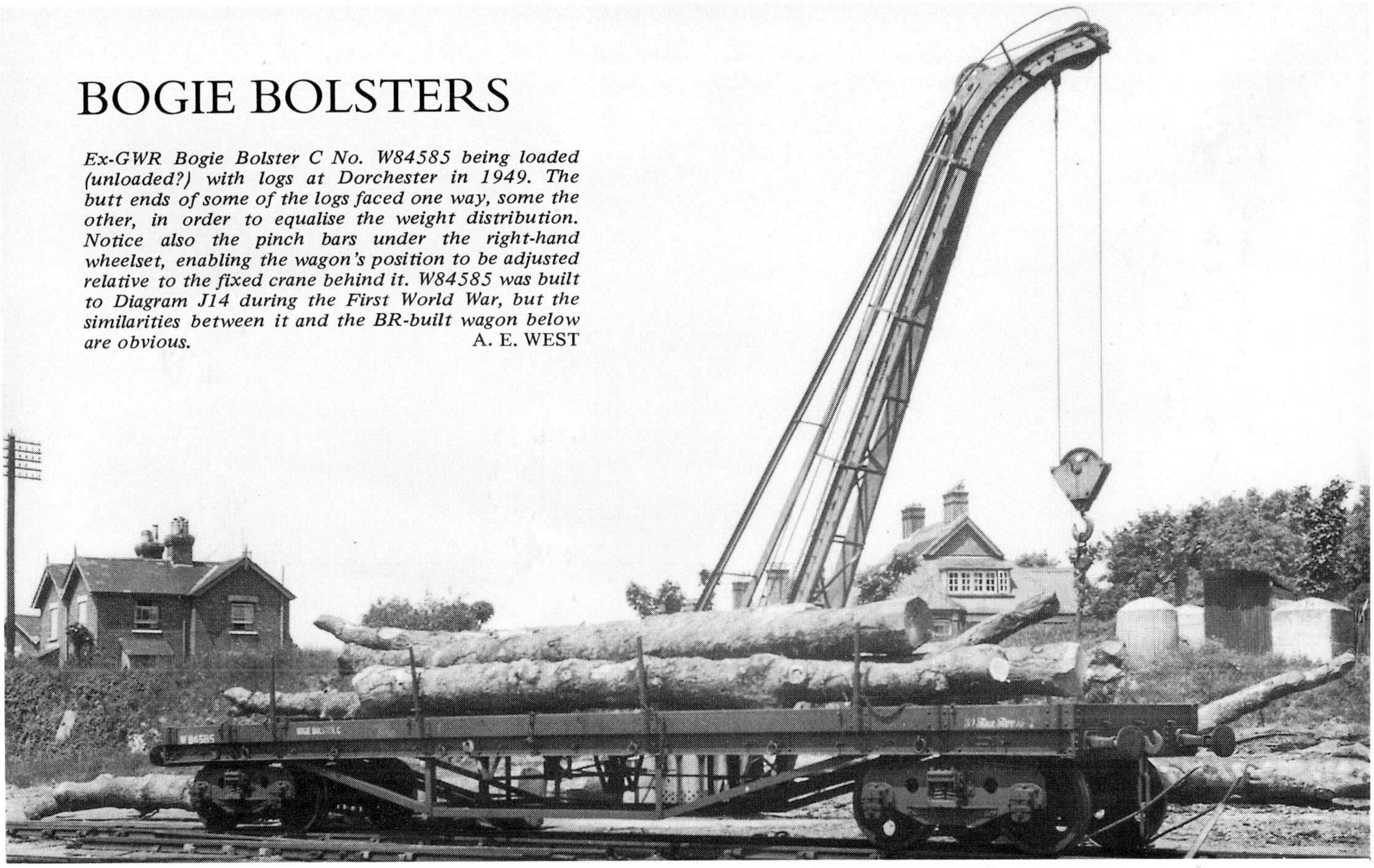

Ex-GWR Bogie Bolster C No. W84585 being loaded (unloaded?) with logs at Dorchester in 1949. The butt ends of some of the logs faced one way, some the other, in order to equalise the weight distribution. Notice also the pinch bars under the right-hand wheelset, enabling the wagon's position to be adjusted relative to the fixed crane behind it. W84585 was built to Diagram J14 during the First World War, but the similarities between it and the BR-built wagon below are obvious. A. E. WEST

B922536 was built over forty years later, and was equipped with roller bearings and vacuum brakes. By the time it was photographed at Immingham in 1995, it had also acquired tensioners fitted to the curb rail to facilitate the use of webbing strops to secure the load as an alternative to chains. AUTHOR

Even if we exclude post-war conversions of wagons designed for military use (Rectanks, Warwells and Warflats), and wagons intended wholly or mainly for engineering purposes, bogie bolsters came in a bewildering variety of sizes, shapes and capacities. Each of the Big Four inherited designs from one or more of its constituents, and went on to build further examples of its own. Many of the pre-grouping wagons passed to BR in 1948 along with their later cousins, some of which were then developed by the new authority into its own standard designs. Whilst some classes were built in large numbers, many of the early or more specialised types were only ever turned out in limited quantities.

Prior to World War II the term bogie bolster seems to have been confined largely to the LMS and the Southern, while the GWR had its Macaws and the LNER its Quads, Quints and Septs (according to the number of bolsters carried by each type). The GWR blurred things a bit by including four- and six-wheel bolster wagons in the Macaw code, although it had standardised on bogie vehicles from an early date, and built very few non-bogie wagons after the start of the twentieth century.

During World War II a new classification system was introduced by which all such vehicles were to be known as bogie bolsters and to be coded A, B, C, or D broadly according to overall length and carrying capacity: bogie bolster As (BBAs) were the shortest, while Ds were the longest. Capacity generally increased in line with length, although bogie bolster Bs were an exception, being all converted Warwells and Warflats with a capacity of fifty tons, the heaviest of all. BR later complicated things further by adding the bogie bolster E, which was shorter than the As but had the capacity of a C. Bolster wagons longer than BBDs (generally 60 feet and over) were built mainly for the carriage of rails, and were coded Borail; although intended primarily for departmental use, they were available for traffic purposes as well: rails have always been an important export product of the British steel industry.

The first Bogie Bolster Ds built for BR were a batch of 150 wagons turned out from Derby in 1949 to Diagram 1/470. This was the same as the final diagram used by the LMS, No. 18C. They were fitted with five fixed wooden bolsters and diamond frame bogies of 6ft wheelbase, with smaller than usual 2ft 8½in wheels. Only one bogie was braked. B941029 appears to have been in overall light grey livery when photographed at Drem in 1963.
DON ROWLAND

The second and many subsequent batches of BBDs produced by BR were based on the LNER's Diagram 205. They were given BR Diagram 1/472, and over 2,000 were built up to 1959. Only the first 200, however, had the LNER version of the diamond frame bogie, as carried here by B941346, built in 1951. These were of 5ft 6in wheelbase, with standard 3ft 1in wheels, and each was independently braked. When photographed at Sellafield in 1964, B941346 had been newly repainted in the 'boxed lettering' style, and seems to have been one of the unfitted wagons treated to bauxite livery at this time. DON ROWLAND

All BBDs built by or for BR were of 42 tons capacity and 52ft length over headstocks, whatever the origin of their design. B941621 was constructed in 1954 to Diagram 1/472, and illustrates the GWR-based plate bogie carried not only by the majority of BBDs, but also by many BBCs as well. ROGER CARPENTER

Below: *On the Diagram 1/472 wagons, the outermost of the LNER-pattern steel and timber bolsters were movable, and this elevated view of 1956-built B942667 at Immingham in 1991 shows a glimpse of the alternative location for the nearest one, together with the four possible positions for each of the stanchions, and the distinctive reinforced buffer guides, another LNER-inspired feature.* AUTHOR

Twelve hundred Bogie Bolster Es were built in the early 1960s with the modern bogies, roller bearings and vacuum brakes that were being fitted to the last of the BBCs and BBDs turned out around the same time. As can be seen from this photograph (taken at Drem in 1963 – B941029 was at the head of the same train), BBEs were quite short, only 32ft over headstocks, but of the same 30 tons capacity as a BBC – later uprated to 32 tons. Here B923532 was flanked by an ex-LMS double bolster and single No. B917414 in use as runners beneath the overhanging load. DON ROWLAND

Four batches of Macaws H/Bogie Bolster As were built to GWR Diagram J25 between 1927 and 1936. Nos. 107105 (seen at Crewkerne in 1948) and W107188 (Eastleigh, 1959) were both from the first lot, while W107344 (Eastleigh, 1950) was from the fourth. A close-up of the bogie of this wagon is also shown.

A. E. WEST

25 Tons. Tare 14.4

In the absence of a photograph of one of the twenty BBAs built to Diagram J30, we can usefully examine its big brother. Although built at Swindon more than ten years later to BR Diagram 1/471, B943080 was essentially similar apart from its greater overall length, down to the 'missing' curb rail above the headstocks. (Wagons built to the same diagram at the same time by Metro Cammell appeared with the curb rail restored.) As with the BBAs, B943080 had three possible positions for the outer bolsters, and featured the lever-type brakes fitted to the J30 wagons. It was photographed in 'as new' condition at Congresbury in Somerset. J. H. MOSS

The only volume-production, steam-era, bogie bolster available in 4mm scale is the Bachmann BBC. This is an original Mainline example, forerunner of the Bachmann model, and represents the bulk of GWR-period construction, though requiring comparatively little modification to reproduce many of the BR-built examples.

Apart from BBEs (and a few other odd code letters relating to conversions for special purposes), in its first twenty-five years BR built only BBCs and Ds. To substantial numbers of both types inherited in 1948, the nationalised authority added several thousand more, culminating in the air-braked Ds (known as BDAs), which are still with us. In model form these are represented by a kit in the Cambrian range, and enterprising modellers may well be able to convert the kit to an earlier prototype; unfitted BBDs were in fact rebuilt to produce the BDAs in the late 'seventies. This and the Lima BBE apart, however, all the traditional bolster wagons available in kit or ready-to-run form are of pre-nationalisation or pre-grouping design.

Of these, only the Bachmann (ex-Mainline) BBC reflects a type produced in really significant numbers, namely the GWR's Macaw B, of which over 1,700 were built between 1907 and 1946. However, for various evolutionary reasons not all of these were the same as the model in every respect: in particular, the first 330 to diagrams J11 and J4 had bar trussing rather than the model's angle pattern (and the J11 had a slightly shorter wheelbase into the bargain); whilst the last 250 to Diagram J28, on which BR's standard BBC design was closely based, had lever-type brakes instead of the model's Dean-Churchward gear as fitted to earlier diagrams, and dispensed with curb rails above the headstocks at each end (though this was a feature that BR soon restored).

The next most numerous type to be represented in model form was another GWR design, the Macaw H (BBA from 1943), which ran to 305 examples. This is the subject of both an etched brass kit from Connoisseur Models and a ready-to-run offering from Hornby: once again, the progenitor of this version was in the Mainline range. Yet another GWR vehicle, the Macaw G, is covered by the venerable Ratio Kit: dimensionally similar to the H, a mere twenty of these had been built in 1911 for the Taff Vale Railway. In fact, the only non-GWR wagon currently available as far as I know to represent pre-1948 designs is Parkside's LNER Quad: this is another pre-grouping vehicle, this time from the North Eastern Railway, and whilst they were rather more numerous than the Macaw G, they couldn't properly be described as mainstream either in terms of design or numbers built.

So the choice for the only bogie goods wagon to be represented in these pages really comes down to either a Macaw B/BBC or a Macaw H/BBA. Either might be seen in a branch-line or pick-up goods context carrying, say, round timber or telegraph poles. The Bachmann BBC has the added benefits of being able to be run in multiple on a main line layout and of being capable of being adapted without too much trouble to produce later variants of the breed: substitution of lever-type brakes, and one or two minor cosmetic modifications to the bogie sideframes, would produce a very acceptable model of wagons of the type built up to 1956.

Nevertheless, I chose the Connoisseur kit of the BBA. Originally rated at 20 tons and later uprated to 25, these were built between 1927 and 1941 to two diagrams: all but the final twenty were turned out to diagram J25, and were fitted with Dean-Churchward brakegear; the remaining wagons were to J30 and had lever-type brakes. The kit is in fact a slight mixture of the two. It has the diagram number J30 etched on the solebar, and lever-pattern brakegear to suit. However, it also has the low sides or curb rails above the headstocks which J30 wagons, like the last of the Macaw Bs, dispensed with; and the numbers quoted in the instruction leaflet are for the J25s.

Removing the curb rails at the ends seemed easier than altering the brakegear (although, as will become clear, I ended up making some changes to this in any case), and so I decided to build the kit as one of the J30 batch, numbered 32710–29. The only photograph I found of one of these, 32728, appears in *GWR Goods Wagons* and in the long-out-of-print *A Pictorial Record of Great Western Wagons*, where it is slightly better reproduced, but wrongly described in the caption as a Macaw B. Both books have additional pictures – with a further overlap – of J25 examples, and an official view of 107361 can be found in both *GWR Goods Wagons* and *Great Western Wagons Appendix*. A photo of 107404 not reproduced elsewhere is in *Pre-Nationalisation Freight Wagons on British Railways*. Finally, outline drawings of both diagrams appear in *GWR Goods Wagons* and *Great Western Wagons Plan Book*. The similarity of detail in many cases between Macaws B and H is helpful in extending the references available.

According to the kit's instructions, the first job is to bend over the top lip or flange on the sides and ends. Because wagons built to J30 lacked the ends, I had already broken these off, but bending the flanges on the sides using only a flat piece of wood and finger pressure as suggested didn't seem to work for me, so I resorted to using a pair of smooth-jawed pliers, and bent them over a bit at a time. I found the brass was quite soft enough to iron out any creases thus caused using the same pliers.

At this stage you may want to consider whether the wagon is to run loaded or empty. Unladen bogie bolsters tended to look slightly banana-shaped (hogged, to use a nautical term), only flattening out when they were loaded. The longer the wagon, the more pronounced was the effect, but even BBAs were prone to it. Having decided that I wanted an empty one, I found it was quite easy to induce a small upward deflection using fingers alone; in fact, it was easy to overdo it: half a millimetre in the centre of the body is about the most that's needed. Of course the solebars required the same treatment once the top and bottom flanges had been bent over. If you're going to do this, make sure you arch them the right way: the etched holes for the lashing rings are nearer the top.

Having tinned the backs of the half-etched solebar overlays, I sweated them into place. At this point I departed from the suggested order of assembly by making and fitting the lashing rings before attaching the solebars to the floor: something told me this would be easier with the solebars separate. The instructions also tell you to form the rings round the handle of a needle file. Well, all my needle files were much too large. I used 30 swg nickel-silver wire wound like a coil spring round a length of plastic rod with a diameter of 1.5mm. This give you a series of rings (you need fourteen) of around 2mm outside diameter. Again, I had no split pins small enough to fit the etched holes in the solebar and overlay, even when these had been drilled out a bit, so I made my own using the 0.5mm brass wire supplied with the kit. The result is neater if you file the wire flat on one side (half-round wire would save this job, though it only takes a few seconds) before bending it over a length of the wire used to make the rings and clenching it to make the eye of your split pin. When cutting the pin away from the main part of the half-round wire, it's a good idea to make one leg slightly longer than the other: it makes it a lot easier to get the pin into the hole.

As well as soldering the protruding ends of the pins behind the solebar, I also soldered the rings to the eyes of the pins with the joint of each ring in the eye itself. This makes the rings appear to hang naturally even when the wagon is handled, and avoids the risk of a ring being pulled apart if it snags on something. Of course, if the wagon is to run loaded, the rings used for the securing chains wouldn't just hang loosely; in this case, it would be best to solder them up only after the chains have been fitted and tensioned over the load.

I noted, but didn't act on, the fact that the two outermost rings on each side are set very slightly higher than the five between them, as the prototype photographs prove. The kit doesn't provide for this, but on reflection I think it might have been possible to simulate it by bending the eye of the relevant split pins up at an angle before fitting them.

It's necessary to cut and file the legs of one pin on each side flush with the back of the solebar, namely the one just inside the right-hand queen post where the V-hanger is located. This is certainly easier to do with the solebars detached. When fitting the solebars, it isn't immediately obvious that it's the backs of them that should be matched to the half-etched dotted lines on the underside of the floor, though this becomes clear by reference to photographs. They are, in fact, considerably wider-spaced than on a normal four-wheel wagon. A modicum of care is needed to ensure that each is simultaneously in the correct position in both fore-and-aft and transverse planes and square to the floor as well. Once they are, the fitting of the headstocks and trussing should present no problems, although I found a little bit of judicious filing was necessary to the ends of both the solebars and the headstocks to get the flanges to mate snugly and the headstocks parallel with the ends of the floor.

The brakegear was the only area where I met any real problems with the kit. To begin with, when I folded up the four V-hangers using the half-etched lines to produce the baseplates by which they are attached to the floor, I found that the hole in the apex of each of the vees was partly obstructed by the trussing, whereas it should have been clear of it by at least a millimetre. Straightening out the vees and refolding them to give clearance wasn't difficult, and I reamed out the holes slightly to take cross-shafts of 0.7mm wire, to which I added a pair of short cranks fashioned from 10-thou brass, intending in due course to furnish these with pull-rods passing out of sight above the bogies.

The etched brake lever guard provided with the kit is of the normal pinhole pattern. Masokits provide an etching for the correct GWR toothed rack which incorporates a stay by which the foot of the guard would usually be tied to the nearest axleguard. On these vehicles the stay rises in line with the lever guard to brace it to the truss behind it. The etched stay is therefore at completely the wrong angle for this, but fortunately the brass is quite soft, and anyone with a sense of adventure and a pair of fine pliers can persuade it to adopt the straight and narrow path without the result looking too much of a bodge.

It was at this point that I realised that the position of the lever guard shown on the drawing that accompanies the kit is rather too close to the queen post: according to the diagram in *GWR Goods Wagons*, which seems to be confirmed by the only available photograph, it should be about 5mm further to the right. This makes the etched brake levers too short by at least the same amount, so I cut and filed a pair of my own from sheet brass. In fact, I made them about 8mm longer to give a spigot by which the right-hand end of the handle was extended to pass through a hole drilled just above the lower solebar flange, into which it was then soldered for added security.

The bolsters and stanchions are white-metal castings. Because the outer bolsters were movable to alternative positions on the real thing, there are also four extra cast stanchion pockets on each side. I drilled blind $\frac{1}{32}$in holes in the tops of these just for the effect, and opened out the dimples on the tops of the bolsters in the same way before epoxying them into position. When I came to look critically at the stanchions, however, they struck me as being rather vulnerable to breakage, so I cut off the posts themselves and drilled the tops of these pockets rather deeper – about 2mm, in fact. The kit includes a length of 1mm brass rod, whose real purpose is a bit of a mystery: it was too large for the brake cross-shafts because the holes etched in the V-hangers wouldn't stand reaming out that far. However, it was just about right for replacement stanchions, except that there wasn't enough meat in the castings to drill them at this diameter. So I turned down (roughly, with a file) 2mm of the end of

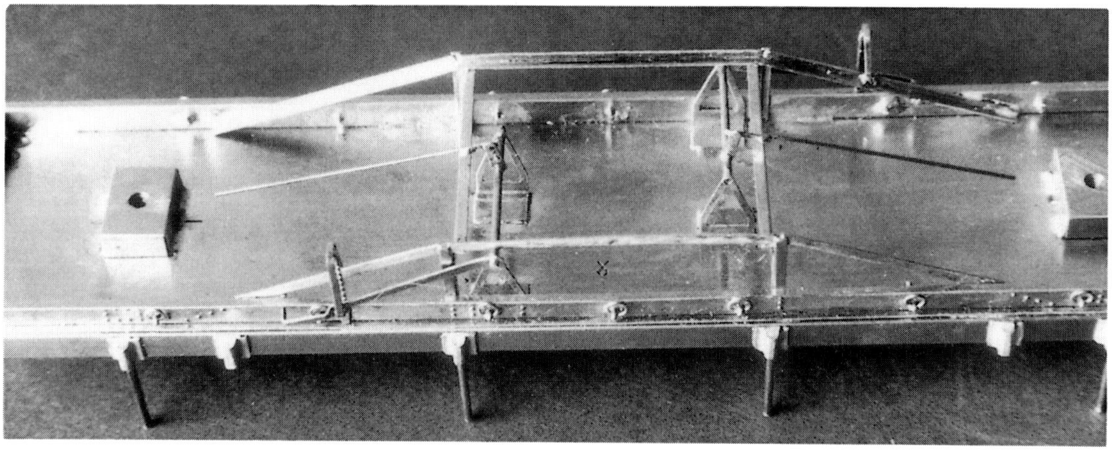

The relatively few modifications made to the Connoisseur BBA kit are described in the text. One area that could stand a measure of extra detail is the bogie sideframes. As the prototype photos show, these were quite heavily riveted, and the faces of the axleboxes weren't as plain as the castings appear. A thin plastic overlay could be used for the axleboxes, and a surprisingly effective way of adding rivets to whitemetal is to impress the visible surface with a punch, a drill or a needle. Other than at very close range, this deception can be remarkably convincing.

each one till it fitted the 1/32 in hole, into which it was then epoxied. At least now they don't bend if you breathe on them. A few lengths of chain glued randomly to the wagon bed completed the superstructure.

The bogies too are whitemetal, each one consisting of two sideframes and a stretcher bar-cum-pivot, which rely for strength and squareness on some rather basic locating lugs where they meet. Holding everything together in a dry run to test the fit of bearings and wheelsets wasn't easy, but after several attempts I came to the conclusion that even with the deepest-coned bearings I could find, there wasn't quite enough clearance for 26mm axles. So I countersunk the bearing holes using a 5/32 in drill bit twirled in my fingers just enough to allow the flanges of the bearings to sit flush with the rear surface of the casting, and glued the bearings in with a touch of Evostik – enough to stop them falling out, but not to make it too difficult to extract them if it turned out that I'd miscalculated.

The instructions offer no suggestions as to how to fix the bogie parts together, though most experienced modellers would probably choose low-temperature solder. The difficulty with this method is the same one that made my dry runs awkward, namely the lack of a foolproof means of locating the stretcher and the sideframe securely enough to ensure that the result is square from all angles while they're soldered together. For that reason I preferred to use two-part epoxy so that I could check the squareness from different directions while the glue went off. For added assurance I pinned the joints with wire passed through a 0.5mm hole drilled in both components, and waited until the first joint had properly hardened before fitting the second side.

The initial care taken to check, and then countersink, the bearings paid dividends in that, with the bogies assembled, the wheels revolved freely with minimal end float or slop. Had they erred a bit in either direction, it's comforting to know that whitemetal parts can always be tweaked a bit, but it's even better to find that it's not necessary.

The bogies swivel on etched boxes inside which you solder a nut before fitting them to the underside of the floor. I found it was necessary to clear the screw holes in both the mountings and the bogie stretchers, and took the advice in the instructions to screw the bolt and nut together while soldering the nut in place, and to oil the thread first to prevent locking everything solid. The notes also advise that it might prove necessary to insert washers between the bogie pivot and the mounting in order to achieve the correct ride height; in fact, I found that the completed wagon did sit about 1/2 mm too low, but more noticeably it also sat a bit lopsidedly. To counteract this, I soldered pads of different thickness to each side of the mounting. Actually, I think I would have packed the body up by this method anyway, even if it had sat squarely, in order to reduce any risk of the body rocking when in motion. Whenever you see a bogie vehicle of any kind waddling down the track it's usually because the pivot area is too narrow, and it pays to widen the bearing surface out as much as possible, at one end if not at both.

Seen at Eastleigh in 1949, Macaw B/Bogie Bolster C No. 84122 had been built to GWR Diagram J4 before World War One. The flat bar trussing would soon give way for new construction to angle iron, but the bogie design remained substantially unchanged for several more decades.

A. E. WEST

PIPE AND TUBE WAGONS

B740904, seen here at Niddrie in 1962, was a Diagram 1/460 pipe wagon, originally built unfitted and later converted to vacuum braking, as represented by the Parkside kit. DON ROWLAND

Perhaps more than any other type dealt with in this chapter, pipe wagons come closest to the definition of specialist vehicles. They originated as an LNER design in the mid-'thirties whose purpose was to carry drainage pipes from the works of the well-known Stanton & Staveley Company near Ilkeston, and wagons to a very similar specification were still being built by BR twenty-five years later for the same traffic. In all, well over two thousand were produced, and they travelled far and wide to wherever new drainage schemes were being undertaken. As the traffic for which they were intended gradually declined, they drifted into more general use, carrying almost anything for which a high-sided merchandise wagon would be used. Many were later transferred to departmental use, where their full-length drop sides were especially valued, a move which prolonged their lives into very recent times.

The LNER-built vehicles were all equipped with that company's style of full vacuum brakegear, and BR constructed an identical batch of 300 wagons in 1949. However, the bulk of post-nationalisation production was to a very closely-related design of LMS origin, also commencing in 1949. The LMS hadn't, in fact, built any of its own, although around the same time an unknown number of its double bolsters was converted to carry pipes from the makers' other works near Chesterfield. Unlike the LNER wagons, the 800 built up to 1954 to the LMS pattern were all unfitted, but with the adoption of vacuum braking on new construction from 1955, the earlier ones were quickly retrofitted, and by 1960 only a handful remained unconverted.

Some years ago a composite plastic and whitemetal kit for the LNER design was marketed by Nu-Cast. Strictly speaking, it represented only the first 50 of these, which were a few inches narrower over the body than those that followed. Examples of this earliest batch certainly outlasted the end of steam, but if you were able to overlook, or compensate for, such minor differences as four inches in width and changes in axlebox design, the kit could have been used for both the later LNER wagons and those built to BR diagram 1/461 as well, which lasted considerably longer. More recently, however, an etched kit for the later vehicles has been released by Connoisseur Models (Pocket Money Kits).

The LMS-style vehicles are covered by a kit from Parkside. According to the instructions it represents the 800 built to D1/460, although since it is designed to be built in vacuum-fitted form, it only covers their life from 1955 at the earliest. However, the alterations necessary to build it in unfitted condition are very straightforward, and it could also be used for the remaining 850 turned out up to 1961 to diagrams 462 and 463 – most of them without any alterations at all except for the fitting of different cleats for sheet ties.

The two best sources of information on BR-built pipe wagons are *An Illustrated History of BR Wagons, Volume One*, and an article by David Larkin on the D1/460 vehicles in the September 1982 issue of *Model Trains*. Volume One of his series *Working Wagons* is also helpful. What is probably the best published photo of a pipe wagon – certainly of an unfitted one – can be found in *Freight Wagons and Loads in service on the GWR and BR, WR*; this shows B740652 as turned out by Swindon Works in 1953, at which time the timberwork of new wagons was still being left unpainted, and it was this vehicle that I chose to model.

All you need to do to build the kit in unfitted form is to omit the vacuum cylinder, remove the lamp irons and axleguard tiebars and change the buffers from hydraulic to spindle – I used 18in RCH ones from MJT. However, the kit benefits from a few other modifications, chiefly in the areas of the solebars and the brakegear. In fact, the only addition I made to the body was the twenty-two small clips over the capping irons on the top edge of the sides and ends, each formed from three scraps of 5-thou strip. These appear to have been a standard fitting on all the wagons in BR days.

In dealing with three of the kits we've looked at in this chapter, I've drawn attention to the fact that higher capacity wagons often had wider, heavier-duty axleguards, and offered some suggestions as to how these may be arrived at. Here, however, we have the opposite case: the solebar mouldings incorporate heavy-duty axleguards (of the type we've seen fitted to the BR plate wagon) which pipe wagons didn't have because, being of only twelve tons capacity, they didn't need them. All the photographs and drawings I've seen show that they were equipped with standard BR axleguards (or RCH ones in the case of the LNER-built vehicles) – look for the six inches or so of vertical profile below the inclined sides, and the vee-shaped openings behind the springs on each side of the central aperture. Fortunately, it's not difficult to alter the mouldings with file, drill and craft knife. You also need to chisel off the riveted hornguide reinforcement on either side of the axlebox.

The solebars themselves are unfortunately rather featureless. In particular, they lack the four triangular body support brackets above the axleguards, and the lower half of the door control spring mechanisms. I compensated for these omissions with 5- and 10-thou plastic; as is the way of things, these fittings don't show up very well on the majority of photographs, but reference to the section on Medfits in Part One may give you some idea of what the door controllers looked like. I also filled in the space behind the downward extension of the central door pillar, which fronted a substantial plate bracket linking it to the solebar.

As is often the case with plastic kits, the brake levers don't really do justice to the complex profile of the real thing, especially on the lifting-link side. I overlaid the mouldings in a few places to accentuate the shape of the original, and contrived to bend and file the bottom link so that it fitted behind the V-hanger as it should. Finally, I anchored the bottom of each of the lever guards to the axleguard with an approximation of a check strap filed from 40-thou strip, and tied the rather weak handle ends of the levers themselves to the underside of the solebar with more noggins of 40-thou which I hope will be fairly hard to detect when the underframe has received its customary coat of dirty browny-grey.

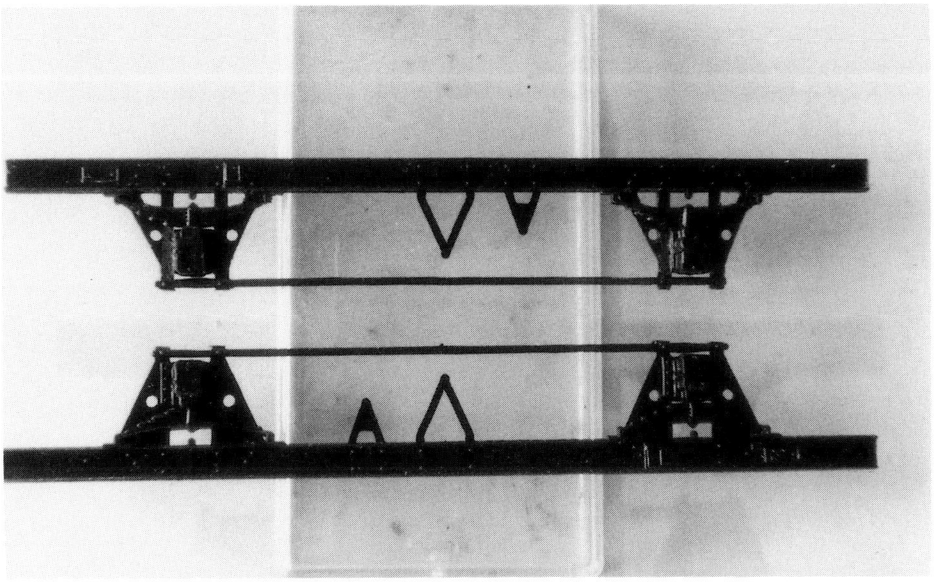

A comparison of the pipe wagon's reduced axleguards (top) with the heavy-duty originals as moulded.

Brakegear apart, there were relatively few differences between the LMS-designed pipe wagon adopted as the BR standard and the older LNER equivalent. The Parkside kit of the former, with its modest modifications, compares with the veteran Nu-Cast kit of the latter (in the process of renumbering to reflect the fact that, strictly speaking, this represented only the very first batch built to this design, a point I had overlooked when I put it together).

Successors to the GWR's Open C (recoded Tube during World War Two) were its Diagram O41 vehicles, which were longer, and classed as Tubes from new. Although this was a BR-built wagon, the four-plank sides and the lashing rings in the tops of the side stanchions, not to mention the toothed brake rack and the distinctive angle-trussing, clearly reveal its parentage. Seen at Worcester in the 1960s, the absence of black patches behind the lettering suggests that, although unfitted, it was in bauxite (except for some unpainted planking). Such aberrations were not entirely unknown at any time, but for a short while after the livery changes of 1963/4, some unfitted wagons did appear in bauxite, and B731011 could well have been one of them.

ROGER CARPENTER

These two tube wagons appear at first sight to be the same, and both were in fact built to the same LMS diagram, No. 1675. The older of the pair, however, M337562, seen at Carlisle in 1960, had Morton brakes and plain side doors, while the younger, 499594, pictured new, had 20-ton slotted link gear and merchandise doors. The vehicle glimpsed to the left of M337562 seems to have been one of the rather elusive ex-LNER fixed-sided tube wagons, in this case unfitted, although both vacuum-fitted and hand-braked examples were built.

DON ROWLAND and HMRS

The 900 wagons to Diagram 1945 were 3ft 6in longer than those to Diagram 1675 although they shared the same wheelbase. M492086 is also seen at Carlisle in 1960. The steel works at Corby was a common return destination for empty tube wagons for many years, although, as here, they were used routinely for a variety of bulky general merchandise as well. DON ROWLAND

Although their code name suggests that they were as dedicated in use as pipe wagons, tubes were in fact always used for a much wider range of bulky general traffics. Nothing exemplifies this better than the GWR's Open C: 1,200 of these long-wheelbase, four-plank open merchandise wagons were built between 1907 and 1939, with much the same kind of evolutionary development that was shown by their shorter contemporaries. Only during World War II were they re-coded as Tubes, perhaps as much by analogy with existing LMS and LNER designs, to which they bore a measure of similarity, as to reflect any significant change in use.

Another pointer to tubes generally being regarded as large open merchandise wagons is the fact that all four of the designs inherited by BR from the GWR and the LMS had small drop doors in the centre of each side, just like standard high-sided opens. Only the LNER bucked this trend at all, bequeathing an eclectic series of designs, one of which had two pairs of cupboard doors, another full-length drop-sides very similar to its pipe wagons, only longer, and a third completely fixed sides with no opening of any kind.

The LNER was also on its own in fitting full vacuum brakegear to some of its wagons, including the pipe wagon lookalikes, of which BR built a further five hundred to diagram number 1/445. A kit is available for this version from Connoisseur Models (Pocket Money Kits). The fixed-sided vehicles came in both fitted and unfitted forms, but like the cupboard-door wagons, which were unfitted, they seem to have been particularly camera-shy. I know of only two published photographs, both of fitted wagons: one in *Pre-Nationalisation Freight Wagons on British Railways* and a second in the February 2003 issue of *Backtrack*. However, although only a hundred of the vac-fitted design were built (numbered 301602 to 301701), examples lasted well into the 'eighties in departmental use.

The GWR's two types of tube wagon, on the other hand, were unfitted and remained so throughout their lives. Nevertheless, both designs outlasted the steam era. The Open C was the subject of an early Ratio plastic kit (of which more anon), and has more recently appeared in cast whitemetal from David Geen, but no kit has materialised for the longer post-war version coded Tube from the beginning. A hundred of these were built by the GWR to its diagram O41, and a further hundred appeared after nationalisation to BR's D1/446. A drawing can be found in *GWR Goods Wagons*, and the best published photograph is in *Freight Wagons and Loads in service on the GWR and BR, WR*.

All the LMS wagons, over two thousand of them, were unfitted as well. Three main diagrams were involved, culminating in the 300 vehicles turned out to D2116 shortly before nationalisation, a further 490 of which were built by BR as their D1/447 – once again, we shall come back to these in due course. The first of the standard designs produced by or for the LMS comprised the 950 wagons built mainly by the trade between 1925 and 1936 to D1675. This (and all subsequent LMS tubes) shared the 17ft 6in underframe that we've already seen beneath contemporary plates and double bolsters, and Ian Kirk took advantage of this in marketing his kit for the early style of tube wagon; as with the double bolster, this is now produced by Colin Ashby. The evolution in brakegear design described in respect of the other two types was evident here as well, coupled in this case with a small, but highly visible, change in the design of the side door: from 1933 'merchandise' or 'sack-truck' doors were fitted, characterised by the angled bottom plank that eased the job of barrowing goods into and out of a

wagon when the door was being used as a ramp onto an adjacent loading dock.

Now, whether the change from Morton to 20-ton slotted-link brakegear occurred at the same time I haven't been able to establish, although I suspect it happened sooner. In any event, all the photos I've seen of wagons with the new door design show the later brakegear as well. But the kit matches Morton brakes with merchandise doors, so altering one or the other seems inevitable. Which you choose is really up to you: if you have a spare lever incorporating the slotted link (the Parkside BR tube wagon mouldings provide two, only one of which is needed for that kit), it's perhaps marginally easier to fit this than to file the angled bottom door plank and hinges flat on both sides. The only extra bit you require for the new pattern of brakegear is the second, smaller V-hanger that supports the main lever, which can easily be cut from 20- or 30-thou plastic sheet. This was the route I took on this occasion, and apart from adding the usual clips over the capping irons on top of the bodysides, it was the only further modification I made to the model I'd built a long time ago from the original Kirk kit when I came to review it critically for this exercise. Had I been putting it together nowadays, I would have incorporated all the modifications I made to the double bolster underframe, instead of just reversing one side of the brakegear moulding as I had done at the time, and adding door springs bent up from strip brass.

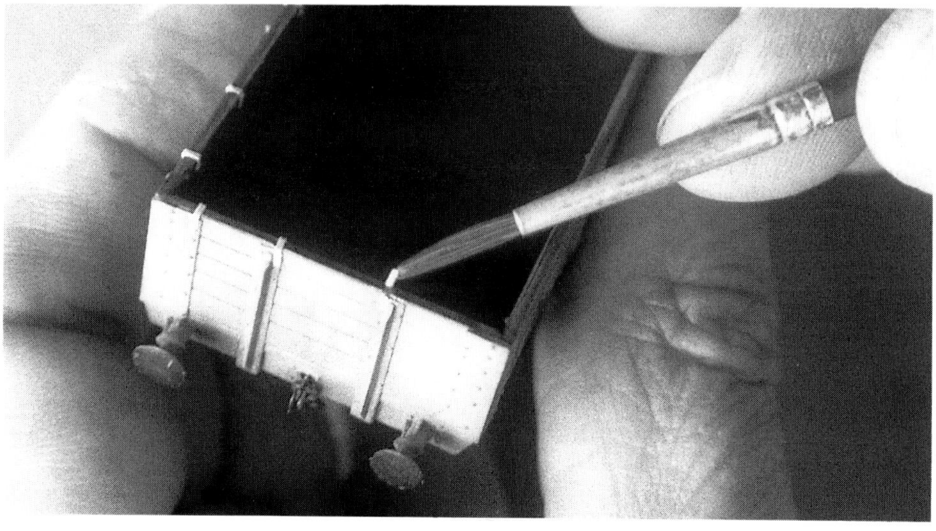

Had I been building this Ian Kirk/Colin Ashby kit of the LMS D1675 Tube today, I would have modified the axleguards and springs in the way I described for the D1949 Double Bolster. As it was, the only fresh modifications I made for the purposes of this survey were the change from Morton to 20-ton lifting-link brakegear, and the addition of the small brackets or clips over the capping irons. These were added in 5-thou, each one in three pieces picked up on the tip of a brush charged with solvent. After a few seconds, the solvent softens the plastic enough to enable the ends of the strips across the top to be moulded to the slightly rounded shape of the top edge of the bodyside, though they still need to be cleaned up gently with a file when set hard. The rather haphazard and untidy positioning of the clips is quite prototypical.

Returning to the Ratio GWR Open C, this model was even older than the LMS tube, having been built, I calculate, at least thirty years ago when the world was young. It had received a partial update since then – really no more than a fresh coat of paint – but when I compared it with the drawings and pictures in *GWR Goods Wagons* I realised that I had incorporated a number of faults into it, partly through my own inexperience at the time, and partly because of flaws in the kit itself. Most obviously, the V-hangers, which should be at 6ft centres, were much too close together, and instead of Dean-Churchward levers I had fitted standard RCH-type brake levers pivoting on the right-hand vee of each pair. And the axleguards came with long springs, auxiliary suspension and axleboxes that weren't much like anything ever fitted to Open Cs.

The body, on the other hand, seemed a fair representation of the real thing. *GWR Goods Wagons* has a table listing the six diagrams involved (including the longer, post-war design), and the fittings that changed as each one was introduced. Bearing in mind my own modelling period up to ten years after nationalisation, I wanted a reasonably modern example of the breed. Diagram O34, the last 'real' Open C, had sacktruck doors, 9in corner plates, exposed floorboard ends and straight-down side stanchions in L-section; all these are different from the kit, and the latter in particular would have involved a fair degree of work, since the kit features the turned-under, T-section pattern fitted to all previous diagrams. The next-to-the-last diagram, O28, also had sacktruck doors, which by themselves would have been a relatively straightforward modification, but in the end I opted for O19, which was built up to 1927, and whose body required nothing more than a few detail embellishments and the substitution of GWR self-contained buffers (of which I happened to have a set in stock) for the spindle type supplied with the kit.

The embellishments apply generally to the first three diagrams, and with one exception to O28 as well, although the retaining clips over the capping irons weren't added until around the time of nationalisation, and the distinctive lashing rings at the top of the vertical side stanchions weren't originally fitted to the earliest diagram, O8. Instead, these had a pair of chain lockers outside the solebars on each side until they were removed in favour of the rings. Neither was featured by Ratio, but the David Geen kit specifically represents the earliest wagons and includes the lockers, together with notes describing the process of their replacement. In both cases, therefore, it's up to the builder to make and fit the rings, and I bent mine up from 30swg nickel-silver wire. Having satisfied myself that I'd got a more-or-less circular ring 1.5 to 2mm in diameter, I opened the ends out enough to slip one of them through a .45mm hole drilled as close as I dared to the top of the stanchion, and then gently clenched them together again. A dab of solvent helped to stop the ring flapping around loosely.

Up to and including diagram O19, the protruding web of the stanchions tapered in towards the top. The rings make it difficult to reproduce this taper accurately, but I did my best to shave a few thou off each one as a token gesture. At the bottom the web turns in under the bodyside before bending through another ninety degree angle to where the stanchion is fastened to the solebar. The horizontal section of the web beneath the body was missing from the mouldings, so I stuck short lengths of 15-thou strip where they should be, rounding off the outer corner with a file once they had set hard.

Finally, I cut off the rather representational door springs and replaced them in metal strip. The idea was to force-fit a tongue on each spring through a slot above the bottom solebar flange formed by joining up a pair of 1/64in holes drilled through the foot of the bracket moulded on the face of the solebar. In a couple of cases, though, the theory fell foul of plastic's well-known tendency to go brittle with age, causing bits of the solebar to fracture and break off as I tried to push the metal through it. A rather larger than usual dab of epoxy fixed the springs in position, and I replaced the broken sections with noggins of styrene. Incidentally, should you have to do this at any time, it's a lot easier to file the damaged area into some kind of regular, right-angled shape than to try to match your repair piece to the uneven profile of the break.

The Ratio Open C in original and modified guises.

A close-up of the revamped model highlights the alterations made to the original. Bill Bedford's etched quadrant on the inner end of the brake lever shaft shows up well.

Below the solebar I replaced everything except for the V-hangers and the four separate brakeshoe-cum-pushrod mouldings, although I did shorten the pushrods by a couple of millimetres or so to accommodate the wider setting of the vees. A cross-shaft joins each of the vees to its opposite number on the other side of the wagon, and cranks roughly in the middle of each shaft are connected by a series of rods to the brake levers at the extreme right-hand end of each side. I didn't try to represent this system in entirety, but I used some of Bill Bedford's etched parts for Dean-Churchward III brakegear for the triangular lever mounting brackets and their inboard counterparts, together with the cranks that convert the rotary action of the shaft between each pair to a pulling force on the operating rods. I also used his etch for the toothed quadrant at one end, which always seems to be the same end as the upper pair of brake pushrods. These parts are about all you can see even on the best photographs of the workings of this highly individualistic brakegear. I would have used levers from the same source, but I felt they were a bit short by comparison with all the pictures I could find of Open Cs, so I filed and bent my own up from 10-thou brass strip cut from a sheet.

The axleguards and the GWR oil axlebox and spring castings are from MJT. Although the axleguards are etched in pairs and designed with compensation in mind, this would have meant removing substantial chunks of the moulded underframe members; since I was building a rigid wagon, however, I cut each of the axleguards out separately together with a portion of the adjoining base. Folded into an L-shape, this gave a more secure fitting than would have been the case if I had just Evo-stuck the bare axleguard to the back of the solebar. Because the system is designed for compensation, it was necessary to pack each unit off the underside of the floor by up to 40-thou/1mm, and using the etched fold lines in this way also guaranteed that the centre of each bearing would be a constant distance below the solebar. As I've mentioned elsewhere, in order to achieve the normal rail to buffer centre height of 13.5/14mm (3ft 5in or thereabouts on the real thing), this gap is generally 6mm or slightly less.

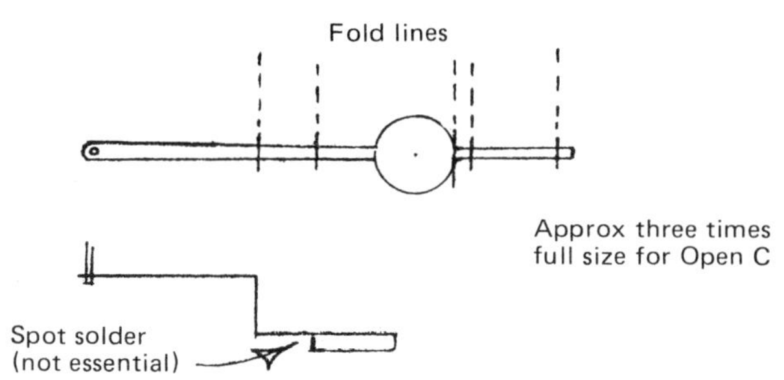

One-piece GWR brake levers

With the alterations touched up and suitably relettered, the Open C/Tube stands in front of two of the vans dealt with in Part Two.

Photographed loaded with wire rod in coil for export at Immingham in 1967 are two BR-built tube wagons. The nearer one, B731194, is an example of Diagram 1/447, unfitted and with unpainted woodwork. Behind it was one of the slightly longer Diagram 1/448 wagons, vacuum-fitted and in bauxite livery. It appears to have been carrying the sub-code 'Batten' to the right of the capacity, signifying that it was one of the many tubes of this design to have been fitted with wooden bearers across the floor. AUTHOR'S COLLECTION

Although BR's standard tube wagon design, diagram 1/448, was closely based on the final LMS version, it wasn't quite the same, being 18in longer in the body and a foot more in wheelbase. Parkside's kit for this wagon allows you to build several variations of the 2,350 that were ultimately produced, with a choice of fitted or unfitted brakegear, two styles of axlebox and two patterns of buffer. As we've seen, however, before settling on this design, BR had built a batch that was identical (in all but one significant respect) to the last wagons turned out by the LMS, and so I examined the kit to see what would be involved in constructing it as the shorter D1/447, and whether it might be possible to build any or all of the last 1,200 pre-nationalisation vehicles from it as well.

Although I couldn't find a drawing for D1/447, a diagram of D2116 is included in *An Illustrated History of LMS Wagons, Vol I*; so, too, is the earlier D1945, which had wooden ends instead of corrugated steel ones, and a general arrangement drawing for this variation can be found in *Official Drawings of LMS Wagons, No. 1*. From these I concluded that about two-thirds of the overall 6mm difference in length is in the panels on either side of the central drop door, with the balance being divided between the two outer panels. Although it's a bit of a short cut, it's possible to remove a millimetre from each of the mitred corners without the reduction in the width of the corner plates being too noticeable. Taking two millimetres off each of the inner panels is less straightforward, if only because of the problem of rejoining the three sections of the bodyside securely once the surgery has been done: on an open wagon there's no scope for reinforcing the joint invisibly, and a plain butt joint is unlikely to be very strong.

The answer in these circumstances was a lapped joint. I started by cutting the side into three down the inside edge of the vertical stanchions between the inner and outer panels, and then carved and filed the diagonal ironwork off the face of the inner ones. The next stage is to reduce by a half the thickness of each panel alongside the cuts over a width of 2mm; this is best achieved by filing and scraping, but isn't made any easier by the otherwise commendably thin bodysides. You need to file away the front of the inner panels and the rear of the outer ones to protect the detail on the face of the latter. Having then rejoined the sections with each one overlapping the next by the 2mm width of the rebates, you can replace the diagonal (now at a slightly different angle, of course) in 5-thou styrene strip, and the vertical bolt-head detail that you've sacrificed on the inside. But first you should consider whether you need to hide the joint line on the inside with a sliver of 10-thou which can be filed smooth when set; on the outside, the fact that the cut was made right next to the vertical ironwork should disguise it satisfactorily.

To shorten the solebars it's best to cut them into three as well so as to preserve the V-hangers in the centre. Because these wagons were built unfitted and stayed that way, you only need to keep the two larger vees and one of the small ones; the second of the small vees and all the adjoining detail below the solebars should be removed. Being less visible on the finished model, it's less critical where you make the actual cuts, but it has to be somewhere between the inboard ends of the springs and the small vertical brackets that correspond with the stanchions on each side of the door. This time, though, it's enough just to cut 2mm out at each place and reconnect the three parts with plain butt joints, because you can invisibly reinforce the repairs with splints or flitch plates of 30- or 40-thou behind the solebars. Take care that the splints don't foul the ends of the transverse ribs beneath the floor – which needs to be shortened by 3mm at each end as well, needless to say.

This brings the axleguards the necessary 4mm closer together, and it only remains to cut a further 1mm off each outer end, although it makes a neater job if at the same time you scrape off the remains of the bracket plate moulded onto the face of the solebars and restore it to its full size in 5-thou.

Shortening the brakegear by cutting out the central tumbler and moving the ends closer together before replacing the tumbler is also necessary, of course. So too is the job of shortening the brake levers: here again, a lapped or rebated joint is stronger, and assurance can be made doubly sure by adding a narrow strengthening splint behind it. Two small modifications not associated with this surgery that can also be made to the levers are to bend and file the short bottom crank on the slotted link side so that it fits behind the V-hanger, and to beef up the handle end with a strip of 30-thou to make it look as if it would clear the axlebox when lowered.

A further modification is needed to represent D2116, the last of the LMS-built wagons. These had axleguards of the type we have already seen beneath the double bolster, whereas the kit has the BR plate variety. With care it would be possible to open up the horse-hook holes into a vee-shape and to add the characteristic bracing strut between the solebar and the inside bottom corner of the axleguard. For the BR period you could fit the rectangular platefront axleboxes supplied with the kit, although all the LMS-built wagons seem to have received split boxes from new, for which an alternative moulding or casting would be necessary. Finally, to go back a stage further to produce a wagon to LMS diagram D1945, new planked ends would also be required.

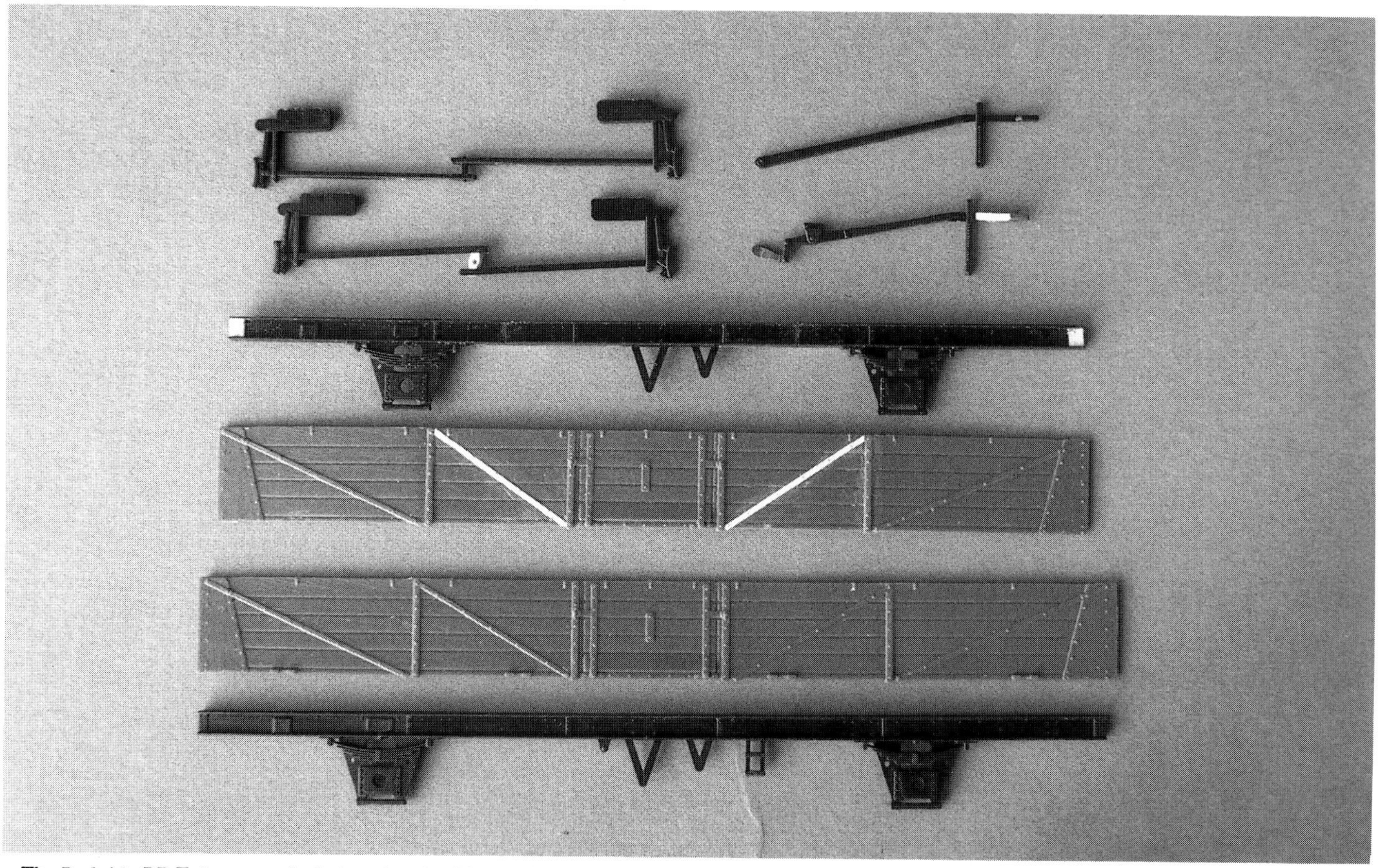

The Parkside BR Tube wagon is designed as the Diagram 1/448, but can be shortened by an overall 6mm to turn it into the slightly shorter D1/447. The reduction in the bodysides is achieved partly by cutting 2mm out of each of the panels nearest the side door, the balance by narrowing the corner plates. Corresponding shortening of the underframe and brakegear sections also reduces the wheelbase by the necessary 4mm.

CHAPTER THREE

BRAKE VANS

LMS 20-TON BRAKE VANS

Comparing this late Midland Railway brake van, photographed in 1961, with vans built during the early years of LMS production, makes the line of descent very clear. Indeed, even the most modern LMS vans bore many of the same hallmarks, especially in cabin design. The likely livery of DM 623 was black with yellow, or possibly white, markings. The 'Not in Common Use' legend relates as much to the absence of side duckets as to the van's transfer to departmental duties.
ROGER CARPENTER

The first departure from the pure Midland design was the introduction of side duckets on the 100 vacuum-braked vans to Diagram 1656 built in 1926/7. Photographed at Nine Elms in 1949, this one appears to have been No. 46.
A. E. WEST

MIDLAND-STYLE VANS

Goods brake vans built by the LMS during its first ten years or so were closely based on the Midland Railway design, and were, indeed, initially turned out to an MR diagram. Naturally enough, various changes took place during this period, and Parkside produce kits for the two most numerous types: diagram 1659, of which 849 were built between 1924 and 1927, and diagram 1657, which accounted for a further 950 vehicles from 1927 to 1931. I chose the latter, which lasted in traffic at least until the mid-'sixties; they were distinguished from their predecessors by flush-boarded end panels, and followed the slightly earlier, vacuum-fitted D1656 vans in having side-duckets (though these may not have been fitted in every case, it seems). The majority were hand-braked only, but the last fifty had through vacuum pipes, together with screw couplings and packed-out buffers.

Apart from the brief notes included in the kit instructions, information on these vehicles comes chiefly from *The LMS Wagon* and Volume One of *An Illustrated History of LMS Wagons*. Photographs appear in Volume Five of the Cheona series and both volumes of Wild Swan's *Official Drawings of LMS Wagons* contain pictures and general arrangement drawings of closely-related diagrams, though not of D1657 itself. But many features and fittings were common to the breed as a whole.

As you might expect, the kit represents the original as it was first built, and, one or two details aside, does so in a perfectly sound and accurate way. Anyone wanting a model of one of these vans in later life, however, should be aware of a number of very visible modifications made to many of them over the years. These were applied in a fairly haphazard manner, and some vehicles survived in more-or-less original condition throughout their life.

M328337, pictured in *An Illustrated History of LMS Wagons*, on the other hand,

Two vans built to Diagram 1657, seen as running in the early 'sixties. M294056 bore similar modifications to those described in the text, while M296579 lacked the extra beading above the ducket and the metal sheathing along the bottom of the cabin sides, but had received vacuum piping at some stage in its life – notice the white pipe indicating this form of braking, rather than full vacuum gear. Whether this was one of the original fifty so equipped is difficult to say, because of the random numbering applied to most of this diagram.
DON ROWLAND

The final flowering of the early, 20ft underframe vehicles was the hundred vans turned out to D 1940 in 1933/4. These had 14ft rather than 12ft wheelbase, as exemplified by No. 297435 seen in its original livery at Cardington in 1939. A. E. WEST seems to have experienced most of them, and it was this one I chose to model. By 1964 it had acquired prominent V-shaped ironwork on its sides, together with rather less obvious triangular brackets at the top inside corners of the verandah entrances – both, probably, to counteract a general weakening of the superstructure as the years wore on. In addition, all the joints of the sheeting above and around the ducket have been beaded over: I'm guessing that flexing of the body in service caused these joints either to leak or to encourage draughts, or both, to the discomfort of the guard inside. Deterioration of the bodyside woodwork is also the likely reason why many vans had the bottom 2–4 inches of boarding sheathed in metal. Lastly, extra bracket work has been applied to the three vertical end posts; some of this is in fact included in the kit, although the T-brackets on the offset intermediate post are not. For strict prototypical accuracy, however, anyone modelling a van in its early years may need to remove the vertical leg of the corner brackets at the top of the outer posts.

Incidentally, the offset centre upright was a feature inherited from the Midland, who fitted it with a lamp iron. By the early 'thirties the LMS had dispensed with lamps in this position, and the lamp iron was duly removed. The last of the diagrams for the 'short' vans, D1940, dating from 1933, lacked this fitting from new, and on these vehicles the middle post was accordingly relocated to the centre line of the body.

The kit lacks a lamp iron in this position, so it would need to be added to any model of these vehicles in their youth. The other eight are moulded onto the sides and ends, but they looked a bit skinny to me, so I replaced the projecting portion with L-shaped bits of brass strip, epoxied into 1⁄64 inch holes widened into a slot by carefully working the drill bit in and out. I say 'carefully' because this is an ideal way of breaking small drills, as I've proved to myself time and time again.

The remaining modifications were added in 5- or 10-thou styrene strip prior to the assembly of the body. I departed from the instructions in glazing the duckets before fitting them, reasoning that it might be easier to add the 5-thou beading around the apertures with the ducket as a separate unit. It was a fiddly job, all the same. And although the instructions recommend building the body around the floor, I followed my usual pattern of making up the shell of the body by first joining each pair of ends and sides to ensure the neatest possible corner joints. In doing this I may for once have been hoist by my own petard, for the floor and roof both ended up being a touch too short. The roof in particular had virtually no end overhang, and rather than taking the body apart and trying again, I extended it with a narrow strip of 30-thou plastic curved to the roof profile in my fingers, and filed to hide the joint when properly dry. According to the general arrangement drawings in the Wild Swan books, the overhang at each end should be 1¾ inches, or just under 0.6mm. I didn't fit the roof permanently at this stage: I felt it would be easier to paint the end partitions of the guard's cabin, especially the window reveals, with the roof off.

While we're talking about the roof, I should mention that the stove chimney is in the wrong place. Although correctly located for the earlier vans, the fitting of duckets caused the stove to be moved, and the chimney should in fact be about 11mm nearer to the end to which it is already closer. In cutting it off and re-attaching it on a small square of 5-thou plastic, I took the opportunity of drilling out the solid top to a depth of about a millimetre.

The roof moulding has continuous rainstrips, with which most of these first-generation vans appear to have been originally fitted. By BR days, however, many vehicles had acquired variations and M328337 was no exception. Each verandah entrance had a separate rainstrip by then; the exact configuration is difficult to tell for certain from the photograph, but it appears to involve two straight legs, a short horizontal one near the end of the roof, and a longer, slightly angled one towards the centre. I filed and sanded off the mouldings and substituted lengths of square-section 10-thou strip in their place.

With the shell of the van body in one piece, I fitted the end partitions of the guard's compartment. One small omission here is the triangular-section fillet in the angle between the partition and the verandah floor, which appears to have been fitted from new on all the short vans, although it may have been an in-service acquisition on some of the later vehicles. I bevelled the edge of a sheet of 20-thou styrene with a file at about 45 degrees, and then cut four short lengths to fit between the door openings and the van sides. At the same time, I made the door bar wearing plates from 5-thou strip; these take the form of L-shaped brackets fitted to the corners of the body just above the verandah floor where the hooked end of the door bar strikes the woodwork when it's released.

The door bars are the only handrails not mentioned in the kit's instructions, and as such are probably its only serious omission. I made them up from 30 swg nickel-silver wire, forming the loop at one end with a fine pair of pliers. An alternative method with thin wire is to bend it round a drill bit or similar held in a vice or forced into a block of balsa. A shorter length of wire, also with an eye on the end, and epoxied into a 1⁄64 inch hole close to the edge of the end partition, formed the fixed ring on which the door bar pivots. At the other end, the bar slots into a sort of open-sided box mounted on the end post; the hook on the bar engages in a hole in the base of the box. I made the boxes up from 5-thou, and I have to admit that because they're so small I left the end of the bar plain and just epoxied it into the slot. What appears to be the projecting end of the hook is just a noggin of plastic stuck underneath the box. I did form the hook on the one bar that I modelled in the open position, but I made it overlength to fit a hole drilled in the wearing plate so that it doesn't wave about when the van is handled.

The rest of the handrails were fitted as per the instructions, although again I used 30 swg wire rather than the 0.45mm wire provided in the kit. According to *Official Drawings of LMS Wagons* all the handrails are ¾ inch diameter: 0.25mm in 4mm scale. Even 30 gauge is a bit too heavy, therefore, since this scales out at 0.32mm – all but one inch. But I felt that anything finer might be just too flimsy, especially for the long horizontal rails on the sides. I centre-popped the holes with a needle in a pin-chuck before drilling them 1⁄64 inch, and held the long handrails away from the body with offcuts of 30-thou sheet while I bent the tails over and epoxied them inside the van – the principle is shown on page 72 of Part One. On the real thing the lower rail is secured by a bracket at its mid-point. The exact form of this is unclear from any of the drawings and photographs I've seen, but examination of a surviving example at the Rutland Railway Museum showed that it was a simple L-shaped piece of metal butt-welded to the rear of the handrail. So I force-fitted a length of nickel-silver strip into a hole drilled below the ducket and soldered the two together – very quickly, for fear of melting things. A short piece of 5-thou plastic formed the leg of the bracket bolted to the van side.

Whether or not I'd made the body slightly overlength by not building it around the floor, the solebars were an exact fit between the headstocks, with no adjustment or trimming necessary except for the removal of the mould lines top and bottom. And only the merest countersinking around the bearing holes was required to accept standard 26mm pinpoint axles with marginal end float when the axleguards were vertical – rather than turned in or splayed out. Not only that, but everything went together square and parallel at the first time of asking.

In the matter of appearance, however, certain details stand a measure of improvement. Perhaps the most obvious area is the springs: according to the evidence of drawings and photographs, the number of plates in the springs of these early vans was generally either seven or eight. The kit has four, and the springs look a bit weedy as a result. However, as far as I know, no-one makes replacement long springs of this type, so I tried scribing them in 15-thou styrene using a pair of dividers. Try as I might, I couldn't squeeze the eight separate leaves necessary for M328337 into the 1.5mm or thereabouts of the springs at their maximum width. So I made do with scribing the top and bottom edges (at a radius that I calculated to be 60–65mm), using these lines as a guide for cutting out the shape and then notching the lower edge progressively to represent the ends of the individual leaves. I scraped the surface of the moulded spring down by the appropriate 15-thou, and applied the new outline spring as an overlay on the old one before rebuilding the top saddle of the axlebox and the buckle in thin sheet.

The completed model of an LMS Diagram 1657 brakevan built from the Parkside kit. Most of the embellishments described in the text can be seen here, including the two methods of building up the springs.

This at least is what I did for the first one I tackled. When I looked critically at the result, it didn't really seem to be worth the effort. So for the other three I just added some extra leaves above and below the moulded springs in 5-thou strip. These springs have only seven leaves, therefore, but I leave you to judge which of the two methods is more effective at the end of the day. Once painted, I doubt whether the difference will be obvious.

The brakegear is a bit rudimentary too, so I added a little surface detail to the shoes, and yoked each pair with 30-thou plastic rod clipped into dimples drilled in the back of each one. L-shaped safety loops epoxied into lumps of 60-thou stuck under the floor, and 30 swg pull rods from the cranks of the hand gear completed my additions. Fortunately, the rather more complicated gubbins that transmitted and equalised the pull of the screw between each set of four shoes remains virtually invisible behind the wheels.

Speaking of wheels, these vehicles were fitted with 3ft 2in disc wheels rather than the 3ft 1½in spoked or three-hole variety commonly seen on goods stock. The half-inch difference is pretty academic in the smaller scales, and I 'solidified' a set of ordinary three-hole wheels using home-made washers of 20-thou black plastic Evo-stuck into the recess between the centre boss and the rim.

One further, possibly unnecessary, modification I made was to replace the continuous bottom footboards and their four supports, which I felt might be rather vulnerable in plastic to handling damage, with metal ones. Because I had some in stock, I used 3mm brass channel for the stepboards themselves, filing off one flange to reduce the width to about 2.5mm, before soldering to each of them four lengths of brass strip with a tongue bent at right-angles at each end: the lower one to support the stepboard and the upper one to slot through a hole drilled in the solebar just above its bottom flange and at the foot of each of the moulded brackets. Note that there is a slight but perceptible angle to these supports, the lower stepboards being set out slightly when viewed end-on. Nevertheless, the width over the upper steps is still fractionally more than over the lower ones.

Lastly, buffers and couplings. I found it necessary to drill out the holes in the buffer guides slightly to accept the combined buffer rod and head mouldings. This seemed advisable when the first one that I was trying to force in pinged away across the room – for once, I found it without too much difficulty. Conversely the slots in the headstocks are too large for scale coupling hooks, so I cut and filed off the moulded face plates before adding styrene blanks (10-thou on the outside, 40-thou on the inside) in which I drilled less generous holes to accept the tails of the hooks with the minimum clearance necessary.

STANIER VANS

In choosing to model the early style of 24ft-long, 16ft-wheelbase van built during the Stanier era to diagram 1890, I'm well aware that this was an interim design produced in 1933/4, numbering only 150 examples compared with 2,500 of the later, more familiar pattern, which continued to be built into BR days. However, this is a particularly distinctive variant of LMS van that has rather more in common with the later standard design than with its shorter predecessors – from which, nonetheless, it is clearly derived.

Its heredity shows chiefly in the dimensions of the enclosed cabin (which in fact barely altered during the life of the company), and in details like the appearance of the duckets and the cabin windows. However, the longer wheelbase, with new suspension arrangements, a change to horizontal timbering in all panels, and above all an extra two feet added to the verandahs at each end, clearly differentiated it from earlier diagrams. Indeed, it was only in the last area that it differed markedly from the designs that followed: on D1890 the entrances remained adjacent to the cabin, with the extra couple of feet enclosed by short, half-height, boarded wings attached to the outer end panel; on all the later diagrams the positions of the entrances and wings were reversed. The later vans could also be distinguished by steel end panels without the central vertical post, by two sizes of prominent ballast boxes beneath the solebar, and in due course by 9-inch wide duckets in place of 6-inch ones.

Etched brass kits have been produced for both the interim and standard designs of 24ft van (from Chivers and Connoisseur respectively), but given my predilection for plastic, it will come as no surprise that I decided to build one from scratch. The two most fruitful sources of information are again Volume One of *An Illustrated History of LMS Wagons* and Volume Five of the Cheona series. The best drawing, by Ken Morgan, has had quite a wide circulation: it first appeared in *Railway Modeller* for July 1970, then in *The LMS Wagon*, and finally in *Modellers' Backtrack* Volume 3 Number 6.

In considering the thickness of material to use for the construction of the body, I reasoned that a sandwich of 20-thou would be appropriate for the end partitions of the van section; (a) to ensure that the window reveals were not too deep, and (b) to allow for the inset door. Thus the outer skin has the windows beside the door cut to exact size (except as described below on the outer edges), plus a door-sized rectangle cut from the centre, whilst the inner skin has over-sized apertures behind the side windows to accommodate the glazing, but

Contemporary with the Diagram 1940 vehicles were those of the first generation of longer vans, the 150 built to D 1890 with extended verandahs. Comparison with earlier vans also highlights the change to longitudinal instead of vertical boarding, and the auxiliary suspension that replaced the swing shackles previously employed. Unlike all the vans that followed, however, these had the verandah side attached to the end screen rather than the cabin. M295065 is seen at Niddrie in 1963 and M296446 at Exeter Central three years earlier. The latter was one of the fifty vans built with vacuum piping. DON ROWLAND and A. E. WEST a correctly-sized hole for the door light. Beading around all the windows was formed of narrow strips of 5-thou.

20-thou styrene was also used for the end and wing panels, which were marked out separately from the van sides – there seemed little point in cutting the sides and wings from one piece, when they are only connected by narrow strips of framing at the verandah entrances. In any case, this enabled me to make the van sides from 40-thou, my preferred thickness for reasons of strength and rigidity. However, using the thinner material for the end panels made it possible to simulate the framing on the inner faces, even though this is partially obscured by the wider cills along the upper edges of the panels, and by the thickened vertical posts, which, like the top framing, need to be built up so that they are about 1.5mm square.

Incidentally, when scribing the planking on the end and wing panels, note that the ends of the horizontal boards don't correspond exactly with the edges of the vertical posts above the waistrail: the planks appear to be set into the corner posts by an inch or so. The same applies to the end partitions of the van section: the easiest way to simulate it here, given the 40-thou thickness of the sides, seemed to be to butt join the partitions inside the sides, and to scribe the outer vertical end of the boarding to correspond with this joint when dry. This meant that the frame of the window above this area at each side would have been very thin indeed, however, and realising this, I didn't try to retain it when cutting out the window apertures, but added it with a sliver of plastic stuck to the inside face of the 40-thou side sheeting once the van section had been assembled. Only then could the beading round the windows be completed, of course.

One small extravagance that I allowed myself was to chamfer the edges of the corner posts. The real things were finished in this way, though it's frankly all but invisible on the model. But for those who want to do it for the sake of the thing, the two inward-facing edges of the outer posts, and all four edges of the inner uprights on the wings were decorated in this way above the waistrail.

When marking out the various components of the body, I had allowed for them all to fit round a 40-thou floor. Thus they were all full depth except for the end partitions of the van section, which of course were 1mm less. The outer end panels, conversely, were deepened to include the 12-inch headstocks, which would be thickened up to 40- or 60-thou between the solebars in due course. Photographs show a narrow gap between the body and the headstocks, which I tried to simulate with a wider-than-usual scribed line between the two. How successful this dodge proves to be will only become evident once the vehicle has been painted.

This form of construction meant that the floor was not a plain rectangle, since it needed to allow for the differing thicknesses of bodyside material. I complicated it further by extending it to the full width of the body at each of the four entrances; I could have incorporated the outer edge of the floor at these points with the bodyside panels (as I had with the framing above the entrances), but it seemed marginally easier to do it the other way. In point of fact, I put together the van section and each of the two end panel-plus-wings assemblies before tailoring the floor to suit. I then used the floor as a frame around which to attach first the van, and then each of the end sections. I had cut out the top framing over the entrances slightly overlength in anticipation, and trimmed them exactly to fit as part of the assembly process.

Before going on to detail the body, I made and fitted the 12-inch solebars, largely to ensure that the structure was as rigid as possible. As described elsewhere, I used 30-thou styrene for the face and added webs of 10-thou top and bottom to arrive at an overall depth of 4mm. With the solebars attached at 24.5mm back-to-back, I thickened up the headstocks between them, drilling them for coupling hooks and buffers when dry. I had no buffers in stock that matched exactly, and ended up taking a file to a set of 1ft 8½in BR heavy duty ones from MJT, reducing the size of

The Diagram 1890 van in an advanced state of completion, but still in need of springs and axleboxes. The geometry of the footboard units, one of which is seen in the foreground, is rather complex: a total of twelve spigots – the central supports have two each – slot into holes drilled in the solebar.

the heads from 15 inches to 13 inches, and thinning down both the heads and the bases as far as I dared to disguise the fact that they are too long. Although I was modelling a vacuum-piped example (M296457 as illustrated in Cheona Vol. 5), all these vans were fitted with 18-inch buffers, the piped ones having a packing piece inserted to increase their length by 2½ inches. By adjusting the thickness of the packing slightly, I finished up with buffers of just about the right overall length.

I always find the geometry of duckets difficult to cope with; although the LMS pattern is rather less awkward to make from scratch than the LNER design, there's a strong element of trial and error in getting them dimensionally close at the same time as you capture the characteristic shape of the original. For this reason I used separate pieces of 30-thou for the three outward faces, filing the horizontal edges to an approximation of the angles required before sticking them together, and relying on the thickness of the material to give enough meat to refine the shape if necessary when dry. The sides are a sandwich of glazing material overlaid with 5-thou in which a 1mm × 5mm slot has been cut for the window. Being less than 1.5mm wide and angled top and bottom to fit inside the shape of the outer face, the sides are fiddly things to make. Although the 5-thou beading round the windows can be relied upon to tidy things up a little, I found it necessary to smooth over the joints with a file when everything had set, and also to clean up the edges that mate with the body to ensure neat contact all round and an overall projection of no more than 2mm from the bodyside.

I did wonder whether to cut a hole behind the ducket, but decided against it: the windows are so small that it's well nigh impossible to see anything through them. So I mounted each ducket on four strips of 5-thou about 1mm wider all round than the ducket itself, and surrounded these on three sides with 10-thou strip for the replacement beading fitted to M296457.

Most of these vans seem to have received this modification during their lifetime. Some also acquired the V-framing fitted to M328337; although M296457 escaped this, it did have additional beading strips over the vertical joints between the horizontal sheeting and the corner posts of the van section, together with several bits of extra ironwork to hold the verandah sides together. These were duly added in 5- and 10-thou strip.

Built at Derby in 1938 to Diagram 1919, M730639 represents the final phases of LMS brakevan development, only Diagram 2036 with wider duckets and Diagram 2068 with both these and deeper ballast weights following in the years up to nationalisation. Photographed at Axminster in 1959, M730639 was built unfitted, but had been vacuum-piped later in life: the low-level pipe suggests that this was done in BR days. A. E. WEST

The roof is a plain rectangle of 20-thou curved by the method illustrated in Part Two, and reinforced with a second lamination of the same gauge underneath, cut into three sections to fit round the partitions. As with the short vans, D1890 seems to have received full-length rainstrips originally, but many vehicles show four separate ones in later days, and M296457 is no exception. It's difficult to tell from the photograph whether they are straight or not, but on balance I think they were probably slightly arched, so that's how I've modelled them.

Handrails were added in 30swg nickel silver wire after the fashion of the D1657 van, with a minor exception in the treatment of the door bars. Instead of the flimsy 5-thou open-sided boxes I had built up on the corner posts of M328337, I cut solid shapes out of 20-thou for M296457 and merely drilled a 1/64 inch hole to accept the end of the bar that I modelled in the closed position. The easiest way to fit this was to thread it onto the bar before epoxying the pivoting end into its hole in the corner of the van section. I was then able to adjust the bar for position as I Mek-Pak-ed the 'box' to the corner post.

Once again, the door bar lacks the hooked end, and the projection below the 'box' is simply a scrap of styrene. The three in the open position do have hooked tails, but this time they are just glued to the wearing plate with a dab of epoxy: in all the photographs I looked at, the hooks are lying flat against the plate and not turned in as the open one appears to be on the model of the earlier vehicle.

As generally with the bodies, the running gear of these interim vans was carried forward to the standard design: larger axleboxes, with vertical rather than inclined faces, plate axleguards, ten-leaf springs, and J-hangers with auxiliary suspension in place of swing-link shackles, all distinguished D1890 from its shorter predecessors (although the hundred contemporary short-bodied, 14ft wheelbase vans to D1940 shared most of these features). This is not particularly good news from the scratchbuilder's point of view, and I rapidly concluded that I was going to have to make everything from scratch, including springs and axleboxes, since I wasn't aware of a source of these components.

So I filed and bent up a pair of axleguard units from 10-thou nickel-silver sheet, and set about manufacturing the rest from styrene. This may sound a fearsome proposition but provided you take it stage-by-stage, it doesn't need to be. I described the principle in Part One, and hopefully the accompanying photographs and caption will illustrate it satisfactorily. The key to it is to build up the component on a backing sheet which then becomes integral with the finished item – although the only visible part of the assembly that it contributes in its own right is the flat of the hornguides on either side of the axlebox.

The auxiliary suspension complicates things a bit in this case: the fresh air between the ends of the springs and the J-hangers persuaded me not to try to glue the vertical pins to the springs before cutting the parts out; instead, I fitted them in place on the underframe as three separate units. I was also in several minds as to how to reproduce the cylindrical dampers beneath the J-hangers: I felt they needed some sort of surface texture to represent the composite nature of the original. In the end I 'turned' a screw thread onto a length of white plastic rod by forcing it through a 6BA nut, and then chopped this up into eight separate pieces, each drilled 0.52mm up the centre to accept pins of 20-thou red plastic rod. But I'm not over-thrilled with the result: plain dampers might have been nearer the mark, after all.

The MJT clasp brake castings I used are designed to fit the manufacturer's own axleguard units, so it's not surprising that they didn't readily match my home-made ones. In particular, they needed to be mounted about 2mm clear of the base of the unit in order to get the shoes centred on the wheels. I laminated two rectangles of 40-thou to fit between the axleguards, and then added a third one that was about 5mm shorter. The ends of the third piece form a shoulder for the back of each casting to locate against, and a right-angled seat into which the casting may be more securely Evo-stuck.

The exact configuration of the brake rigging in the middle of the underframe isn't perfectly clear from either the drawing or any of the photographs, although in principle it's similar to that of the earlier vehicles. Unfortunately, the drawing gives only a side elevation, the photographs show it only in

Four stages in building up spring and axlebox assemblies from scratch. Top right: *the spring outline, shaped in 40-thou and marked to show the position of the notches representing the individual leaves or plates, is offered up to the plain outline of the axlebox on its 10-thou backing sheet.* Top left: *having been notched and cut out, the spring is added to the backing sheet; reinforcing ribs in 10-thou have been applied to the sides of the axlebox.* Bottom right: *the spring hangers and auxiliary suspension units have been added, and the backing sheet cut away round them. These will remain separate from the axlebox/spring unit until after fitting to the underframe, but they and the spring ends have already been drilled to accept pins of 20-thou plastic rod.* Bottom left: *detailing of the axlebox has been completed, and this too has been cut out; only at each side of the box is the backing sheet visible in its own right, forming the riveted plate reinforcement for the hornguides.*

A feature common to LMS brake vans generally was the hinged sections of the lower footboards, which could be folded back to give access to the axleboxes. These two photographs of the same vehicle, M731243, taken at Immingham in 1991 and 2000, conveniently illustrate both the hinged flap in position, and, after removal of the footboards, the complex bracketwork needed to support them and to compensate for the inevitable weakness attributable to the design. AUTHOR

The completed Diagram 1890 van with and without the roof in position. All-plastic models usually benefit from some added weight, hence the piece of lead flashing glued to the cabin floor. Because the verandah end units were made separately from the cabin, keeping the whole thing square when they were all put together was a bit of a trial.

silhouette, and on the later vans it's hidden behind the ballast boxes. In essence, there appears to be some kind of rectangular, U-shaped framework (if you can have such a thing) suspended around the centre of the unit, the exact purpose and design of which elude me, though I take it that its prime function is as a safety guard to prevent any bits of the gear that may become detached from dropping into the four-foot. I fudged it as well as I could on the model, and await further enlightenment.

Finally, the footboards. On a scratchbuilt model there's no excuse for using anything but metal for these, and for the lower ones I made use of the same brass channel that I had for M328337. The top steps have no toe-boards at the back, and plain 10-thou sheet metal sufficed for these. The outer support bracket for the top steps is attached to the corresponding ones for the lower footboard, and to avoid the risky business of soldering these together in situ on the model, I made all the stepboards on each side as a single unit. The result is a bit unwieldy and easily distorted by handling, but once epoxied into position seems firm enough. The centre supports for the lower stepboards aren't bolted directly to the solebar as on the earlier vans, but stand away from the face, to which they are attached by separate rectangular brackets. On the model, therefore, each of these has two legs that slot into holes close to the upper and lower flanges of the solebar, whereas the three that support each of the upper footboards have only one.

A feature of all LMS brakevans is the opening flaps in the lower stepboard in front of the axleboxes. This required a complicated set of supports bracketed off the axleguard. Knowing my limitations, I steered clear of trying to reproduce these, but anyone who likes a challenge might find the accompanying photographs helpful.

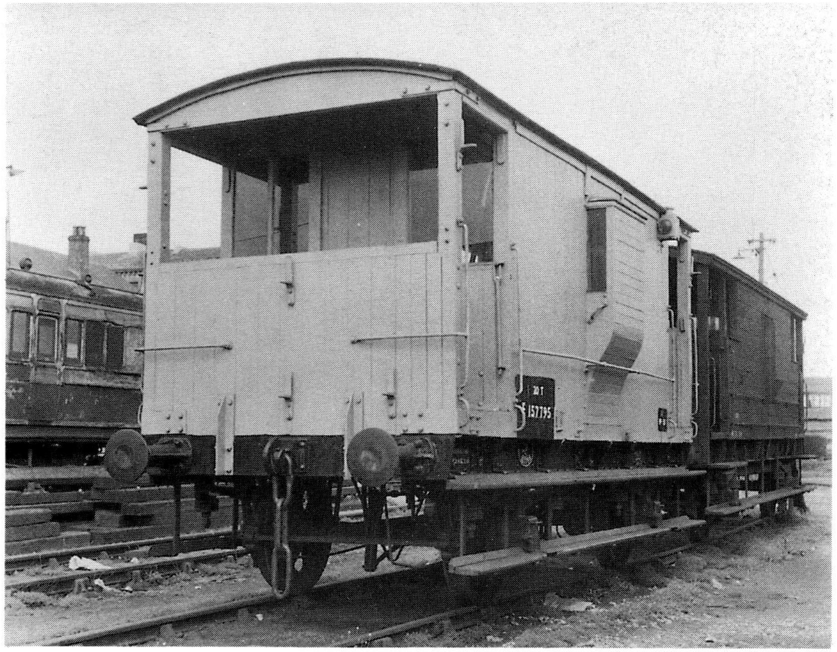

The first generation of LNER brake vans was developed from a North Eastern Railway design, and already the similarity of the superstructure to the standard British Railways style is apparent, as may be seen from this selection of photographs taken between 1951 and 1962. Around 1,600 were built up to the mid-'thirties to two diagrams, both of which were for vans of 19ft over the headstocks and 10ft 6in wheelbase. Whereas the earlier ones had wooden duckets and end stanchions, however, these were replaced in later construction with steel fittings, but over the years many older vans received more modern features. E140537, for example, was built with wooden duckets and end posts, and both E157795 and E157797 would have had wooden stanchions originally. E167915, on the other hand, had a steel ducket from new, but retained wooden end posts; it had also acquired BR axleguards (as had E157797), and bridging pieces welded across the gaps in the vertical handrails, a common BR-period modification. The BR alterations to the upper lamp iron layout favoured by the LNER are also evident.
ROGER CARPENTER, A. E. WEST and HMRS

LNER/BR BRAKE VANS

Looking at brake vans in Peter Tatlow's *A Pictorial Record of LNER Wagons*, I was surprise to find that the first of the long-wheelbase vehicles that were ultimately destined to develop into BR's standard design were produced as early as 1929. By the time construction ceased in 1962, BR had added to almost 2,000 built by the LNER over 4,500 more, the last survivors of which are still around forty years on, albeit in very specialised use.

By comparison with the prototype's life history of threescore years and ten, the Dapol, formerly Airfix, kit for the BR version is barely middle-aged. Still, forty years or so is a long time for any kit to have lasted, and in common with its contemporaries from the same stable, it betrays its pioneering status in some of its basic design features and a certain coarseness of detail, in which it has been overtaken by Connoisseur Models' (Pocket Money Kits) etched brass equivalent – see articles by Tim Shackleton in *MRJ* No. 133 and by Steve Banks in *Model Rail* for February, 2002. An even more recent arrival is Dave

A scratchbuilt model of an ex-LNER Toad E, built long before the release of the Parkside kit. Kenline cast whitemetal axleguards were at the time the nearest approximations I could find to the correct pattern.

Bradwell's etched underframe kit for the Dapol/Airfix plastic body. Moreover, there's a good deal of competition in this field from the ready-to-run players, among which the latest Bachmann version, while not without its faults, takes some beating.

All the same, as I hope to show, the original kit still has the potential to produce a good scale model and, being plastic, lends itself to conversion to earlier variants, and to the straightforward correction of a few slight mistakes in the initial pattern-work.

Not surprisingly for a design that was in production for so long, quite a number of evolutionary changes in detail took place over the years, too many to list fully here, in fact. One of the more obvious ones was the adoption of concrete ballast slabs during World War II instead of the iron ballast used previously, leading to the built-up end platforms that replaced plain steel decks flush with the tops of the solebars. I believe this also led to a slight increase in the overall height of the vehicles: certainly the BR-built vans were 1¾ inches higher than the iron-ballasted LNER ones, and comparing photos of LNER vans with iron and concrete ballast, the floor thickness in the verandah entrances on the latter definitely looks greater. Another change

The LNER's other brake van design, introduced in 1929, retained the same style of cabin, but mounted on a 24ft, 16ft-wheelbase underframe. E178705, built in 1935 and photographed in 1950, was typical of the first phase of construction. E242170, built five years later and pictured soon after a works visit in 1962, was very similar except for the addition from new of angle trussing under the solebar and a few other minor in-service modifications including the relocated upper lamp irons and handrail bridging pieces noted earlier. Glazed cabin doors and concrete ballast (both these vans have iron ballast between the frames) would follow over the next few years. Unlike the earlier short vans, almost all of which were unfitted throughout their lives, all those built for the LNER in this extended form had full vacuum brakegear from new.

A. E. WEST and DON ROWLAND

during LNER days was the addition of small, angle-iron trussing under the sole-bars – omitted, as it happens, on the Airfix kit.

In its standard design BR extended the short footboards favoured by the LNER to full-length ones, with the addition of horizontal handrails above the end platforms. A little later, single vertical handrails appeared on each side of the verandah entrances in place of the split ones fitted previously, and around the same time upstanding vacuum pipes were replaced where appropriate with low-level ones (the LNER had built only fully-fitted vans of this design for itself, but BR built vacuum-piped and unfitted ones as well). In due course, roller bearings and Oleo buffers became standard on all new vehicles.

A fuller account of this evolution can be gleaned from a combined reading of *A Pictorial Record of LNER Wagons* and Eric Gent's *British Railways Brake Vans and Ballast Ploughs*, and I would strongly suggest that anyone contemplating a model of one of these vans of whatever period would benefit from studying both. Other useful sources of photographs and information are 'Cheona' Volume 5 and *Working Wagons* Volume I, and the May 1983 issue of *Model Railway Constructor*, which also contains the only detailed published drawings I've seen of the standard BR vans. Most recently, Steve Banks' article in *Model Rail* is also a helpful source of prototype photos and information.

LNER 20-TON VAN

I chose to model E278704 as illustrated (in pre-nationalisation garb) in *LNER Wagons*. As a 1946-built van, this has the concrete ballast common to all the BR vehicles, the glazed cabin doors which earlier LNER ones lacked, and pressed-steel axleboxes very similar to those on the kit. In fact, the only differences I can see between 278704 and the first BR-built vans, the 290 vehicles turned out in 1949 to Diagram 1/500, are the design of the axleguards, the position of the upper lamp irons (which may not have changed immediately after nationalisation – see below), and the absence of the characteristic cut-outs at the verandah end of the ballast slabs; these came in very shortly before nationalisation.

This was one of the first things I altered, jamming chunks of 2mm × 2mm styrene into the slots with plenty of solvent, and filing the joints flush when everything had set hard. At the same time I filed a good millimetre off the ends of the floor moulding: although I've seen a few photographs where the ends of the ballast slabs were level with the headstocks as on the kit, on the vast majority of both LNER and BR vans there was a distinct ledge 3–4in wide along the top of the headstocks. 278704 was certainly like this.

While doing this, I sliced and filed the moulded handrails off the end platforms, and then proceeded to do the same with those on the cabin and verandah sections, re-scribing the planking where necessary. There were, incidentally, minor variations in the layout of the cabin-side boarding on the original vehicles, complicated further by in-service repairs, but I decided to ignore the difference between 278704, which has 33 verticals including the inner corner posts, and the kit, which has 30. I also ignored the fact that the duckets appear to be set a trifle low: since they are moulded integrally with the sides, this would not be easy to correct.

Finally I removed the moulded lamp irons, the projecting ones from the outer corner posts because they are impossibly thick, and the single ones on each verandah screen because the later LNER vans (and the early BR ones) had two in this position. The lamp irons on the corner posts became standard on all vehicles during the BR period, and those inherited from the LNER in due course acquired them as well, but prior to nationalisation the latter had carried a single upper one high up at one end of each cabin side. Some of the early BR vans followed suit in this respect when first built. I know of no source of etchings for the particular pattern of lamp irons used by BR on the corner posts, and when I came to fit them I resorted to cutting and filing them out of thin brass sheet to the pattern illustrated in the accompanying diagram.

Before beginning the assembly of the vehicle, I glazed the cabin windows. The mouldings are rather thick, and to reduce the depth of the window reveals I filed the backs of the cabin end partitions down to about half their original thickness where it shows. I also glazed the duckets; this was

SR/BR corner post lamp irons for brake vans

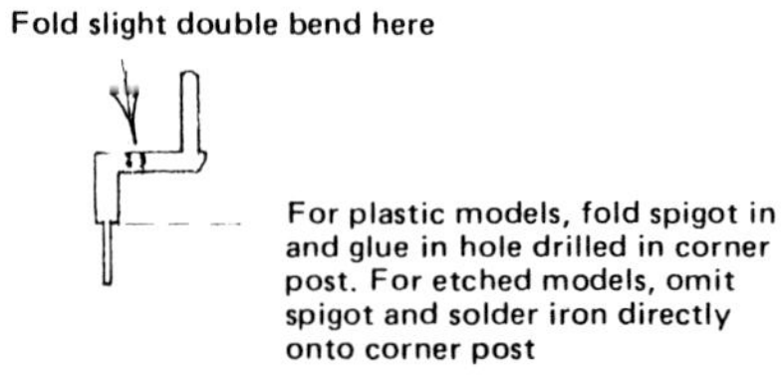

made rather easier by filing away some of the thickness of the plastic adjacent to each window at the same angle as the sides of the duckets – hopefully the photograph will illustrate this more clearly than I seem to be able to describe it in words.

The final preliminary job before assembly was to file away the three prominent circular moulding marks on the outside of the cabin end partitions, and to re-scribe the planking after I'd done so. I suppose I should have done the same with those on the inside of the verandah screens; these are rather less obvious, but they do show up from some angles I now realise.

Assembly of the body followed the instructions until I came to the roof. The moulded roof is a good millimetre thick, and looks wrong as a result, so I made a new one out of 20-thou styrene, pre-curved as described in Part Two. I stiffened it by adding a second thickness of the same material underneath, divided into three to fit between the curved tops of the four transverse body sections. If you choose to retain the original roof, you may wish to consider whether the curve of the moulded rainstrips is not rather exaggerated. Certainly most vans seem to have acquired any one of several different patterns during their lifetime, and 278704 had a much shallower outline from the start. Whatever the truth of this, one definite fault with the roof is the position of the stove chimney, which should be towards the right-hand end of the van when viewed from the side to which it is nearer (which always seems to have been the same side as the vacuum cylinder on fitted vehicles). Finally, the moulded torpedo ventilators are a bit approximate. On the new roof I fitted cast whitemetal ones from MJT of the elliptical pattern favoured by BR and latterly by the LNER. Earlier company vans had had the larger circular sort.

To facilitate painting round the end windows at a later stage, I left the roof unattached for the time being, and turned my attention to the underframe. The solebars, axleguards and springs are a pretty fair representation, but I felt I could improve on the vestigial body support brackets, and carved these off with the intention of replacing them in due course with styrene for the four triangular plate ones on each side, and metal strip for the two outer ones. The axleguards fitted to the LNER vans were closer to the RCH pattern than the BR standard plate version, and I cut the vee-shaped slots below the springs to convert them. And although the moulded axleboxes are close to those fitted to 278704, I gently filed the faces back to simulate the sloping fronts of the LNER type, adding a sliver of 10-thou to represent the handle at the top.

The kit was never designed to accept scale pin-point axles and bearings, of course, and I found it necessary to drill out the holes in the axleboxes until the bit was on the point of breaking through, and then to countersink the holes to take the bearing flanges by a good millimetre before the wheels would revolve freely. The next stage would have been to pack the solebars out, but this would have increased the width over the footboards, which I had reason to believe from previously-built examples was already inclined to exceed the prototypical 34mm, so I was keen to avoid this if I could.

As already mentioned, all but the first few batches of LNER-built vans were fitted with angle-trusses below the solebars. These, for some reason, aren't included in the kit, which must rank as its chief error. I soldered mine up from 1mm brass angle, and epoxied them in place against some small plastic tabs stuck to the rear face of the solebars. On one side the moulded V-hanger can also be used for support, though I found it necessary to thin it down a bit to get the trussing to sit squarely. Strictly speaking, the vertical web of the angle should pass behind the solebar, with the flat riveted to the underside of the lower flange, but the relative thickness of the materials involved made this difficult, and I compromised by filing away the vertical web flush with the bottom of the solebar.

I could have made the trusses from styrene strip, but it wouldn't really have solved this problem, and my experience with similar fabrications elsewhere is that they would tend to be a bit weak. In this case, however, they would be protected by the footboards, so they would probably be less vulnerable to damage.

Something that isn't immediately obvious until you come to fit the truss on the vacuum cylinder side is that the V-hanger is slightly off-centre, and correctly so. Other than the cylinder itself, however, this is where faithful reproduction of the prototype stops, for there is no cross-shaft, inner V-hanger or actuating lever, and the piston in the cylinder is far too short. I extended the piston by sleeving it with brass tube, bent up a lever from brass strip (sized to put a slight angle on the mounting of the cylinder which all LNER fitted vehicles seem to have featured), and cut a second V-hanger from 30-thou plastic, joining it to the moulded one with a wire cross-shaft.

The double clasp brake shoes in the kit are correct for all but the earliest of the BR-built vans, including unfitted ones, but the LNER used single shoes, so I Evo-stuck a set of cast ABS ones to the underside of the floor. This requires a degree of modification in the way of cutting and filing a slot in one of the moulded ribs in each location and the addition of a bit of 30-thou strip to provide a pad for the casting to sit squarely on. In my usual rudimentary style I yoked each pair of shoes with 30-thou plastic rod, and fitted wire safety loops epoxied into lumps of 60-thou stuck under the floor.

As with the brake shoes, the 1ft 6in spindle buffers in the kit are fine for BR vans built up to 1957, but the LNER vehicles had 1ft 8½in ones. I filed away the rather heavy moulded bases from the headstocks and drilled the holes out to accept ABS cast buffers to the RCH fitted stock pattern, though as usual I filed down the spigots before doing so: if you don't, the holes in the headstocks have to be so large that plastic ones would be significantly weakened. Because the end platforms had already been trimmed back to create the ledge referred to earlier, the tops of the headstock mouldings are exposed, revealing a row of rivet heads on the real thing, which now need to be added in noggins of 10-thou plastic.

Finally, the upstanding brake pipes carried by all the LNER vans represent another departure from the kit. I felt they were too prominent to get away with the plain bent wire I normally use, and if I'd had any in stock I would have fitted cast brass or whitemetal pipes. But I didn't, so I soldered a few wire collars and strip metal brackets to my usual bent paper clips, which look okay if you don't examine them too closely. It's difficult to be certain, but it seems that the upstanding pipes were always to the right of the drawhook when viewed end-on. This is the opposite way round to the low-level ones, so the holes in the headstocks intended to receive the kit's moulded pipes need to be plugged with a rounded, slightly tapered, strip of 40-thou.

Some of the holes in the solebars for the footboard brackets are also surplus, by reason of the shorter steps carried by the LNER and early BR vans. Shortening the moulded footboards is complicated by the fact that the supports aren't evenly spaced: whilst you can happily chop 10mm off the right-hand end, losing the outer support in the process, if you do the same at the other end you lose two, since the second one in is closer to the headstock at that end. What you have to do is to chop out 10mm *astride* the second support and re-attach the end section, drilling a new mounting hole 4mm to the right of the second one. This again is, I hope, a lot easier to work out from the photographs than it is to describe.

On one side of the vehicle two more of the solebar holes are in the wrong place. On both the LNER and BR vans the two central footboard supports are slightly offset in relation to the centre line of the van side. The two sets of moulded footboards are identical, which means that this pair of supports appears offset to the right on both sides. On the real thing, however, they were offset towards the same end, and according to all the photographs I've studied, and the tacit evidence of the drawings in *Model Railway Constructor*, this was always to the right when looking at the non-chimney side, and to the left on the chimney side. On this side, therefore, they need to be removed and replaced about 4mm to the left, on the opposite side of the adjacent triangular body support brackets.

I didn't realise this until after I'd fitted the altered footboards, so on the one side I had to cut the two supports out in situ and replace them in Plastikard. I had initially considered whether to substitute metal footboards for the moulded ones, as I had on the Parkside LMS van, but this time had contented myself with thinning down the toe-boards along the backs of the steps and chamfering the rear edges of the over-thick supports. At the same time I filed the small gaps in the lower toe-boards to clear the axleboxes, something that was common to all the later vans of this design. The earliest LNER vehicles had a complete gap in the footboard, bridged by a flat metal tie.

Thinning down the supports does make them rather weaker, and to counter this flimsiness I glued a surreptitious bit of 30-thou under each of the axleboxes abutting the rear edge of the lower steps. This had the desired effect of stiffening things up. but clearly this dodge wouldn't be compatible with compensation, and to be honest, given all these various alterations, and the very heavy appearance of the support brackets in particular, a complete set of metal steps would have been more satisfactory on most counts.

Shorter footboards reduce the number of handrail sections you need to make by four, since there were none along the end platforms on these vehicles. But that still leaves twenty-eight, plus another twelve bits of metal for the door bars. These were quite similar to the ones on the LMS vans, except that there was no hook on the end: in the open position the bottom of the bar located in a fixed ring about a foot or so above the floor, and the loop at the top was elongated to allow the guard to lift the bar to engage and disengage it – not that he always bothered, it seems. Incidentally, according to photographs, it looks as if the door bars proper were of slightly heavier gauge rod than the rest of the handrails, but the loop at the top was not. I did experiment with slightly thicker wire, but the loop looked wrong, and the technology of reproducing the dual thickness eluded me, so in the end I used 30swg for everything, as I had on the LMS vans.

A couple of other points about the handrails that aren't immediately obvious: I was initially puzzled to see that some vans appeared to have three small grab handles around the ducket, while some had only two (or one, or none, as many did in later life). In fact it seems they all started off with two on one side and three on the other, the three being on the same side as

These views show most of the modifications and additions made to the Airfix/Dapol kit to adapt it into a late-LNER example. The elevated view illustrates in particular how the plastic has been thinned down to reduce the depth of the window reveals in the duckets and the cabin end panels, while the underneath shot reveals the brake gear variations and the additional angle trussing.

the chimney, which also had a further small grab rail next to it. Now I can understand that the two beside the ducket would have been helpful when cleaning the small windows, but since there were no steps as such, exactly how the higher one helped in gaining access to the roof (if that's what it was for) is a bit of a mystery – to me, anyway. Or did the handrails themselves double as rather widely-spaced and precarious steps?

Second, the horizontal handrail along the van side below the ducket was in three sections on all the LNER vans, and on the first batches of BR ones, although often the only clue is the shadow cast by the rails on a sunny day.

The method of fitting was much the same as for the LMS vans, except that the end of the outer sections of the long horizontal rails on each side was touch-soldered to the vertical handrail on the cabin corner-post. Again, I used a piece of plastic of appropriate thickness to support each one clear of the bodyside while it was soldered at one end and epoxied at the other. The securing brackets at the ends of each handrail were tiny discs sliced off the tip of a rounded strip of 20-thou square plastic.

Two photos contrasting the finished van unpainted, and painted in weathered bauxite. In the upper shot the nearer footboards have been left off to show the running gear more clearly. It's on this side (the chimney side) that the two middle supports should be repositioned left of centre – see text.

BR 20-TON VAN

B950884, pictured new in 1950, embodied the earliest modifications made to the LNER design after nationalisation: longer footboards, BR axle-guards and double brakeshoes are the most obvious, together with the absence of vacuum brakegear. It still had LNER axleboxes, however, and, remarkably for a van built almost three years into public ownership, it had LNER-style lamp irons as well. This is the only picture I've seen of a BR-built van with lamp brackets on the cabin sides, although since one of the diagrams reproduced in British Railways Wagons *shares this feature, 950884 probably was not unique in this respect; it was no doubt modified before long. Regional branding was discontinued from 1957.*
CTY. PAUL BARTLETT

Having been brought up, so to speak, with the Airfix kit of the BR brake van, I had for a long time assumed that many, perhaps most, of the breed had been built with full vacuum brakegear as typified by the kit. I was vaguely aware that some were unfitted, as well, but it wasn't until I read *British Railways Brake Vans and Ballast Ploughs* that I realised that, with the sole exception of Lot 2051 (the 290 vans turned out in 1949 to diagram 1/500, which were effectively to LNER specification, and did have full vacuum brakes), BR supposedly built only unfitted or vacuum-*piped* vehicles. So why, I wondered, did Airfix include a vacuum-cylinder in their kit?

Eric Gent's statement to this effect is supported by Steve Banks, by Roger Silsbury (in *Model Railway Constructor* for May 1983), and by David Larkin in his Data Sheet on these vehicles, although confusingly the second two don't agree entirely with the first two, or with each other, on which lots were unfitted and which were piped. Only Don Rowland (in *British Railways Wagons*) suggests that some of the lots which were officially only piped did in fact receive the full works. And there is a measure of photographic confirmation to back him up. Positive evidence is admittedly thin on the ground, but there is a sprinkling of pictures clearly showing vacuum cylinders spread across the whole life of the vehicles from the early 'fifties to the 'nineties. Other photographs show V-hangers, with or without cross-shafts, but no cylinders, indicating that they had either had the full gear, which had been removed, or had been intended to have it. Most published pictures, however, show vans in later life, so in these cases it isn't possible to be certain whether they were built fully-fitted, or retro-fitted.

But it's a curious thing that without exception all the vans I've noted with either full vacuum brakes or partial fittings come from the seven lots that Don Rowland says were built fully-fitted. And one of those lots begins with B952516, the number Airfix chose to supply in transfer form with their kit all those years ago ...

Where the truth lies I can't say. Between them the published authorities agree on only nine of the sixteen lots (other than Lot 2051): five unfitted and four piped. I wanted a piped van, which, to be on the safe side, gave a choice therefore of Lots 2136, 2206, 3227 and 3394. The last two were turned out in 1959 and 1962 respectively, which made them a bit late for my chosen period, while Lot 2136 retained more of the LNER-inspired features I had incorporated in E278704 than Lot 2206, which had single vertical handrails, four-pane doors and low vacuum pipes. At least, according to Eric Gent it should have had low pipes, but the only two photographs I found of vans from this lot actually showed upstanding ones: B951267 and B951270. But at least they were clearly white-painted, which proved that they were indeed only vacuum-piped. I chose to model the latter, which was still in relatively original condition when photographed at Birkenhead in 1982 (*British Railway Goods Wagons in Colour*, p. 79).

Not surprisingly, many aspects of the construction of the model mirrored that of the LNER-built version. But there was a number of variations as well, not all of them well-documented, it seems. Take the end panels of the van section, for instance: the change from two to four panes in the doors is fairly obvious, and this required

Photographed soon after building in 1953, B952125 seems to confirm fairly clearly that some standard BR vans were fitted with full vacuum brakegear from new, whatever the records might say. Brakegear apart, a number of detail changes, particularly to the handrail layout, had taken place since B950884 was built, and the only significant ones still to come were the introduction of roller bearings and Oleo buffers in 1956 and 1957 respectively.

I. VAUGHAN
CTY. PETER SMITH

Seen in the early 1990s, B953867 and B955101 (unfitted and converted to air piping respectively) represent the final variation of BR vans. They had undergone a few repairs, particularly to the verandah screens, and were in different liveries: freight brown in the case of B953867, and red and grey for B955101. The plain panel above the duckets on these vans appears to have been a standard feature on later vehicles, and was a common modification to many older ones.

AUTHOR

only the addition of two short horizontal glazing bars cut to fit the apertures once the panel had been thinned and glazed as previously. Less evident is the fact that all the BR-built vans, except, I think, those produced to diagram 1/500, had plain panelling, presumably plywood, rather than matchboarding for the lower half of these end partitions, including the doors. The kit is therefore strictly correct in this respect only for vans built to the full LNER specification. In fact, if you accept the need to file the ugly moulding marks away, this relieves you of re-scribing all but the edges of the sections of panelling.

Another point – admittedly a detail – that Steve Banks mentions, but which isn't highlighted elsewhere concerns the horizontal handrails on the main bodysides. As with the LNER vans, these were initially in three sections, with the rails turned in and bolted to the woodwork near the bottom corners of the ducket. BR apparently perpetuated this feature even after the split vertical handrails beside the verandah entrances had been combined into one. Several photographs of vans from Lots 2206 and 2207 show evidence of this, and only from Lots 2349/50 is a single continuous rail fitted, with small L-shaped brackets welded to the back of it in the same positions.

Speaking of the vertical handrails, whilst the outer ones at each end were the same overall length as the split ones of the earlier pattern, those on the inner side of the entrances were longer, extending below the bodyside where they were turned under and fastened to an L-shaped bracket beneath the floor. On the model I made this bracket purely cosmetic: in fact, it's a small rectangle of 10-thou threaded onto the bottom of the handrail which extends through a hole drilled in the solebar, behind which the tail is secured with a blob of epoxy. The bracket can either be Mek-Pak-ed to the van body or epoxied to the wire, or both.

Combining the outer vertical handrails into one led to a minor change in the fastening of the horizontal grab rail that ran from the verandah screen to the headstock on all vans with full-length footboards. Hitherto the inboard end had been bolted to the side of the corner post in the gap between the two vertical rails. From now on it was generally attached to the face of the screen. Not always, however: an exception, which is illustrated here, was B953867, which had this rail kinked about a foot away from the screen to bring the end outside the corner post, as before. Several others have been noted between B953442 of Lot 3012 and B954219 of Lot 3129.

Above the solebar the only other differences from the LNER version were the retention of the kit's single lamp iron in the centre of the verandah end panel (though again replaced in brass strip), and the addition of a rectangle of 10-thou plastic in each of the four cut-outs in the ballast slabs next to that panel. Photographic evidence confirms that the deck plating beneath the concrete was continuous in these areas.

Completion of the underframe is in some respects a simpler operation than it was for the LNER model. For a start, of course, you don't have to shorten the foot-

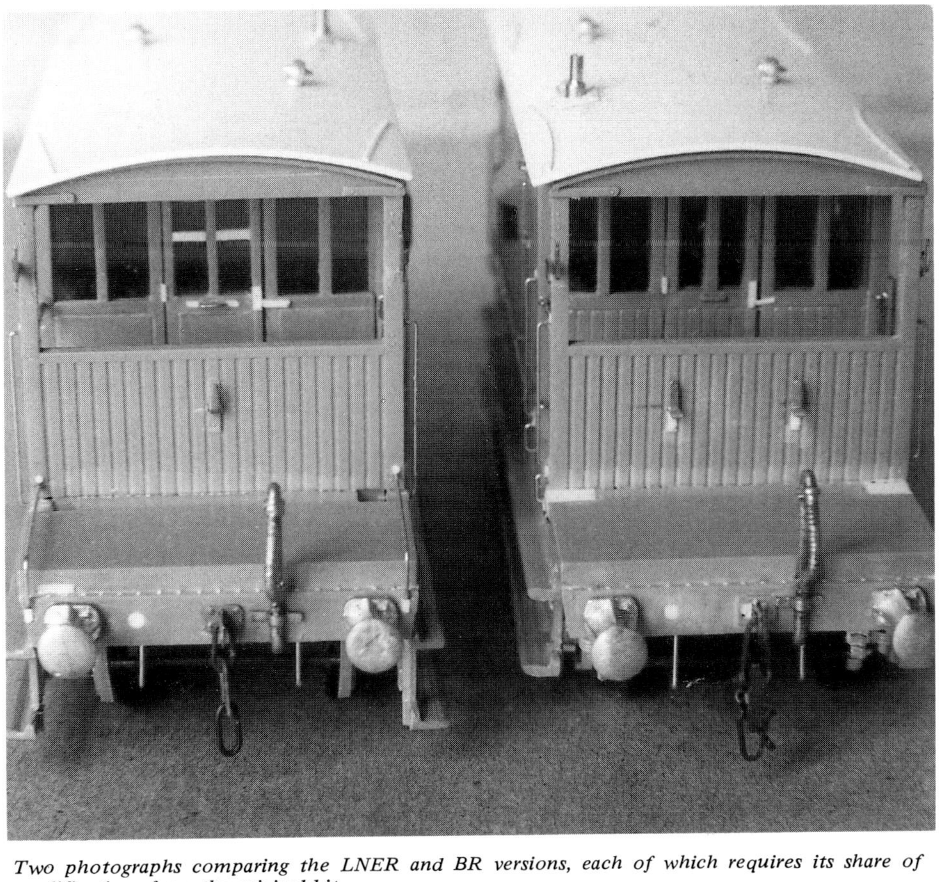

Two photographs comparing the LNER and BR versions, each of which requires its share of modifications from the original kit.

20 T
B951270
XP
19-7

boards, although as before I thinned them down considerably, and anchored them to the underside of the axleboxes. Even so, the need remains to reposition the two central supports on the chimney side as described for the LNER van. And you should be aware that there are at least three common layouts for the end supports, which might also require surgery (or further justify replacing the footboard mouldings with metal ones). On B951270 they were the same as the kit, with the two left-hand supports on each side quite close together. But the position of the second one in at each end did vary, so as always it pays to follow a photograph of a particular vehicle.

With a vacuum-piped van like B951270, there's no brake rigging visible except around the wheelsets, where the kit's moulded brake shoes can be used. The instructions recommend fitting these to the backs of the solebars before attaching them to the underframe, but I left them until later to be sure of getting them in line with, and as close as possible to, the wheels. This turned out to be the right thing to do, since the moulded locating pins were rather too far away from the tyres of scale wheels. Getting the shoes within spitting distance of the wheels did require a bit of trimming and packing, however: trimming away about 20-thou of the ends of the underfloor cross-members, and packing the brake mouldings away from the solebars by 15-thou, and off the floor by 20- to 30-thou.

As moulded, the axleguards don't have the holes in them to facilitate horse- or capstan-shunting. These were drilled $^1/_{32}$ inch, and enlarged slightly by working the drill bit in and out in the pin chuck. Finally I decided to test the theory that plastic trusses would be adequately protected from handling damage by the footboards in front of them, and made them up from 10-thou strip. On balance, I think metal ones are better, if only because of the risk that over time the plastic ones may develop a tendency to warp.

GWR 20T BRAKE VAN

As in other areas, the Great Western went its own way in brake van design. While the other members of the Big Four were building double-ended vehicles with side duckets, the GWR stuck to vans with a single verandah at one end and no proper means for the guard to be able to look along the sides of his train, or watch for signals, from the comfort of his cabin. He also had to go outside to apply the brake. These differences were to result in the design being phased out of main line use from the late 'fifties on safety grounds, and in their relatively early withdrawal from revenue-earning service entirely, although they soldiered on in departmental use well into the 'eighties at least.

Only in this latter guise did they tend to stray far from their original home territory. For most of their life not only were large numbers allocated to particular yards, but in many cases also to specific workings, these details being painted on the sides. In BR days most of them were also branded R.U. (Restricted User) and Not in Common Use. I believe the second inscription came later, and I haven't personally seen photographic evidence of its being applied to mainstream GWR vans before about 1957. Whether it coincided with their being withdrawn from long-distance use, therefore, I'm not sure, but it seems likely. A few other designs from other sources bore the same legend, no doubt for similar reasons, but no type seems to have been accorded the blanket coverage received by GWR vans in this respect.

The history of GWR brake vans prior to nationalisation is amply documented in *GWR Goods Wagons*, backed up by *Great Western Wagons Plan Book*; an article by James Snowdon with photographs and drawings in the May and July 1976 issues of *Model Railway Constructor* is also very useful. BR period photographs are plentiful in Cheona Volume Five, and the small batch of vans turned out by BR to the final GWR diagram is covered in *British Railways Brake Vans and Ballast Ploughs*.

The long-established Ratio kit represents the 24ft long, 16ft wheelbase vehicles built from 1912 right through to 1950. That said, it doesn't exactly fit any of the eight diagrams issued for general-purpose vans of these dimensions, and anyone wanting a model of diagram AA19 in particular might be well advised to look at the etched brass offering from Connoisseur Models. However, being plastic, the Ratio kit does lend itself to the alterations required to turn it into an accurate model of any of the post-WWI designs. It's probably best-suited to diagrams AA15, 18, 19 and 20, covering the period from 1918 to 1943, and the transfers accompanying the kit in fact represent at least three of these.

W35409, a standard unfitted AA23 van, is seen at Birmingham in the 'fifties. The livery appears to be a rather dark grey (there are no black patches behind the lettering), although as one of the last vans to be built to this diagram around the time of nationalisation, this is not unlikely. But why someone should see fit to chalk the running number in the next panel to the perfectly clear painted one is something of a mystery.

The 74 vans built to BR Diagram 1/502 soon after nationalisation were identical to those turned out by the GWR to its Diagram AA23. One of each is seen here in the mid-'sixties (although the photographs are undated, the insulated van seen in both shots was in fairly clean ice-blue livery, introduced in 1963/4). Originally unfitted, both had been vacuum-piped and repainted in bauxite, and both had lost their sanding gear, although W68483, at least, retained the levers that operated it.
AUTHOR'S COLLECTION

Such is the family resemblance of all 'modern' GWR designs, however, that enterprising modellers have used this kit as the basis of most of the twenty-odd diagrams applicable from 1888 onwards; an article in the September 1977 issue of *Model Railway Constructor* illustrates this point very well.

For my own purposes I chose the very last of the 20-ton diagrams, AA23, which doubled as BR's 1/502. In this choice I was influenced to a degree by the existence of an article in *Model Railway Journal* No. 92 by John Hayes, in which he describes the construction of a diagram AA15 van from the same kit (i.e. towards the other extreme of the age range), and also by a picture in Volume Five of the Cheona series showing W35960, an AA23 vehicle built in the mid-'forties and allocated to Coton Hill Yard at Shrewsbury, which I deemed appropriate for my forthcoming layout set in the Wrexham area.

As I studied the various sources, I soon became aware of a number of significant differences between AA23 vans and their predecessors, not all of which are spelled out in words of one syllable. The straight-down side stanchions and modified handrail fastenings are fairly obvious. Less

W35232 is another AA23 van, seen at Radley in 1963. It too had been vacuum piped and re-painted, but this time had kept its sand pipes.
P. J. GARLAND

W114764, photographed at Yeovil in 1959, was an AA20 van with a number of detail differences from the AA23 vehicles: the turned-under bodyside stanchions and the attachment of the handrails are two of them, as is the higher level of the stepboards (most AA20 vans had these in the lower positions of AA23, but it seems that this may not have applied to the earliest vehicles built to this diagram). A. E. WEST so the lower height of the stepboards adopted during construction of AA20. And it takes a keenish eye to spot that the steel sheeting over the lower bodysides is four inches deeper on AA23, a fact that I only verified for certain by comparing preserved examples on the Gloucestershire Warwickshire Railway. The sheeting on the end was extended to match, although I think it had already been deepened by about 2½in from around AA20.

As others have done before me, I began by removing the moulded handrails from the bodysides. It takes time to do this neatly, and even with careful sanding it's virtually impossible to achieve an unblemished finish – as I discovered when my home-made chisel (a ground-down screwdriver) managed to gouge a groove in one place. Fortunately, the separate wire handrails, when fitted, help to conceal any minor irregularities.

Because of the deeper steel sheeting on the van side the upper line of rivets is in the wrong place, and therefore also has to be removed. The bottom row is in the right place, but there should be seven between each pair of vertical stanchions instead of five as moulded. I don't think I would have worried unduly about this had I not already been sacrificing a fair amount of the moulded detail, but it seemed a shame to spoil the ship for a ha'porth of tar, so off they came as well. Incidentally, the top row is correct as moulded in having only five in each section.

The wider steel cladding requires a corresponding adjustment in the side and end planking immediately above it. Measurement of W35357, the AA23 van at Winchcombe, indicated that there is a narrow, 1in-wide, infill strip immediately above the cladding, surmounted by a 4in-wide plank, on both sides and end. Most of the rest of the boarding is around 6¾in/6⅞in, except for two 3¾in planks near the top. These may be the result of a repair: they aren't evident on W35960, but it seems that the 1-inch and 4-inch boards were common to many of the vans built to this diagram. The angle at which most photographs were taken means that this area is obscured by the upper handrail, however, so it's hard to be certain.

Anyhow, I scribed two fresh lines about a scale inch apart, and removed the faint moulded mark on the sides that indicates the top of the steel sheeting. The result is a slight compromise, because there isn't quite enough room to get 26 inches of steel plate and five inches of timber below the lowest of the moulded seams, but it will have to do. Again the handrail helps to confuse the issue on the model, as it does on the real thing from most viewpoints. And I chickened out of including the 4-inch board on the end, where the moulded planking doesn't line up as it should with that on the sides.

At the same time as removing handrails and rivet detail, I also took off the moulded lamp irons, buffer bases and coupling face plates, together with the turned-under side stanchions up to a millimetre or so above the bottom edge of the van sides. At this stage the only other modifications I made to the body parts were to add a sandbox operating lever in brass strip and a Suffolk latch in wire to the partition between the verandah and the van proper, and to overlay the flat rainstrips above and below the windows in the other end of the van with 10-thou strip. Photographs show these to have been triangular in section, and beefing them up in this way enables them to be scraped to the correct profile when everything is dry. I also glazed the windows with 10-thou plastiglaze, and chamfered the bottom of the corner angles of the body at both ends to simulate the cut-away found on all the modern vans; a small triangle of 10-thou was added to reinstate the bottom flange of the headstocks.

Before I could assemble the body, however, I had to stick the two underframe halves together (for once, I followed the kit's instructions to build the body round the floor, chiefly because the sides are in three sections). I found that the two didn't mate very well: not only were the edges slightly curved, they were also feathered or tapered, so they only met along the upper edge in the middle. A few strokes of a file cured that, but for extra rigidity I glued a strip of 20-thou to the underside of one half so that it overlapped the joint and formed a rebate for the other half to fit into. Only then, with the two halves butted squarely against each other (but not yet stuck together) could I check the clearance and alignment of the wheelsets. In fact, the axleboxes needed only a very modest

The verandah detail of W17244 (another van to Diagram AA20 now preserved on the Gloucestershire Warwickshire Railway) was typical of several variants of the GWR brake van family. AUTHOR

amount of drilling out before the bearings went deep enough for the wheels to revolve freely, and no other tweaking was necessary to get the axles parallel in both planes, and square to the longitudinal axis of the underframe.

Since, unlike John Hayes, I was not incorporating suspension or compensation in my model, I didn't need to remove axleguards, axleboxes or springs, though I did carve the mountings for the footboard supports off the solebars, and removed the moulded axleguard tie-bars, since none of the post-AA13 vans seem to have had them. Moreover, the kit comes with five-leaf springs and round-top, GWR-style axleboxes, whereas the later vans had nine-leaf springs of a noticeably flatter profile, and RCH-pattern boxes (W35960 had gone a stage further by 1964 in having a set of BR-style boxes at one end). I doctored the mouldings to suit, using a 10-thou overlay for the springs with the appropriate number of notches along the bottom edge, and altering the shape of the axleboxes to a fatter, squarer outline. The new spring saddles above them are just noggins of 10-thou stuck at an angle between the top of the box and the buckle; from an oblique angle you can see daylight behind them, but this won't be obvious from any normal viewpoint once everything has been painted. Finally, the shackles at each end of the springs are dumb-bells of 10-thou with a touch of relief detail to simulate the ends of the bolts.

One further point to note before sticking the underframe together is that the brake standard is not, as the instructions state, on the centre-line. In fact, depending which diagram you are modelling, there are three different positions for it, all offset to one side or the other, but all a constant 2ft 9in or thereabouts inside the verandah end. For AA23, the offset is about a foot to the left of the centre-line when seen from the van door.

Once the underframe has been assembled, the body can be pieced together around it. Like the underframe halves, the sections of the bodysides are moulded with a slight bevel or taper; if you file these square, as I did to ensure sounder joints, you may find that the roof is a touch overlong. In my case I discovered when I offered it up that the delicate verandah end posts with their hooped top frame were being forced outwards, and I had no choice but to shorten the roof, at the same time carving about ¾mm away from the rebated underside where the hooped frame locates.

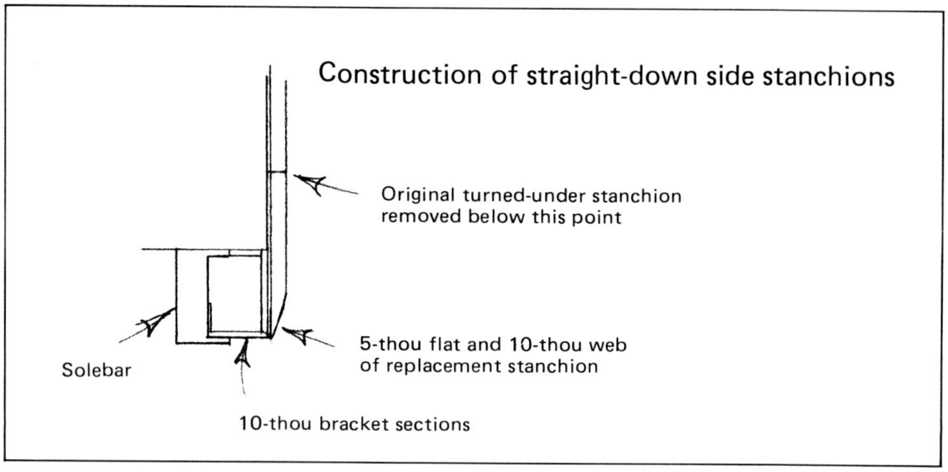

While we're talking about the roof, it's worth noting that according to the drawings in *Great Western Wagons Plan Book*, the chimney was moved about 18in further from the end of the vehicle with effect from diagram AA20. So I cut the moulded one off and substituted a new one soldered up from two gauges of brass tube, using a slice of 4mm diameter sprue as the rather prominent mounting block.

Back with the bodysides, the wooden verandah doors slot between the steel sheeting of the van and verandah sides. The kit has them with relief framing on the outside, and plain on the inside, whereas the framing is on the inside and only the pattern of the planking relieves the outer face. The doors are also slightly inset, although only by half-an-inch or so, which is the thickness of the steel sheeting of the verandah side plus that of a length of angle-iron that acts as a stanchion-cum-doorpost, which the door overlaps. However, the edge of the floor below the door is flush with the sheeting on either side. The easiest option seemed to be to make new doors out of 20-thou styrene, with 10-thou framing on the inside. The thickness of the moulded 'steel' verandah side persuaded me to limit the representation of the overlap – the true width of the door, in other words – to the framing alone.

The fittings inside the verandah varied somewhat from diagram to diagram, although the brake standard and a pair of sandboxes were common to all the general purpose designs. These are provided in the kit, but the sandboxes are rather small, and free-standing, whereas on all diagrams save the vacuum-fitted AA21 they are incorporated into a transverse bench that spans the full width of the outer end. (On AA21, the space between the sandboxes is occupied by the brake cylinder.) Up to and including AA18 there were two lockers in addition, one on each side next to the doorways.

I made up the transverse bench out of 20-thou, and new sandbox tops to sit in each corner. The linkage between them, together with the operating lever, was cobbled up from brass and styrene. Finally, I fitted a scribed overlay in 10-thou to represent the floorboarding, and drilled through it and the floor beneath to accept the brake standard.

With the body and the underframe now in one piece, I was able to replace the turned-under side stanchions I had earlier removed with the straight-down ones fitted to AA23. I used a combination of 10-thou (for the vertical and horizontal bits of the bracket itself, together with the web of the stanchion), and 5-thou (for the flat of the stanchion and the small angle of the bracket bolted to the face of the solebar): five pieces in all, plus a sixth bit of 10-thou to form a ledge of sorts for the upper end of the bracket to locate upon. Hopefully the accompanying diagram will illustrate this more clearly than I can in words.

One small detail present on all the later vans but missing from the kit is the triangular gusset plates beneath each corner of the roof. These came in round about AA19: although they're not shown on the diagram reproduced in *Great Western Wagons Plan Book*, all three AA19 vans pictured in Cheona Vol 5 had them when they were photographed in the 1960s.

Buffers and brakes were fitted using ABS cast parts. RCH 18-inch 4-rib buffers were standard on the later vehicles, but the only one visible on W35960 appears to have only two ribs, so I bodged a set to match. On reflection, it's quite likely that some or all of the other three would have been standard RCH ones, but there's no way of telling from the photograph.

I wasn't over-impressed with the moulded clasp brakes supplied with the kit, and whilst the ABS castings I used were nominally of LNER pattern, they have a more satisfactory chunky look about them. As usual, I yoked each pair with 30-thou plastic rod clipped into the blind holes thoughtfully cast into the backs of the shoes, and added safety loops from narrow n/s strip force-fitted into holes drilled in the transverse ribs of the underframe.

All GWR vans, and at least some of the batch produced after nationalisation, were equipped with sanding gear, and the sandpipes to each wheel are quite prominent. According to the general arrangement drawing of one of the earlier diagrams reproduced in the *Plan Book*, they were of $1\frac{3}{4}$-inch diameter. The nearest wire I had in stock was 24 swg (22 swg would have been closer), which I bent to shape, filing the bottom at an angle parallel to the rail surface. I then wound a length of 33 swg wire round it to make the rod that braced the pipe to the underside of the headstock, and soldered the two together. Pipe and brace are epoxied into suitably-sized holes drilled in the floor and up into the headstock.

As mentioned earlier, both upper and lower footboards began to be set closer to the ground part-way through the production of AA20: four inches in the case of the bottom ones. For this reason alone some alteration of the supports would have been necessary, since the kit has them in the higher positions. In any case, however, the design of the supports changed with diagram AA18 from four forged rods on each side to four lengths of angle-iron; the change was highlighted by the fact that whereas the rods had been bolted to the face of the solebar, and having curved elegantly over the lower flange, dropped vertically to the footboard, the new supports were mounted behind the solebar and descended at a rakish angle. Rather unexpectedly, AA19 and all subsequent designs reverted to two supports of each pattern, the outer ones becoming once again vertical rods. The moulded supports on the kit, while a bit nondescript, more closely resemble the older style.

Since the replacement supports could only satisfactorily be made in metal, I felt, I was tempted to make the footboards themselves in the same way, as indeed John Hayes does with the lower ones in his *MRJ* article. I did use metal for the short upper ones, soldering two lengths of n/s strip to a piece of 20-thou n/s sheet and epoxying these spigots into holes drilled just above the lower solebar flange. The upper stepboards are level with the flange, so the bits of strip need to be double cranked to fit. Unlike the moulded ones supplied with the kit, the top steps have no toeboards at the back; they are also mounted slightly off-centre in relation to the doorway above them, and coincidentally one of the moulded brackets for the lower stepboards is in exactly the right place, directly beneath the corner post of the van section. This did me no good at all, because I had already removed both the centre ones in anticipation of the new angle-iron supports for the lower footboards, which don't need them. But it was a simple job to apply a couple of bits of 5-thou, which also served to obscure the holes drilled to attach the top steps.

In the end I retained the plastic mouldings supplied for the lower footboards. But I didn't fancy the idea of just gluing them to the new metal supports, and decided to help the joints along with some vertical wire pins soldered into the ends of the supports where they project beneath the footboard. The pins mate with holes drilled in the footboard itself, and getting all four supports the right length and at the right angle to ensure that the footboard is straight and level takes quite a lot of tweaking. I used 24 swg wire for the outer supports, epoxied into holes drilled just

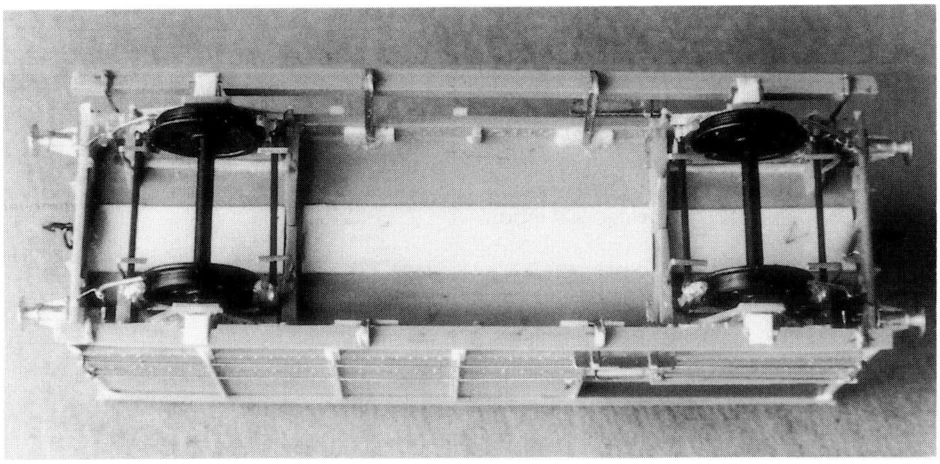

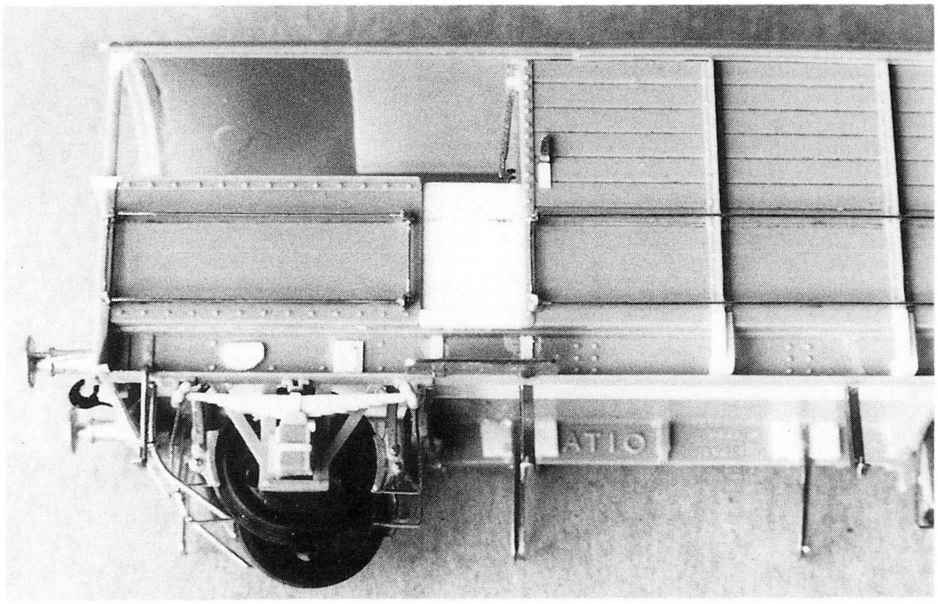

Because the Ratio kit for the GWR brakevan combines certain features from more than one diagram, some alterations are almost inevitable whichever version you choose. AA23 and D 1/502 vans probably require the greatest number of modifications, however, as this series of photographs proves.

above the lower solebar flange, and clenched flat at the bottom so that they could be drilled for the wire pin. For the two centre supports 1mm brass angle was mounted behind the solebar between two slabs of 40-thou; one web of the angle was filed away to make a spigot that would be forced into a hole drilled in the floor immediately adjacent to the solebar.

The drawings suggest that these lengths of angle-iron all faced one way, whichever side of the van they were on: looking at the projection of the angle behind the footboard, the web that points across the van is at the verandah end. The three you can see on the photograph of W35960 are certainly like this, so I assumed they all were, but in practice the orientation of the supports varied from vehicle to vehicle: any of them can face in either direction, it seems.

The drawings also show that the footboards narrowed progressively over the last couple of feet or so. This is difficult to detect on photographs, and on most of the preserved vehicles I've looked at, they don't. I'm inclined to put this down to the likelihood that the timbers have been

replaced at some time; anyway, I chamfered mine in accordance with the drawings.

Finally, as with the LNER and BR vans, I stiffened the footboards a bit by sticking a semi-invisible piece of 10-thou across the gap between the underside of each axle-box and the footboard outside it.

I used the same 1mm brass angle for the sixteen handrail brackets. Having drilled two 1/64 inch holes (for the 30 swg nickel-silver wire I was planning to use) close to the end of the strip of angle, I then filed the webs away over a length of about 3 or 4mm to form a spigot to fit another hole in the van side. I thought for some time about how best to fit the handrails themselves, and ended up epoxying two diagonally opposed brackets of each group of four into their holes and soldering two bits of wire cut to approximate length, one short and one longer, into each of the other two in an L shape. I did this with the spigots jammed into a lump of balsa to avoid any risk of the plastic melting by trying to do it in situ.

With the wires now trimmed to exact length, I was able to thread the shorter leg into its fixed bracket at the same time as I was locating the soldered bracket in its hole, and then to spring the end of the long handrail into the other fixed bracket with a pair of tweezers. Rather than soldering the free ends of the rails into place, I used a dab of epoxy, again for fear of causing damage with a hot iron.

Unlike the earlier diagrams, there are no intermediate brackets on AA23 to secure the long handrails to the vertical side stanchions on the van body. Instead, where the web of each stanchion was notched to locate them, the handrails were simply welded into place. Securing wire to plastic in this fashion on the model presents obvious problems, but it seemed the best way to try to keep the handrails straight, and I'm hoping that the touch of epoxy I applied at each notch will do the trick. At least all the handrails are straight and parallel even if, despite my efforts, I managed to get the top ones ½ mm higher on one side than on the other.

The first design of brake van adopted for new construction by the Southern was the ex-SECR 'Dance Hall', which was duly given SR Diagram No. 1560. DS55500, seen at Eastleigh in 1962, was a 1927-built vehicle that showed few changes from pre-grouping example S55467 photographed three years earlier at Exmouth Junction. The absence of side duckets told against these vans (S55467 had already been branded 'Not in Common Use' for this reason), but many like DS55500 went on to lead long and useful lives in departmental service: a very respectable 1923-built vehicle was seen in this guise at Barrow-in-Furness(!) as late as 1985. A. E. WEST

SOUTHERN RAILWAY 25-TON BRAKE VANS

Not surprisingly, in view of its smaller share of the country's traffic, the Southern had fewer brake vans than each of the other members of the Big Four, and new buildings during its lifetime could be counted in hundreds rather than the thousands built in particular by the LMS and LNER.

Nevertheless, its modest total included several diagrams and three distinct designs of vehicle, from the SECR-style vans of diagram 1560 to the impressive bogie brakes of diagrams 1550 and 1580. But the bulk of new construction, extending from the late 'twenties through to nationalisation, was accounted for by three diagrams of 25-ton vans similar in layout to the long-wheelbase LNER vehicles: a short cabin on a 24ft over headstocks, 16ft wheelbase underframe, but noticeably narrower across the body, and with offset duckets; the horizontal planking and 15-inch solebars were also distinctive. A 15-ton version with shallower solebars for branchline working completed the range.

Though they were obviously fairly rare beasts outside their own territory, odd 25-tonners, and even bogie vehicles, could turn up almost anywhere from time to time, at least during the BR period.

Unlike the brake vans built by the other members of the Big Four, the standard design eventually worked out by the Southern looked to owe little to pre-grouping practice, although the underframe was in fact taken directly from D 1560. 1929-built S55532, already over thirty years old when seen at Stockport in 1962, was an example of the earliest version, Diagram 1578, evidenced by the left-hand ducket and the footboards bracketed off the face of the solebar (c.f. DS55500). Subsequent modifications include the removal of the sandboxes (leaving the telltale battens on the verandah screen), the addition of a second window in the cabin end to the right of the door and through vacuum piping. By comparison, S55583, built a year later to D 1579 and seen in 1959, had a right-hand ducket and footboards attached to the bottom flange of the solebar. It too had been vacuum-piped by BR, and both vans had wagon-type axleguards rather than the heavy-duty plate variety fitted to all but the earliest of these vehicles.

J. A. G. H. COLTAS, CTY. STEVE HALL and A. E. WEST

Also to D 1579, S56175, dating from 1933, retained its sandboxes when photographed in 1951. So, too, in 1948, did S56355, built in 1943 to the same diagram, although now with alternating wide and narrow planking and enlarged, two-pane windows next to the cabin doors. Notice the two, slightly differing styles of sandbox.

A. E. WEST

S55129 represents the final development of the SR style, Diagram 1582, and was turned out at the time of nationalisation. Built without sanding equipment, it also had redesigned brakegear, involving two sets of V-hangers with cranks on each attached to a central pulling bracket at the foot of the brake column.
ROGER CARPENTER

(Incidentally, though I shall go on referring to them as '25-ton vans', many of the later ones were in fact rather lighter than this.)

Two kits are currently available for the 25-ton vans. One, in etched brass, was originally produced by Derek Mundy under his Model Signal Engineering trade name, and has since passed to London Road Models. It represents the version with even-planked bodywork and duckets offset to the right, plate axleguards, and footboards bracketed off the bottom of the solebars. These were built to diagram 1579, although later batches under this number had bodywork with alternate pairs of narrow and wide planks, a change which also took place with other varieties of Southern van (see Part Two, Chapter One). Diagram 1578, which preceded it, covers a small number of vans with the duckets on the left, W-axleguards, and footboards attached to the face of the solebar. These would be relatively straightforward modifications to the kit; representing the later uneven-planked bodywork, which was shared with the final diagram, 1582, might be more difficult. Diagram 1582 also had different brakegear, and lacked the sanding equipment featured by all its predecessors.

The second current kit, Cambrian's plastic version, is more flexible in offering parts that cover all three diagrams, and having previously used Derek Mundy's kit to build an example of D1579 (of which more anon), I decided to model one of the initial D1578 vehicles. I chose S55982, a good photograph of which appears in Cheona Vol. 5. Prior to the recent publication of Volume Four of *An Illustrated History of Southern Wagons*, which contains photographs and drawings of this and other variations, the only other published pictures I had found of these vans were of S55556 in the January 1971 issue of *Railway Modeller*, and of S55953 in *British Railway Modelling* for October 2001, in articles by Terry Gough and David Larkin respectively. Other sources include *Model Railway Constructor* for May 1967, and David Larkin's Data Sheet on brake vans, as well as both sets of kit instructions, of course.

Incidentally, there are a few apparent errors and inconsistencies between the various sources, especially when it comes to the numbering of the D1578 vehicles, and it's difficult even to be sure how many of them there were: probably not as many as the ninety claimed by Cambrian. For example, both David Larkin and Derek Mundy place S55556 in D1579, when the photograph in *Railway Modeller* clearly shows it to have been one of the early series. Indeed, the notes included in the etched kit were silent on the very existence of a separate diagram for these. And Cambrian don't even recognise S55556 as falling in any of the number series used for the 25-ton vans, although I think this is only a misprint.

The confusion seems to stem from the fact that some of the D1578 vehicles are apparently intermingled with the first batch of D1579. Volume Four of *Southern Wagons* states that there was a total of eighty vans built to the earlier pattern, but even here a complete number series is lacking. With these vans especially, therefore, the old adage of modelling to a specific photograph is particularly valid.

The instructions for the Cambrian kit start with the underframe, as do the modifications necessary for anyone building one of the earlier vehicles. The kit is moulded with the later solid plate axleguards; to convert these into the earlier W configuration, the notes tell you to cut the V-shaped holes above and below the springs, but they don't mention the need to file back the edges first: these guards tapered more, and the bottom seven or eight inches on each side should be vertical. There is an assumption stated or implied in some of the sources that only D1578 vans had wagon-type axleguards, but photographs prove that these were also fitted to some of the early D1579 vehicles as well, among them S55574 and 55583.

As already mentioned, all but the last of the 25-tonners were equipped with sanding gear, but the abandonment of this on all new vans from 1947 signalled its progressive removal from all or most of the older ones over the next few years – although not in many cases from the 15-ton or bogie brakes, for some reason. On some vehicles the former position of the sandboxes was shown by battens that remained attached to the verandah screens. These aren't to be seen on S55982, but I'm assuming that the other tell-tales, the holes for the pipes in the decking below the boxes, were still visible. The floor moulding makes provision for these, and the positions for drilling them are marked on the underside.

Modellers of the Southern Railway period should be aware that not all the sandboxes fitted to these vans were the same as the ones included in the Cambrian kit: the plain type borne by S56175, built c.1931, and illustrated here still with its sandboxes in place, preceded the possibly more familiar 'upturned vee' style as typified by the plastic kit. The notes enclosed with the etched kit do refer to this change, and also illustrate the slightly tortuous layout of the sandpipes.

Assembly of the underframe is made more difficult by the absence of any very positive location for the solebars on the edges of the floor. The mating surfaces are chamfered at 45 degrees, which makes it rather too easy to get one end of a solebar higher than the other. Worse, you can finish up with each pair of axleguards not properly aligned and the axles askew instead of at right-angles to the longitudinal axis of the underframe. The risk of this can be minimised by attaching one solebar first, leaving it to set, and then matching the other one to it, but there is still an element of chance in deciding exactly where to put the first one, and more than usual care is needed at every stage in making sure that all is square and parallel in every plane.

Another sensible precaution is to ensure that the wheel bearings aren't too tight a fit so that if necessary you can prise them out and adjust them (as described in Part One). I made the mistake of force-fitting mine, and was able to remove one only by attacking the face of the axlebox with a hammer and punch. This left an ugly hole which I then had to plug with a suitably-shaped noggin of plastic, filed flush when set.

Speaking of axleboxes, those provided in the kit have vertical faces approximating to the large BR open-fronted boxes fitted to a lot of the vans in later life. However, many, perhaps all, of the 25-tonners originally had axleboxes with inclined fronts, and 55982 certainly retained these when photographed in 1954. A few strokes of a file, plus a little added surface detail, effected the transformation.

One very visible result of the kit's method of attaching the solebars to the floor is the joint line close to the edges of the end platforms where the components meet. On the real thing the deck plating extends right the way across to the outer edges of the solebar flanges, but the kit doesn't represent this very satisfactorily. I concealed the joints with narrow strips of 10-thou plastic which I sanded smooth and flush with the surface, but this rather accentuates the thickness of the top flange. In reality the combined thickness of the flange and the plating is little more than an inch.

Although, as I say, the fitting of the solebars to the floor moulding isn't exactly foolproof, I must have got it about right because the ledges behind the headstocks, which are designed to slot snugly between the backs of the solebars and under the floor, did just that, and ended up nice and square into the bargain. The buffers are each built up from three pieces: the guide, which is integral with the headstock; the head, which incorporates part of the ram; and the remainder of the ram, which also includes the rim around the end of the guide. As moulded, the ram is a touch wider than the guide, which looks a bit odd, but is easy to remedy with a file when the assembly has set. And if you're using scale coupling hooks, you may agree that the slots in the headstocks are rather generous. I stuck a 40-thou blank behind the hole and replaced the face plate with a new one in 10-thou, before re-drilling both to finer tolerances.

The instructions recommend leaving the detailing of the underframe until after the completion of the body. Because the kit offers so many options, this is where things start to get complicated. Some of the parts are cleverly moulded on both sides, so that by reversing them you have two choices of planking or ducket layout. This required the removal of some of the rivet detail on the inside of the even-planked cabin sides so that the van end partitions mated cleanly and securely with them. I also felt it was advisable to file away the rivets on the inside face of the verandah screen corner posts to ensure that the doors fitted snugly, and to tidy up the slightly distorted ducket mouldings with a file before adding them. This is all relatively straightforward once you've made up your mind which bits you're using, and which way round they want to be.

The hardest part to get right, I found, was the choice of cabin end partitions. Not only did the door and window layout vary according to the ducket position, later vans had a revised window design, and all, or nearly all, the vehicles had extra windows added after nationalisation. And of course they mirrored the planking variations as well. All in all, a potent recipe for confusion, but to try to make some sense of it, I think the train of events went something like this:

(a) The cabin doors were always slightly offset from the centreline of the partition towards the nearer ducket; all the doors were glazed with a single pane.
(b) In addition to the door light, another window, initially a single pane, was provided in the wider of the two resulting panels beside the door, that is, away from the nearer ducket. Another way of looking at this is: left-hand ducket, left-hand window; right-hand ducket, right-hand window.
(c) From the time of the change to uneven planking, new vehicles had this second window enlarged to fill the whole of the panel between the door and the corner post. In the process it acquired a central vertical glazing bar.
(d) Finally, starting about the time of nationalisation, a third window was cut in the smaller of the two panels, i.e. between the door and the nearer ducket. Whatever the size of the second window, this was always a single pane of about the same dimensions as (b). Because of the offset door, however, it filled the whole panel.

All these options are available in the kit, although in some cases only by using a blank to fill in a moulded window opening or by cutting a new one. The photograph of S55982 doesn't show clearly whether this particular van had acquired the third window by 1954, when it was taken, but I'm assuming that in any case it would have done so by my own modelling period of 1957/8. I used Plastiglaze for both the partitions and the duckets. Because there's a narrow frame round each of the ducket windows, I stuck a slightly oversized rectangle of glazing on the outside, hoping that my hand would be steady enough to simulate the frame by painting neatly round the edge when the time came. It was only after I'd fitted the duckets that I realised that they don't project quite as far as they should from the van side. Coupled with a marginal shortfall in the width of the cabin itself, this means that the completed body is about 1.5mm narrower than it ought to be. If I were to build the kit again, I think I would seek to

Two views of S56200, another D1579 van, seen at Axminster in 1956. It had clearly gained the extra window in the cabin end (the one to the left of the door), but for some reason seems to have had the door light itself blanked off. The original window had a 'No Smoking' sign on it; economical re-use of secondhand glass, perhaps, or could there have been a connection with the fuel depot in the background? The photographer has noted also that this was one of the ex-SR vans to have had the cabin ends painted in red oxide. A. E. WEST pack the duckets away from the sides with 30-thou before fitting them.

A few detail alterations and additions were made to the body in order to match the model to 55982. The label clips were moved from the right-hand panel of the cabin sides to the left; three small washer plates were added in 5-thou on one side of the cabin – I'm pretty sure that these denoted the presence of spare lamp brackets on the inside; and three lamp irons (the central one replacing the kit's single moulded one) were fitted to the verandah screen. These were made from L-shaped bits of metal strip and 5-thou plastic as described on page 27 of Part One. Most of the vans had three when new; those with sanding gear had the middle one mounted on the sandbox. In most cases only the central one was retained after removal of the boxes, now bolted directly to the screen, but 55982 (and 55583) kept all three, at least for a while. Finally, the moulded lamp irons supplied for the verandah corner posts were discarded in favour of home-made ones cut and filed from thin nickel-silver sheet as with the LNER/BR vans.

In common with the GWR, the Southern fitted proper half-height doors, or gates, to the verandah entrances of their vans. Those in the kit have moulded lugs at one side designed to fit behind the narrow panel projecting from the cabin side. I felt that these resulted in the doors being recessed rather too far into the opening, so I filed them away: in any case, the doors that I modelled in the closed position needed a bit of trimming to fit the gap. The problem is compounded by the fact that the projecting panel is set in a little from the vertical stanchion alongside it: in reality they should be flush with each other, or almost so. I attempted to correct this by overlaying the panel with a narrow strip of 5-thou, having first plugged the moulded grab handle holes, for reasons I will explain shortly.

Whether you model the doors open or closed is a matter of choice. Most of the photographs you see of brake vans of all types tend to show one or more of the entrances with the doors (or the door bars, as the case may be) in the open position. However, the majority of pictures also show brake vans parked in sidings, and therefore probably illustrate the guard's inclination to leave them open when alighting. In use, I have no doubt that they were supposed to be shut for safety reasons, and logically, therefore, that's probably how they should be modelled. All the same, I like to show both alternatives, and on S55982 I opted to have both doors on one side closed, and on the other side open.

The kit's only provision for handrails is a series of blind holes incorporated in the cabin side mouldings, plus a recommendation to use 20-thou plastic rod, which isn't supplied. My experience with using plastic rod for handrails is that it's difficult to get the straight bits to stay straight over time, so I would always use wire for preference. In any case, 20-thou is a bit hefty, but the next available size down, 10-thou, would be too thin. I used 28 swg nickel-silver wire to start with, although I changed to brass for the vertical rails for reasons which will become clear.

Because I was using a thinner gauge material, I plugged all the moulded holes with 20-thou square strip, filed round, and redrilled the holes 1/64 inch when the plugs had dried and been trimmed flush. This enabled me to adjust the position of the holes slightly to allow for the fixing lugs that were forged in the ends of each of the rails. In the case of the horizontals these were represented by noggins of 5-thou once the rails had been epoxied into place, but the vertical grab handles were a bit different. Instead of having the lugs in line with the rail, they were offset at ninety degrees. So, while the fixing bolts were in the centre of the projecting panels/corner posts, the rails themselves were much closer to the edges of the doorways – virtually on top of them, in fact. This made mounting the rails in the conventional way almost impossible, especially where the doors were open, and I could think of no other workable solution than to bend the wire through three right-angles at each end in the space of about 1½ mm. This was too much for the rather brittle nickel-silver wire I was using, and after several breakages I switched to brass. Being softer, this is easier to bend, but, for the same reason, is more inclined to become distorted in service.

Little needs to be said about the roof, although care should be taken to ensure that the stove chimney is on the correct side and at the correct end: it needs to be above the ducketless panel in the opposite half of the cabin to the handbrake wheel, whose position is marked by the orientation of the brake gear beneath the underframe. All this is referred to in the notes, and the relative positions are marked on the undersides of the roof and the floor, but as I was intending to leave the roof unfitted for the time being to facilitate painting, I though it was wise to put extra register marks under the roof and inside the cabin to remind myself which way round the roof should go.

The kit provides torpedo ventilators of the elliptical kind, which were by far the most common fitted to these vans, but 55982 had circular ones, so I used a pair of cast whitemetal vents instead. I also replaced the stove chimney supplied, which has a distinct taper, with one fabricated from two sizes of brass tube.

Surveying the appearance of the completed body with the roof held in position, it occurred to me that, in addition to being rather narrow over the duckets, it looked a bit squat as well, certainly by comparison with the finished etched brass kit alongside it. Checking the overall height from end platform level to the highest point of the roof, which according to a general arrangement drawing I happened to have, should be about 7ft 3in/29mm, it scaled out at only 27mm, a full six inches too low. I have to say that I had inadvertently exaggerated this by filing the bottom edges of the side and end mouldings square to obtain a good joint, but I'm sure I took off no more than a fraction of a millimetre.

Part of the trouble seems to be that the kit makes no real effort to reproduce the 4in-wide metal frame that surmounts the bodysides immediately below the roof; the top edge of this is barely hidden by the overhang of the roof. While the thickness of the roof moulding can be adapted to represent the rather narrower frame on the ends, with a slender strip of 15-thou following the curve of the roof to simulate the overhang, above the sides it's prominent enough to need a strip of 40-thou attached to the top edge of the cabin side mouldings so that it projects slightly outside the line of the body detail. Overlays of 30-thou on the top, and of 10-thou on the face of the verandah screen above the opening, raise the end profile to match. I didn't alter the height of the cabin end partitions because the roof moulding is quite rigid, and with the roof in place the tops of them can't be seen from any normal viewing angle, but I did attach a couple of styrene blocks to the underside of the roof to fit snugly between them and so fix its fore-and-aft position.

Of course, this only makes up about half of the shortfall. The other 3 inch deficit is harder to pinpoint. On the sides it seems to be in the area of the top plank, which is barely half the width it ought to be, but on the ends I fancy that it's the verandah screen which isn't high enough. This has implications for the height of the doors as well, and the combination makes an easy solution impossible, especially at the advanced construction stage I'd reached. Armed with 20/20 hindsight, what I think I should have done is to have added material above the sides and below the ends earlier on, but it was too late for that. So I left well alone and turned my attention to completing the underframe detail.

The eight brake shoes locate onto pips moulded on the backs of the solebars. However, this results in their being both too low and too far away from the wheels, so I stuck them directly to the solebars inboard of the pips and clear of the floor by about a millimetre, using strips of 40-thou stuck to the underside of the floor, both as spacers and to make a sounder joint. There are cups moulded into the backs of the shoes to take yokes of 30-thou plastic rod, though no provision is made for safety loops, which on these vehicles were fairly conspicuous, being metal strip instead of the more usual rod. I used brass strip a little under a millimetre wide, force-fitted into chunks of 60-thou stuck to the underside of the floor.

Apart from a couple of batches built for the army during World War II, none of the 25-ton vans received fitted brakegear. In his brakevan data sheet, however, David Larkin provides a list of the large number that were vacuum-piped by BR in the years after nationalisation; S55982 wasn't one of them. Later still, survivors acquired air pipes as well: the kit makes provision for both options. But in my case no more brakegear was required than the moulded V-hangers under the centre-line of the cabin. One of these is plain and the other incorporates the pull-rod from the brake standard in the cabin above, together with the lever that turns the cross-shaft between the V-hangers. The second one should of course be fitted beneath the brake wheel, whose position varies according to whether you're modelling a left-hand ducket van or a right-hand one. Again, cups are moulded in for the ends of the cross-shaft, but the one on the combined V-hanger and pull-rod moulding ends up on the wrong side for a left-handed vehicle like S55982, and needs to be drilled

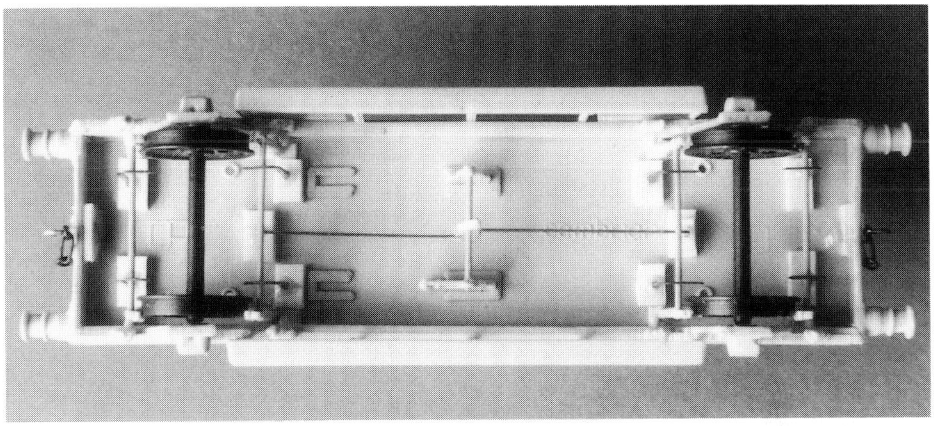

through to fit the shaft. For good measure I added a rocker half-way along the shaft, together with wire pull-rods towards the wheels; the hidden ends of these are bent up and epoxied into more 60-thou lumps stuck to the floor.

As mentioned earlier, two different styles of footboard supports were fitted to these vans: the vast majority had plain, flat ones fixed to the bottom flange of the solebar by triangular brackets, but diagram 1578 had angle-iron supports riveted to the solebar face. The kit offers both options, but reference to the photograph of S55982 – the only clear picture I had at the time of what the angle-iron sort looked like – suggested that the mouldings of the earlier type of bracket didn't really do justice to the original. Understandably, the angle-iron is represented as solid square bar, and the hollow, three-sided nature of the bracket itself would be difficult to reproduce in plastic in this scale, certainly without an unacceptable loss of strength in the finished assembly. As it is, the rigidity of the footboards owes as much to the contact between the short upper steps and the solebar flange, together with the fact that the outer supports can be glued surreptitiously to the faces of the springs, as it does to the brackets themselves. But I felt that with care I could simulate the shape of the brackets more satisfactorily by adding slivers of 5-thou behind, alongside and in front of the moulded ones, even if the result is probably a gnat's whisker overscale. Unfortunately, the kit compounds the deficiencies referred to earlier in the height and width of the cabin by being 1.5mm too narrow over the bottom steps, and this does tend to make the finished vehicle look a little pinched.

Clearly, it's in areas like the footboards that an etched kit scores over a plastic one, and I had no misgivings about the strength of the supports in the Model Signal Engineering kit (mine had been bought when the range was still being handled by Derek Mundy himself). As with most of the etched wagon kits I've come across, however, some of the more elaborate details tend to be simplified, and a measure of scratchbuilding would be necessary to rectify this. This is particularly true of the rather complicated ironwork on the sides just above the solebars, and even lamp irons went unprovided for in the etched parts, and unmentioned in the notes, except for being shown on the line drawing they include. So it's rather a pity that some of the nicest detail in the kit, the stove casting, the brake standard assembly and the etched sanding lever, should be virtually invisible inside the cabin.

However, a significant plus point in terms of detailing is that the rivets that decorate the thin overlays are half-etched from the rear, and need to be pressed out using a not-too-sharp, pointed tool of some kind – I used an old set of school compasses. This method produces nice crisp results provided care is taken to keep them all about the same size, and the only problem I found was that, even though I followed the instructions to work on a sheet of card on a firm, flat surface, I couldn't prevent the thin brass strip from curling upwards in the process. Despite careful straightening, I found it well nigh impossible to iron out all the creases completely, and the odd ripple can still be seen if you know where to look.

That said, the instructions proved a reliable guide, and I departed from the recommended order of doing things in only one or two details. Preferring to work on a flat surface wherever possible, I attached the frames for the doors and windows before bending up the van body and soldering it to the floor. DS56108, a 1931-built example of diagram 1579 of which I had a couple of passable slides taken at Wakefield in the early 'eighties, and which I was using as my model, had had the usual modification of an extra window cut in the end partitions, so I drilled a 1/16 inch hole in each one and enlarged these with files into a rectangle. Framing to match the etchings supplied for the other openings was cut from scrap material.

I also added the verandah gates and vertical handrails to the body side framing overlays before attaching these to the van: I felt it might be hard to get at the back of the overlays with the iron otherwise. To disguise the thinness of the gates and verandah screens, I soldered additional strips of metal along the inside top edges. This also helps to hide the rather basic system of attaching the gates by hanging them on the tails of the outer vertical grab rails. (For this vehicle, although I was using 28 swg wire as recommended in the notes, I had made no attempt to bend the rails in order to offset them in the way described earlier: when I built this kit, I suspect this was a detail that eluded me.)

Turning to the running gear, each of the axleguards is a separate etching; this could be asking for trouble in the way of axle alignment, but happily the correct fore-and-aft positioning is ensured by lining up etched register marks on the base of each axleguard with corresponding ones on the floor. Even so, the instructions wisely counsel you to tack solder the second of each pair in place until you're absolutely sure that everything is square. Springing the axles in and out, and making sure they revolve freely without too much slop, is eased by not butting the axleguards too tightly against the solebars: it is enough to solder just the foot of the L-shaped etch to the floor.

The cast whitemetal axlebox and spring assemblies need to be separated from a carrier casting which prevents damage to the rather delicate J-hangers; the instructions recommend soldering scraps of brass strip behind the solebars to save them from being bent by rough handling in service to which the outer ones, at least, would be particularly susceptible. When I came to fit the castings, however, I found that the holes in the backs of the axleboxes didn't line up with the bearings. In fact, they were a mile out (well, a good millimetre), certainly more than could be remedied by drilling the holes out to 3/32 inch as suggested in the instructions. Nor was filing down the tops of the J-hangers to the merest sliver enough either. Even flattening the curvature of the springs with a pair of pliers didn't do the trick. In the end, I had to take out each of the bearings and enlarge the holes in the axleguards downwards by about half a millimetre – luckily the van had previously sat a bit low, so the only adverse effect is the slightly scrunched-up look of the castings, and the fact that the bottoms of the axleguards are completely hidden by the axleboxes, which they shouldn't be. Had I suspected this problem earlier, a more satisfactory solution would have been to pack the bases of the axleguards off the underside of the floor by 20- to 30-thou.

Another slight problem I encountered (and both of them may have been rectified since) was that the pre-formed brass roof was rather too narrow. It's clear from photographs that the edges of the roof overlapped the van sides by a perceptible margin, whereas the one supplied was barely flush on either side. So I made up another from 15-thou styrene sheet, curved as described on page 4 of Part Two, and reinforced underneath with a second lamination of similar thickness. Once again, I left it loose pending painting.

One other minor addition I made in plastic was the wooden boarding of the verandah floor. Both this and the cabin proper were floored out in 2in deal boards on top of the steel deck, so I shaped and scribed two pieces of 30-thou styrene which I Evo-stuck to the visible areas inside the gates.

A selection of shots of the two Southern brakevan models described in this section. The Cambrian plastic kit has been built up as a D 1578 example, while the one-time Model Signal Engineering etched version represents the slightly later D 1579, the principal differences being the positions of the duckets and the footboard mountings. The comparative height of the cabins will be noted, as will the differing depth of the solebars. Neither exactly reproduces the unusual 15-inch ones used on the 25-ton vans; on the etched kit they are a bit too deep (which may be careless folding on my part, but it's a point to watch), while the overscale flanges on the plastic model tend to accentuate what are already slightly shallow representations of the original.

Wheeled loads are relatively straightforward to model, although the ropes and chocks that go with them (and without which realism suffers markedly) complicate matters somewhat, certainly if you like to make them removable. Even if you're happy to compromise in this respect, however, and settle for permanent loads, the complexity of these three examples would be a challenge to reproduce in full in the smaller scales. Plate wagon B935050 was photographed at Wrexham in 1968, Lowfit B453327 at Edinburgh around 1960, and (opposite page) ex-LMS single-plank wagon M460105 at Kentish Town in 1951. DAVID LARKIN, DON ROWLAND and A. E. WEST

CHAPTER FOUR

FINISHING TOUCHES

WAGON LOADS AND SHEETS

As modellers, it's perhaps easy for us to forget now and then that the railways have never run trains just for the love of it, but to move people and goods from place to place. Time was when almost every item of merchandise that moved in this country went by rail, only the canals and coastal shipping offering any real alternative, with the horse and cart used for initial collection and final delivery over short distances.

Now one of the objectives of any transport undertaking is to avoid as far as possible valuable assets standing idle. Large numbers of empty wagons in sidings are not something any railway operator wants to see, and moving them around unloaded should be minimised at all costs. That said, it was often necessary to reposition empties to their next loading point, so unremunerative journeys were in many cases unavoidable. This was especially true of wagons designed for a particular purpose, such as ore hoppers, brick wagons and minerals. And it must be said that in steam days wagons did tend to stand around doing nothing for long periods of time: by the 'sixties, a handful of loaded journeys a year were all that the average high-sided merchandise wagon could expect.

Nevertheless, the aim was to move wagons under load as often as possible, because only then was money being made. So a large proportion of the make-up of most mixed goods trains on any main line would have consisted of loaded wagons, and those of us who operate a main-line layout should reflect this. Pick-up goods trains are a bit different. In the context of local goods yards, it would be unusual to find many where the inward and outward traffic flows were sufficiently balanced to enable visiting wagons to run loaded in both directions on any significant scale. So modellers who feature this kind of operation – which is probably most of us – have an extra problem if they want to simulate realistic goods working, namely the need to model wagons that can be run both loaded and empty.

Happily, there are quite a few vehicles that look the same in both cases: vans, tanks and covered hoppers, to name a few. Even Conflats would rarely be seen on the move without a container on board, though whether the container itself is loaded or empty is another matter, of course. But with all such vehicles, most of us would be satisfied with placing them in a position where they might be loaded or unloaded when no-one's looking: a goods shed, loading dock, crane, oil depot, etc.

Open wagons and their multifarious loads are less straightforward, but a good many of them can be made removable if you're happy to put up with the big hand from the sky now and again. Even this can be avoided in some cases: loading minerals and hoppers with a measured amount of free-flowing material from an overhead

There's no great science to these removable loads designed for mineral and hopper wagons, but what matters is how the finished load looks when it's in place, and how easy it is to put in and take out. Simplest of all is the coal load whose removal is demonstrated with the aid of B556306, the fitted mineral described in Part One.

chute is a feature that regular exhibition-goers will have seen quite often over the years, and is something that has obvious applications if you include colliery screens or quarry loading bunkers on your layout. Emptying such wagons on stage by any method other than tippling is less easy, and along with working container gantries, wagon turntables, capstans and shunting tractors, mechanical contrivances of this kind are sometimes less than entirely convincing in operation.

Not that this is necessarily a reason to avoid them, but my own preference is for a less technical solution to the problem, which is rather wider in application, but requires a greater suspension of disbelief in the onlooker – or, at least, a willingness to look the other way for a moment or two. So in the next few pages I shall deal with reproducing some of the more common types of traffic that are visible when in transit, and offer suggestions as to how they may be made removable should you choose to do so.

⋆ ⋆ ⋆

Coal has long been one of the most important traffics on the railways of this country, and few goods yards were without a siding or two dedicated to receiving it. But it has always struck me as slightly odd that so many of us should turn a blind eye to the fact that a wagon that comes in loaded ought to go out empty.

Making a realistic-looking heap of coal isn't difficult, and there's more than one way of doing it. Balsa can be carved easily enough with a craft knife into a shape with one or two mounds in the middle and shallow dips at the edges and corners. Alternatively, thickish card can be shaped similarly in your fingers, with narrow darts cut at the edges to enable it to be bent in two directions at once; a layer of gummed parcel tape (more permanent than Sellotape) will stiffen it up and ensure that it keeps the intended profile. A coat of black paint or indian ink will darken the surface nicely. Or you could use some other easily-shaped material such as tubular pipe insulation foam as John Hayes recommends in *The 4mm Coal Wagon*.

To make it easily removable, aim for a load that will fit quite loosely into the wagon: a gap of half a millimetre round the edges won't show unduly, and will enable it to be put in and taken out without catching. The simplest way to get the load out that I've found is to mount it on a central base that is about a third of the length

Another refugee from Part One is the LNER 13-ton wooden hopper (still unpainted twelve years on), for which a coupling hook – or any bit of bent wire – is used to engage in the slot in the top of the load. Notice how unobtrusive the slot becomes once the material has been glued to the bare surface, except when seen from directly above.

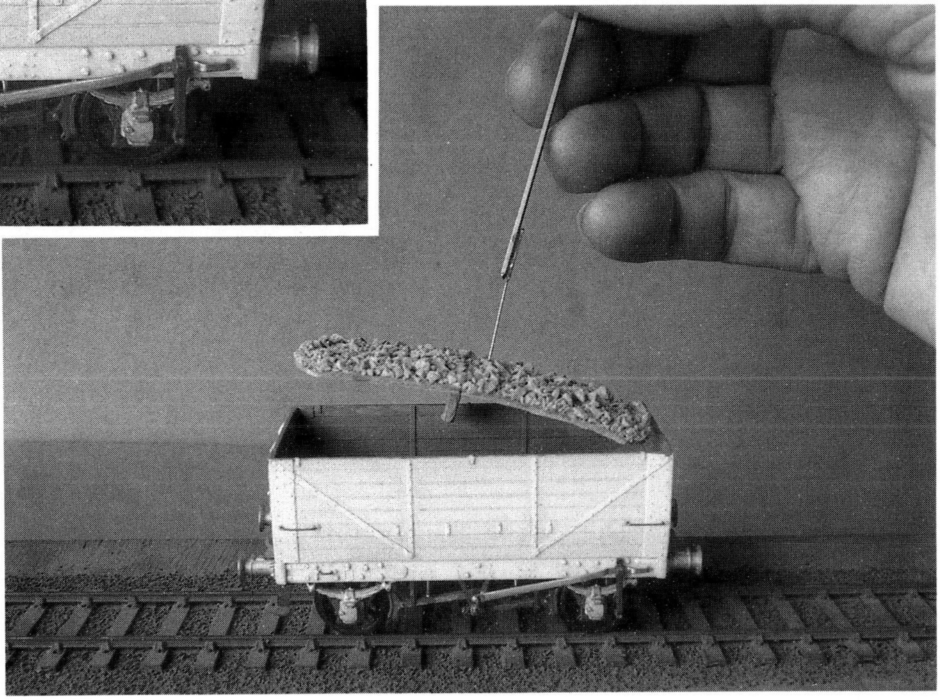

of the wagon – long enough to support the load without wobbling, but short enough to allow you to depress one end with a finger and get hold of the other end as it pops up. (Two hands are advisable unless you're uncommonly dextrous, because you'll probably need to hold the wagon down to stop it derailing as you remove the load.) The base can be a lump of wood or a U-shaped piece of card stuck to the underside of the load, or it could, of course, be integral with the whole thing if you're using balsa or insulation foam.

Other methods of taking the load out include the use of a magnet, with a small piece of metal under the surface, or a hook engaging in a slot in the centre of the heap; if you use three-link couplings, a shunting pole becomes a dual-purpose tool. Either way, the need to limit the size of the base is dispensed with. This kind of solution is necessary in any case with hopper wagons, where the internal shape of the body generally precludes the pop-up method. In most cases a hopper load doesn't need support in the centre, since it can rest on the sloping ends of the body (sometimes quite low down: denser ores, such as some imported iron ores, will load a wagon to capacity long before it's full – see the photographs on pp. 59–61 of Part One of the *The 4mm Wagon*). However, I usually glue some kind of tab beneath the load, which makes it easier to hold on to while painting and adding the surface material. I also write the wagon number and/or type on the underside to make sure it goes back into the one it was made for.

Although artificial loads and materials are available in many cases, to my mind nothing looks as good as the real thing, be it coal, coke, ore or stone. I know that someone living in the far south-west or the north of Scotland might not have ready access to, say, North Wales limestone, but these materials, or a close match for them, are generally pretty easy to come by. My own lumps of golden brown Oxfordshire ironstone (for a Banbury–Brymbo ore train) were picked up off the towpath of the Oxford Canal a few years ago, where they'd been used to repair the surface, but the same sort of thing from a field in North Lincolnshire would pass muster just as well.

The first job is to crush the material to size, most easily achieved by putting it in a plastic bag and hitting it with a big hammer on a stone or concrete surface. Then, if the stuff was normally screened before loading, as with coal or stone, grade or sieve it into three or four sizes, from smalls (almost dust in 4mm scale) to 12–18in lumps. Don't go overboard with this: a little goes a long way, and one smallish nub of coal will make more than enough for a respectable trainload. Try to avoid the sort of coal that splinters into flakes, but don't worry unduly if it looks too shiny at first: it should dull down soon enough, but a bit of matt black paint will speed things up if you prefer.

I've tried various adhesives to stick the product to the load surface. Most of them work well enough, but white PVA wood glue is one of the easiest to use, being water-soluble and clear-drying without looking too shiny when set. Smear a generous layer onto the surface, then sprinkle the material over it; if necessary, fill any bare patches by adding extra lumps with a pair of tweezers; you may need to add more drops of glue first, spotted on with an old paintbrush or cocktail stick. Try not to let either the glue or the material overlap the edges or block the slot in the top, if there is one (you'll find that this is now well-disguised from any angle but directly above).

A few traffics carried in bulk in open, unsheeted wagons are less easy to represent with the real thing crushed small. For example, the Cambridge Area S4 Group's layout 'Pampisford' convincingly uses sesame seeds to stand in for sugar beet. But on the whole, the nearer you can get to the genuine article, the better.

The same goes for other materials, such as timber, both sawn and in logs. Once upon a time you could make nice planking by cutting into strips the kind of matchbox that was made of thin sheets of wood held together with a gummed paper wrapper, but these seem to be a thing of the past. Veneers, thin ply or obechi strip could be used, but their colouring suggests hardwoods, and most timber carried in open wagons seems to have been softwood, so of late I've switched to the small square or round wooden boxes that some French cheeses are sold in. The stripwood used for these is mostly less than a millimetre thick, and it cuts cleanly with a sharp blade following the grain. Even so, for the thinnest boards you may have to resort to strips of plastic, suitably painted.

Sawn timber was generally loaded a plank at a time into high-sided wagons, often with the trailing end overhanging; (timber banded in fair-ended bundles is a product of the 1960s and later). The photos hopefully show how a removable load may be built up on a styrene former. Unfortunately, a snag with making this kind of load removable is that, except for very short journeys, the timber would normally be roped down (see the picture on page 22 of Part One). I haven't so far cracked the problem of representing the ropes on a removable load in such a way that they would stand up to repeated handling. I've experimented with soft iron wire finishing at, but not bent round, the buffers, cleats and stanchions that the ropes were normally tied to, but if it's soft enough to be workable, it's also soft enough to distort easily. In any case, it doesn't look much like the real thing; for a permanent load, waxed button thread is more manageable and looks better: a touch of epoxy ensures the knots stay knotted.

Securing a load of pitwood is less of a problem, because it wasn't always roped. The diagram shows two standard methods of loading: with upright logs at each end braced by those stacked athwartships in the centre, or, if the props were too long to permit this method (over seven feet), stacked in a similar way to sawn timber, and then roped 'as necessary'. These at least were the principles; in practice, there were several variations on these themes: for example, two colour photographs in '*The Heyday of Steam in South Wales*' (Derek Huntriss; Ian Allan Ltd, 1996) clearly show pitwood loaded in other ways.

Cocktail sticks stuck round a balsa or styrene core are an obvious method of

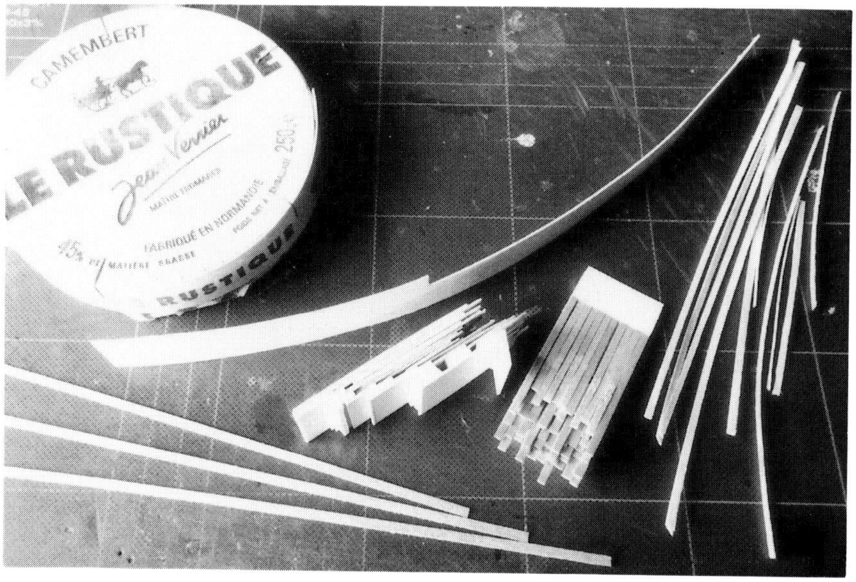

An unlikely source of the raw material for a load of sawn timber is the thin stripwood used to package certain French cheeses. This cuts cleanly, and has the advantage of looking more like newly-sawn softwood than some other alternatives like obechi and thin plywood. Whichever you choose, you can economise on its use by building up the plastic base that makes the load removable – perhaps rather more neatly than shown here, although as long as all you can see when the load is in the wagon is timber, tidiness is rather incidental. The load on the right needs at least one more tier of planks to complete it.

A load of timber sitting in the ex-LNER steel Hyfit whose construction featured in Part One. On its left is a Ratio GWR open with another timber load, this time roped down using button thread. Roping, unfortunately, seems incompatible with making the load easily removable.

simulating such a load, although for strict prototypical accuracy they're a bit too regular in diameter. Matchsticks with the visible parts filed round or half-round would do as well, and offer scope for a bit of variety in size. Bearing in mind, however, that pitwood wasn't necessarily stripped of its bark before use, thin woody twigs from the garden would be my preference. I've had good results with a number of varieties, including beech, willow, birch and escallonia, all of which produce fairly long, thin and reasonably straight twigs. If you select old growth without sap and strip off the bark, you're left with something that looks rather like poles that haven't had all the bark removed in tones of reddish-brown, grey and straw. Judging from photographs, it seems that pit-props were normally in the range of 4–9in in diameter, and weren't as a matter of course graded to size before dispatch to the colliery.

Logs, too, are a load that is best made using natural materials. Again, a fossick

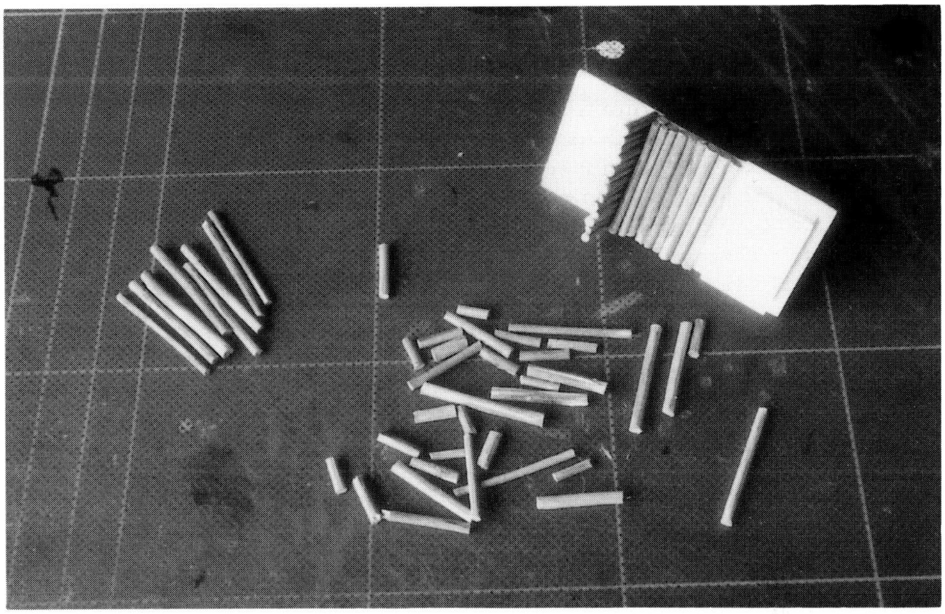

To make the load of pit-props, pieces of twig were cut into three lengths: longer ones athwartships in the centre, medium length ones almost vertically around the perimeter of a raised styrene block at each end, and short ones on top of the blocks. White PVA was used to glue them all in place.

31. **PITWOOD AND PIT PROPS.**

The traffic differs in shape, length and girth, and the following diagrams are supplied as guides to good and safe loading.

Standard High goods or Mineral wagons must be used.

Pitwood loaded crosswise must always be kept at least 4 inches below the rave of the wagon.

Diagram 1.

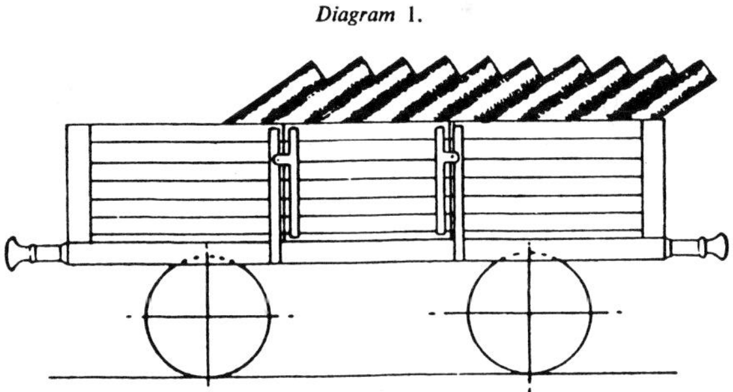

When loaded as in diagram 1 and a wagon with an end door is used, the lower end of the load must be towards the fixed end of the wagon.

The bases of all props must rest upon the wagon floor.

Loads to be roped as necessary.

Diagram 2.

Alternative method for lengths not exceeding 7 feet.

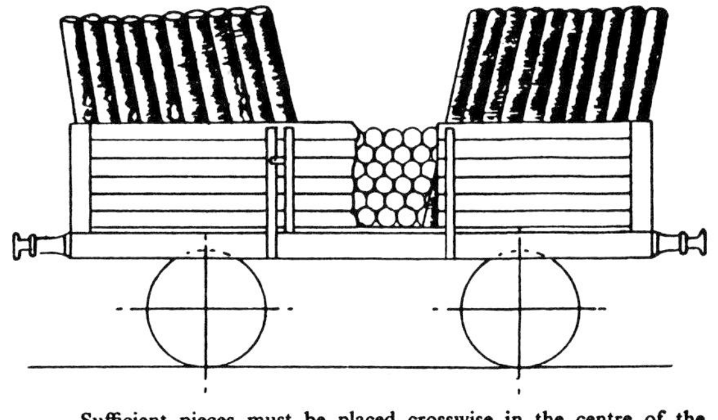

Sufficient pieces must be placed crosswise in the centre of the wagon from the bottom to well tighten the load.

An ex-LMS Diagram 1674 double bolster seen loaded with logs at Eastleigh in 1949. Methods of making such loads removable, chains and all, are discussed in Chapter 2 where these wagons are looked at in detail. A. E. WEST

round the garden with a pair of secateurs should identify some suitable sources of straightish twigs between 6mm and 12mm in diameter. Aim for woody shrubs or trees with bark that's not too figured, too rough or too smooth, and with the colour of old wood; a bit of green mossy growth on the surface does no harm. Try to avoid those with side-shoots that are too closely or too evenly spaced. You might be surprised at how many species these criteria rule out, but you could try plum or field maple as likely starting points. For best results, the ends and any intermediate shoots should be trimmed with a piercing saw or similar.

Logs were, or course, chained onto the bolster wagons that usually carried them, and look naked without some kind of fastening. I've discussed chaining, albeit with a load of steel, under the heading of the LMS double bolster, and suggested a way in which such a load might be made removable. However, I'm the first to admit that my solution is a rather complicated one, and you might get away with reeving a set of chains round the load, and directing the ends, soldered up solid as per container chains, towards the nearest shackle points. How far this refinement would stand up to regular handling would be my main reservation.

* * *

Another load that was often unsheeted in transit was bricks, either when carried loose in high-sided wagons or palletised in Palbricks. Plastic sheet suggests itself as the most obvious way of reproducing both. The rather neater outline of a palletised load, where the bricks were banded together (with narrow strips of 5-thou for the scale banding), can be a group of simple 40-thou box shapes, with the upper

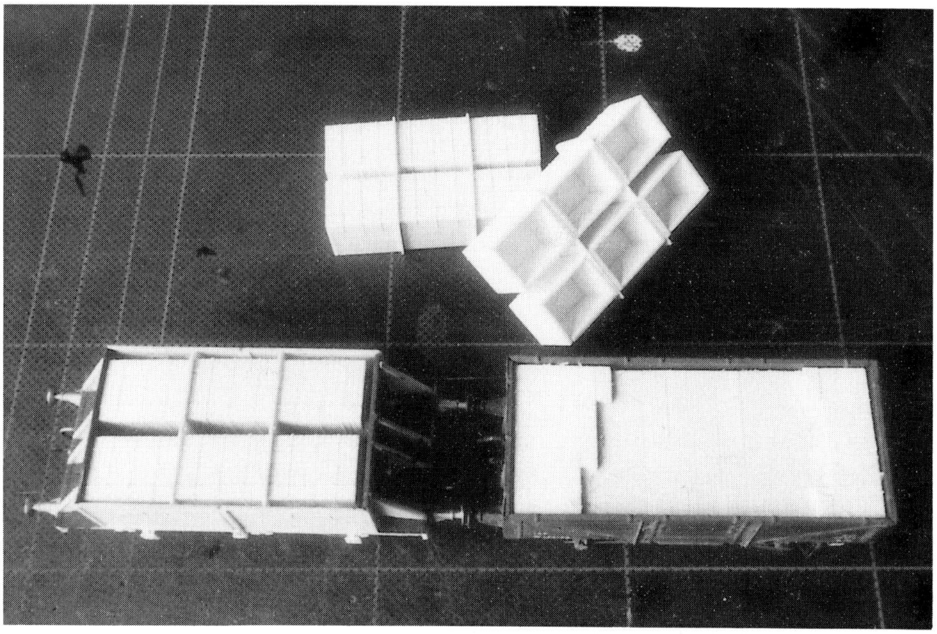

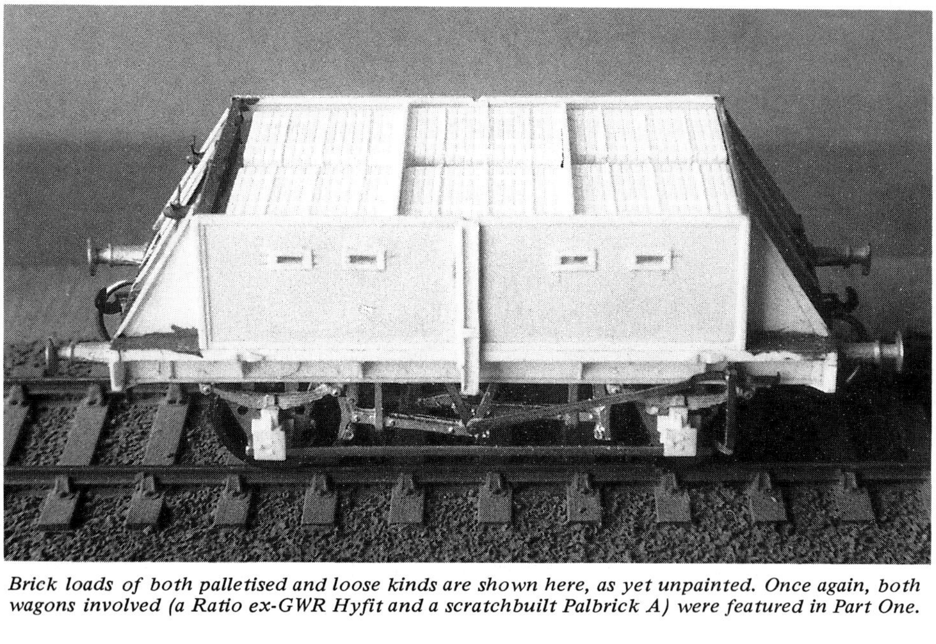

Brick loads of both palletised and loose kinds are shown here, as yet unpainted. Once again, both wagons involved (a Ratio ex-GWR Hyfit and a scratchbuilt Palbrick A) were featured in Part One.

surface and visible edges lightly scribed to simulate the joints in the stack – no need to reproduce the actual pallets since they can't be seen. They were, I believe, generally 3ft by 4ft, the latter dimension being the longitudinal one when stowed on the wagon. Palbrick Bs were wide enough to accept pallets that were 4ft square, but only just; some wagons (not only Bs) had the side panels lined with what looks like strips of rubber tubing, presumably as some kind of cushion for a tight-fitting load. Another feature of loaded Palbricks was the use of transverse wooden dividers between each pair of pallets, no doubt for much the same reason. I'm not certain that these were de rigueur in all cases, but in 4mm scale they make it easier to get to grips with a removable load using, for instance, a coupling hook engaging in a small hole near the top.

A load of loose bricks can be made using the same sort of former as described for coal, but flat in this case, of course, and with the top surface scribed to represent bricks stacked on edge. Whether they were always loaded in this way, I'm not sure: the only good photograph that I've found is in David Larkin's *Pre-Nationalisation Freight Wagons on British Railways*; this appears to show all the bricks on edge, and stacked fore-and-aft at the ends and transversely between the side doors. It also shows part layers at each end of the wagon, a feature that can be seen as well in each of the three loaded wagons visible in the picture on pp. 4/5 of Part One of *The 4mm Wagon*.

Part layers of this kind should be represented with 60-thou sheet, just about right for the width of the average brick; the top surface should be scribed in a 1mm × 3mm grid pattern. After scribing, you may wish to roughen the surface a little: not all bricks are completely smooth, and a brushful of solvent washed onto the sheet and quickly dragged out with the ball of your finger will add just a hint of texture to the material. The best quality bricks were bedded on layers of straw for protection. A few short strands cut from the end of a piece of old-fashioned sisal string can be secured using solvent, though they will probably need re-emphasising with a touch of straw colour after the bricks themselves have been painted. Try a pinkish version of bauxite for this, but use it thinly, and don't aim to cover the surface too evenly.

The Palbrick A in the middle of the raft of these finished wagons is a hybrid: a Crownline etched body married to a Parkside plastic underframe.

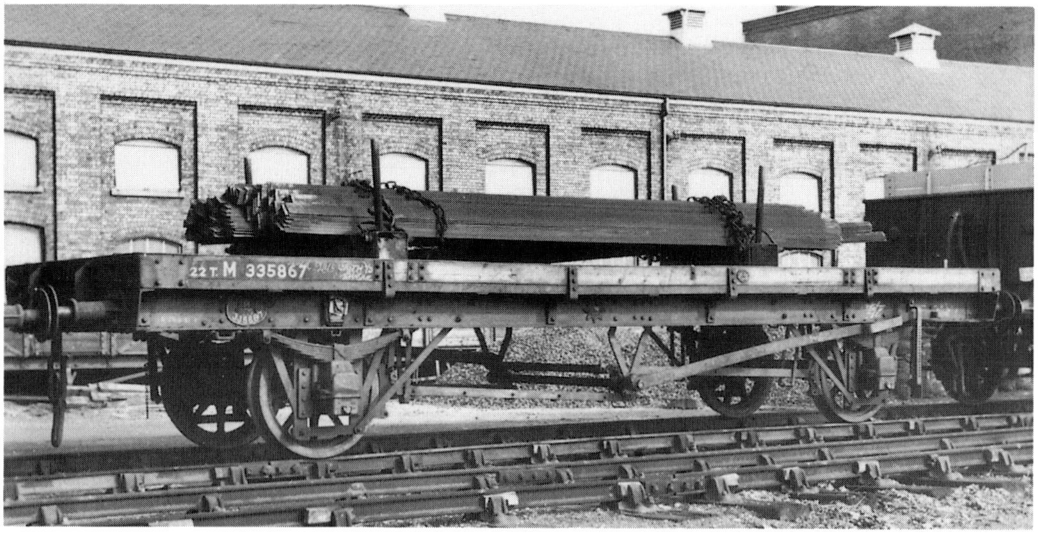

Yet another D1674 double bolster, this time loaded with steel angles. Here again, the chaining involved is covered in Chapter 2.
A. E. WEST

Two loads of steel which don't require complicated securing are wire rod in coil when carried in high-sided wagons, and strip coil held in place by heavy wooden cradles. B725152 was a standard D 1/050 Shock High, and B916818 a converted D 1/402 single bolster. Notice the early Dowty hydraulic buffers, and the fitting of screw couplings and axleguard tie-bars to a wagon that was never vacuum-braked.
DAVID LARKIN

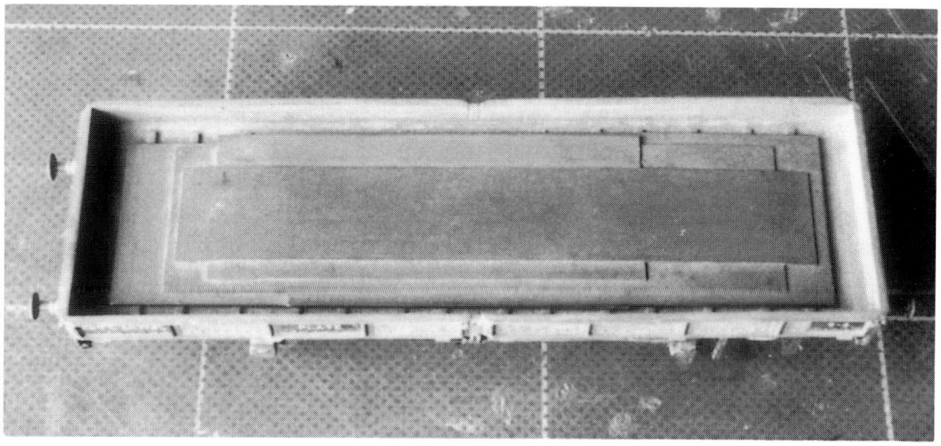

The load of steel plates in these plate wagons are rectangles of 10-thou styrene painted grey. Semi-matt paint was used to simulate the slight sheen of new steel; superficial rust was represented by stippling a little yellow and bauxite here and there.

Steel came in a multitude of shapes and sizes and, generally speaking, only the best strip and wire coil was routinely covered in transit. Not the least variable was scrap, which in model form can be loaded and unloaded like any other bulk material. Whitemetal turnings or drill swarf, bits of tinplate and wire, and even odd lumps of cast whitemetal are all fair game, but try to avoid recognisable shapes like reject loco chimneys, and go easy on the old wagon wheels.

While you might have some difficulty in reproducing complicated shapes like sections of interlocking sheet piling, most of the more common profiles like tubes, pipes, billets, channel and I- or H-beams can be sourced in either plastic or metal from suppliers of modelling materials. Steel plate can be cut from styrene or from sheet metal of any kind – if you can get hold of it, steel banding strip doesn't even need painting, and goes rusty naturally, which most types of steel do quite quickly when unprotected. Assuming that you will have to paint your loads, however, excellent results can be obtained with Humbrol Metal Cote No. 27003, perhaps enhanced with a bit of dry-brushed rust here and there.

Steel in coils, whether strip, wire or bar, is probably something you will have to make yourself. Thin sheet is most easily represented with strips of 5- or 10-thou plastic wound round a piece of tube and secured with sparing dabs of solvent at intervals. Wire rod in coil is one of the commodities covered in a series of articles by Martyn Welch in issues 65 to 72 of *Model Railway Journal*. As well as some of the other loads referred to here, he also describes the making of cable drums and sacks (though the latter would almost invariably be sheeted in transit).

From the modeller's point of view, steel loads have in many cases the added advantage that they don't need securing, at least when carried in certain types of wagon. Pipes and tubes were stowed loose in those vehicles specially designed for them. Plates, billets and pig iron could all be carried loose in wagons with sides and ends, especially plate wagons. And wire rod in coil was unsecured when loaded in high-sided vehicles or ones equipped with cradles specifically for that purpose. Bolster and trestle wagons were a different matter, however: in the period under review, loads were almost invariably chained down on these vehicles.

Mention of the need to protect items such as sacks carried in open wagons brings me finally onto the subject of sheeted loads. In addition to a number of commercial products that have been marketed over the years by manufacturers such as PC and Smiths, do-it-yourself wagon sheets have been made by enterprising modellers from materials as diverse as cheap, two-ply toilet paper and adhesive masking tape. For permanently sheeted loads I would be quite happy with the commercial products, suitably weathered. For the dyed-in-the-wool d-i-y enthusiast, I would suggest the kind of metallised paper used to line the packets of certain brands of loose tea or to make sachets of sauce mix, for example. In both cases these should be scrunched up into a ball, then flattened out again just enough to keep the irregular pattern of creases typical of much-used tarpaulins.

Pursuant to my theme of be able to run wagons both loaded and empty, however, I like sheets that are rigid enough to be taken off and replaced without risk of damage. The only material I know that is sufficiently soft to be bent easily to shape, particularly in the way a real sheet is folded over the end of a wagon, yet is stiff enough to retain that shape when handled, is the kind of alloy from which toothpaste tubes were once exclusively made. Nowadays these are mostly plastic, although at least one toothpaste still comes in metal tubes at the time of writing. So too do glues like Evostik and Copydex, food products such as tomato paste, and, I believe, certain medicinal preparations. For the time being, therefore, this material is still readily available, relieving me of the need to experiment with possible substitutes, such as the various grades of foil used for prepared ready meals and takeaways.

Apart from its ability to withstand handling, the rigidity of this stuff is such that it can be moulded to the outline of a load such as a crate, or a heap of some bulk commodity like sand or lime, without your having to make the load itself. Even the dips in a sheet that collect rainwater (varnish or PVA glue) can be reproduced, and despite its being flattened out initially with a knife handle or similar tool, it retains the wrinkles and creases that other materials are able to simulate. In fact, the only disadvantage I can see in a removable sheet is that you sacrifice the opportunity to reproduce the sheet strings that hold it in place, should you wish to go that far.

Toothpaste tube also comes in handy for making pantiles. But that's another story.

The origins of the removable sheet for this scratchbuilt ex-Midland Railway 10-ton open wagon are not hard to work out. Although toothpaste generally comes in plastic tubes these days, a number of other products are still sold in the traditional material. Once bent to shape, this takes and keeps paint pretty well, even allowing for being taken off and put back on regularly. The ex-LMS 5-plank wagon is another kitbuilt product covered in Part One, this time in whitemetal from ABS.

Whilst it was not common to see mineral wagons sheeted in this way, this Diagram 1/109 Minfit (built 1959 and carrying the post-1964 code in this view) was one of several noted at Wrexham in 1970. From my own observations, southbound trains of sheeted minerals were a regular feature of operations in the area.
DAVID LARKIN

8F No. 48673 is seen climbing Gresford bank with just such a load around 1960. AUTHOR

Another use for wagon sheets noted on occasions was to ensure the watertightness of covered vehicles such as vans, containers and even cattle wagons. These examples were all photographed on the ex-SR lines around Exeter in 1958/9. Notice that the sheets were stencilled with two dates: the earlier of these records when the sheet was released into traffic, and the later is the date when it must be returned for checking, repair and reproofing as necessary. BR stipulated that these dates were to be painted in white and yellow respectively. A. E. WEST

BR WAGON LIVERIES THE FIRST TWO DECADES

Although the range of wagons studied in this series covers a much longer timespan than the twenty years after nationalisation, I have decided to limit myself to this period for this overview of livery details for two reasons. First, because pre-1948 colour schemes are generally covered by the publications relating specifically to wagons built by each of the Big Four and their predecessors. Conversely, relatively little has appeared in any coherent, readily available form covering the years from 1948 onwards, which, as with locomotives and coaches, saw an evolution of policy which, once settled upon, took time to apply, and was even then never immune from further tinkering either officially, or because of day-to-day re-interpretation by those responsible for implementing official policy in real life. And second, because it happens to be the period with which I'm most familiar.

In looking at the ways in which goods wagon liveries were applied in principle and in practice during these years, I have relied chiefly on the following sources:

(a) *British Railways Standard Liveries*, a leaflet dating from 1949 distributed by Messrs A. W. Hambling & Co. summarising the schemes initially adopted by the recently-formed Railway Executive for all locomotives and rolling stock. This information was substantially reproduced in *Railway Liveries – BR Steam 1948–68* by Brian Haresnape and Colin Boocock, published by Ian Allan Ltd in 1989. Similar, though not identical, details subsequently appeared in articles by John Emerson in *British Railway Modelling*, starting in October 1999.

(b) Contributions to the Journal of the Historical Model Railway Society by David Larkin, Paul Bartlett and others, contained chiefly in Volume 16, issues 4 to 10.

(c) David Larkin's data sheet FLG/1, which gives a summary of all the colours applied to the BR wagon fleet over the first thirty years or so after nationalisation.

(d) A large number of general railway books and periodicals including, but by no means limited to, all those specialised 'wagon books' listed in the bibliographies here and in Part Two. Especially useful, of course, are clear

W35935 was a Diagram AA23 brake van seen at Oswestry shortly after nationalisation in an overall coat of BR grey. It seems that the GW practice of painting wagons from top to toe in the same colour may initially have been carried over in a few cases into the new administration. Another example, in this case of a loco coal wagon, can be found in Cheona, Volume 1, but W83854, on the other hand, had clearly received a coat of regulation black, with either yellow or white lettering. The markings were, however, in GW style – notice the white stripe on the solebar denoting brakes on both sides, and the italic tare weight in the right-hand corner. But the uniquely decorative, and totally inappropriate, XP branding must be someone's idea of a joke.

HMRS

photographs of clean vehicles, particularly colour shots, but given the fact that goods wagons were hardly ever cleaned externally, these aren't very thick on the ground.

★ ★ ★

In essence the paint scheme adopted by BR for its wagon fleet was dull and uninspiring: grey for non-vacuum-fitted vehicles, orange-brown (bauxite) for those with automatic brakes or through vacuum pipes, and white for insulated vans and containers. Underframes and running gear were to be black.

This straightforward statement immediately requires a degree of qualification. To begin with, white paint was scarce after the war, and stone colour was initially specified as a substitute, though to what extent it was actually used is problematical, since few examples seem to have been recorded. The scheme makes no mention of crimson, which was flirted with for certain special-purpose vans, and was to be used more widely for uninsulated covered containers. (In 1949, all containers, except insulated ones, were to be bauxite, although open containers seem to have been 'unfitted' grey from the start.) Black as a body colour is another that isn't mentioned, perhaps because it was reserved for non-revenue-earning stock such as engineers' vehicles and loco coal wagons.

It's significant that the whole of the 1949 colour scheme for goods stock is specifically noted as 'provisional', and it isn't surprising that it took a few years before everyone started singing from the same hymn book – more or less. In the interim it seems inevitable that some workshops persisted with pre-nationalisation painting policies, perhaps using up old stocks of paint in the process. This could well be the explanation for the newly-repainted LMS unfitted van in bauxite in 1949 pictured on page 37 of Part Two, and for odd views of ex-GWR vehicles with grey underframes and running gear.

It may also go some way to explaining the confusing evidence over the shade of grey that was intended for unfitted stock. In the Hambling's leaflet, which gives every indication of having been culled from official sources, it is referred to as 'dark battleship grey', a description repeated by F. J. Roche in annotating the wagon drawings he was preparing around that time, which later appeared in *Historic Wagon Drawings in 4mm Scale* (Ian Allan Ltd, 1965). From this it appears that a shade of mid-grey, or even darker, was originally proposed, perhaps conditioned by stocks of paint inherited from the two members of the Big Four who had favoured a darkish grey, the GWR and the LNER.

In the early days of nationalisation, the shade of grey used for unfitted wagons was often dark enough to make the white lettering stand out clearly without black patches behind it. Single bolster B910564 was brand new when caught at Feltham in March 1950 and the photographer specifically described the body colour as dark grey. Apart from a small grey patch towards the right-hand end, the solebar, headstocks and below were black, but it wasn't unknown at this time for the body colour to be extended to the solebars, perhaps in imitation of pre-1948 practice. Diagram 1/142 13-ton hopper B400680, photographed at Carlisle in 1950 exemplifies this, in this case with a black patch for the maintenance details above the right-hand axlebox.
A. E. WEST and ROGER CARPENTER

For how long such a shade was used isn't clear, but it seems to have lightened progressively almost from the start: although there was considerable variation, the prevailing colour soon became quite pale indeed – so much so that in a black and white photograph it can sometimes be difficult to distinguish from unpainted timber. However, it was always different from the grey used for the roofs of vans and containers; this also varied, but even the lightest shades quickly assumed a much darker hue in traffic.

Lettering and other markings were mostly white, except that yellow was used with crimson and on some black departmental wagons, and insulated stock had black inscriptions. The provisional livery scheme makes no mention of the need to highlight markings on unfitted vehicles with black patches (except in one specific connection). This is in line with the early use of a darker grey, and became necessary only when lighter shades began to be used. The exception mentioned throws up something of an anomaly. Although the 1949 schedule states that underframes were to be black, the lettering diagrams included with it require certain mainte-

As lighter shades of grey became more prevalent, it proved necessary to highlight the lettering with the familiar black patches, as shown here on coke hopper B447711 when new in 1955. Except for the bottom of the end stanchions, and, again, a small body-colour patch on the solebar, underframe and running gear were both regulation black.
HMRS

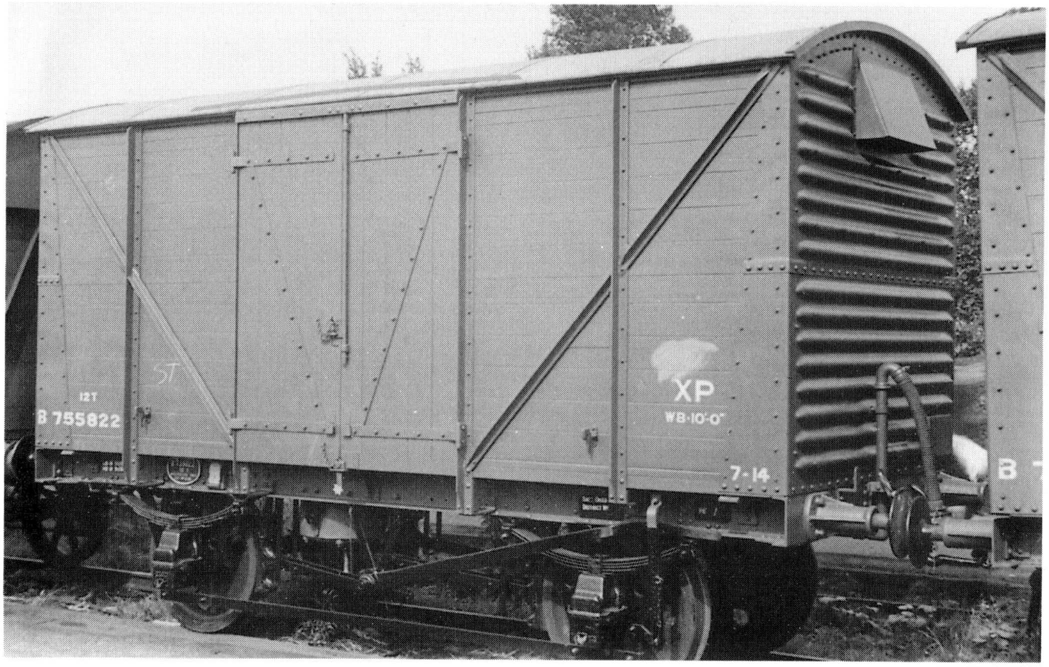

I commented in Part Two that the bauxite-painted solebars of B891054, the restored LMS-pattern cattle van on the Severn Valley Railway, were unusual. I've since realised that it may not have been as unusual as I had thought; some other cattle vans of the same design were painted thus when new, and this shot of a brand-new D 1/208 van proves that not only cattle vans, and not only Derby-built vehicles, could be seen with body-coloured solebars. B755822 was built at Wolverton in 1951, and appears to have gone a stage further by having a bauxite vacuum cylinder as well. And surprisingly, a photograph in Cheona Vol. 3 shows another new Wolverton-built van painted in identical style as late as 1958.
ROGER CARPENTER

nance information to be shown on the solebar in white on a black panel. This only makes some sort of sense if the solebar were to be painted body colour, as indeed some were in the early days. Interestingly, the instructions reproduced in *British Railway Modelling* do specify grey for the solebars of unfitted wagons with steel underframes. Conversely, on some vehicles that did have black solebars, the information was carried on them on body-coloured patches; all the more reason to regard these early proposals as provisional.

Dark patches weren't considered necessary on fitted vehicles either, but, unlike the changes introduced in the light of experience with hand-braked stock, this was to remain constant throughout. Only in connection with certain special instructions were these sometimes highlighted by a black background, and here yellow lettering could also be seen.

* * *

Before we consider other aspects in more detail, or examine individual wagon types, we should look at the changes that were introduced from 1963/4 in connection with the development of BR's new corporate house style. While these were hardly earth-shattering, the most noticeable in the freight context was probably the adoption of a pale turquoise (ice-blue) for insulated vans and containers in place of white; rather oddly, both black and white lettering was used with the new colour. The other two principal colours, grey and bauxite, remained much the same, though minor variations emerged as time went on; ultimately, grey was phased out entirely in favour of freight brown, a flatter, less orangey, version of bauxite.

Some aspects of lettering also changed, with the main markings in a slightly revised alphabet style grouped within white-lined boxes. These were in much the same general position as formerly, although the left-hand corner inscriptions now included the tare weight, and painting and repair information moved up from the solebar to replace it at the right-hand end (often on a black panel, even on fitted stock). The XP branding, where appropriate, was now usually left of centre and con-

A pair of shock-absorbing vans both built to BR diagram 1/209 (though notice the variations in brakegear and body construction material) are illustrated here to show the difference between early and late (1964 onwards) markings for such vehicles. Newly repainted in 1962, B850815 had an unusual end layout for the vertical white stripes (spray-painted using a stencil, it seems, at least on the doors), and both the headstocks and the cover plate for the solebar-mounted shock-absorbing gear were body colour. B851116 had the newer style of markings except for the absence of a box for the codename, capacity, tare and running number.
DON ROWLAND and DAVID LARKIN

tained in its own box. These at least were the broad intentions; in practice, old and new markings were often intermingled.

A minor change to the lettering of the larger steel minerals and hoppers used for coal traffic that was actually introduced a few years later might also be mentioned here, namely the addition of suffix letters to the running number. These were intended as a clerical aid to National Coal Board staff to help them identify the capacity of particular vehicles; they were K for 21-tonners, L for 24-tonners and N for 24½-tonners. Occasionally they appeared on other wagon types, such as iron-ore hoppers, but this was accidental.

From 1963 the three bold stripes denoting shock vans and wagons became three almost square blocks, though they remained white and in the same positions as before. And uninsulated covered containers, for which bauxite had finally become the standard colour, began to appear with the 'boxed arrow' symbol accompanied by the legend 'door to door'.

At the same time engineers' vehicles became olive green with white lettering. Black had in fact been dropped two or three years previously in favour of gulf red, a colour that wasn't all that different to bauxite, at least when weathered, and was several shades darker than the bright geranium red used for breakdown trains. In practice, however, all three colours could be seen alongside each other for many years to come.

This mish-mash of styles also characterised the re-liverying of revenue-earning stock, and any favourable impact the changes might have had on BR's customers must inevitably have been dulled by the attenuated and disjointed process of

Similarly, these two open wagons bear early and late shock insignia. Here, however, B720069 had been comprehensively relettered, while B721806 is seen in completely original guise.
ERIC KEMP and AUTHOR'S COLLECTION

Although built at Ashford in 1957, the special instructions on this Palbrick A were in pure GW style. However, because the removable plywood panels were often refitted upside-down, or the wrong way round, or even to the wrong wagon, it soon became the norm to put the lettering on the fixed steel buttresses at each end. Palbrick C No. B462639, seen at Bo'ness Junction in 1963, not only shows why this was deemed necessary, but also conveniently illustrates the sections of rubber tubing (secondhand vacuum brake hose?) used as cushioning material on some of these wagons.
DON ROWLAND

Contrast the neatness of the markings on the new Palbrick A with the hotchpotch borne by this LMS-pattern fruit van seen much later in life. It bore evidence of numerous repairs, even to the extent of having had its door patched with plywood sheeting from another vehicle and adorned with a cast plate salvaged from an LNER van. And one of the scoop vents had been refitted the wrong way round!
HMRS

repainting, which saw, for example, insulated fish vans running cheek by jowl in both white and ice-blue, and both so dirty that it was hard to tell which was which. A glance at the covers of Part Two should illustrate this more effectively than mere words. In truth, the prevailing colour of the railway freight scene remained what it had been for a long time: a sort of grimy grey-brown. Except perhaps for the bright yellow livery now worn by the road motor fleet, the casual observer would have been hard put to notice any change.

* * *

Returning to the earlier years of nationalisation, it's possible to see numerous inconsistencies which in an ideal world the Corporate Image programme might have harmonised. Take a detail like the black patches that were introduced behind markings on unfitted wagons as lighter shades of grey were adopted: whatever neat, square-cornered shapes these might have been in theory, in practice they varied tremendously, as did the position and dimensions of the markings themselves. In retrospect, it seems as if it was left to the whim of the individual painter. On wooden-bodied wagons the patch behind the capacity and number was often three or four planks high, with the right-hand border following the diagonal ironwork. Oval patches, behind the tare weight especially, weren't unknown. Sometimes the patch behind the bottom-door vee was omitted altogether. Two separate patches for capacity and number were often seen, particularly on steel mineral wagons, and so on.

The quality of the lettering varied too. Hand painting was the rule (although the use of stencils wasn't uncommon, especially in later years), and the strict dimensions and style of the official Gill Sans medium typeface, outlined in the accompanying schedule, were widely ignored in practice, though perhaps less by the signwriters at BR's own works than by those employed by private wagon repairers. Even so, there were variations at all levels; on the Western Region, for instance, the use of GWR-style italics for the tare weight of new wagons as well as older ones persisted well into the 'fifties. And a range of sizes and styles (italic and upright, capital and lower case) could be used for special inscriptions (*Not to be Loaded with Containers*; *EMPTY TO PARK ROYAL*; NOT IN COMMON USE, etc.).

Rather less obvious than marking variations was the seeming indecision over what colour to paint headstocks and solebars – less obvious only because after a short spell in traffic it was difficult to tell the colour that had been used in any case. This was especially true of headstocks and buffer guides: leaving aside vehicles like shock wagons and hoppers, where the distinct separation of body and underframe meant that these parts were overwhelmingly* painted black, a straw poll of almost two hundred vehicles of other types in published photographs where the subjects are clean enough to be able to distinguish colours with reasonable certainly, suggests that 'official' black headstocks were in the lead only by a neck, with body colour being used on over 40% of the sample. Statistically, there appeared to be no bias towards fitted or unfitted stock, and the percentages seemed much the same in the late 'sixties as in the early 'fifties.

*Overwhelmingly but not exclusively, as one or two of the accompanying pictures clearly show.

These two Conflats both show instances of non-standard lettering. In the case of ex-LNER Conflat M E1 75797, seen at Millerhill in 1962, this was purely because of the narrowness of the bodyside, a necessity acknowledged by the rules governing such markings. No such excuse with B707823, photographed at Kirkcaldy in the previous year. Examples of stencilled lettering, and lower case script, together with a much smaller than usual code name, make for an interesting combination. Fresh Meat container BM10149B was in red with yellow lettering. DON ROWLAND

As mentioned elsewhere in the text, many GWR brake vans bore not only the name of the yard where they were based, but also details of the regular workings to which they were allocated. Few were decorated as comprehensively as Diagram AA21 van W17423, however, seen at Carmarthen in 1959.
DON ROWLAND

For some reason, brake vans quite often received body-coloured solebars throughout the period under review. In these three photographs a standard unfitted BR van is seen being propelled into Wrexham General station in 1966, an ex-LMS Diagram 1890 van is seen similarly engaged at Royton Junction in 1958, and an ex-LMS Diagram 1657 brake was standing outside Northwich shed in the late 'fifties. All seem quite freshly repainted, and had grey solebars; in the latter case even the coupling, and, I think, the footboards, had received the same treatment.
AUTHOR, HMRS and A. W. V. MACE

We are on slightly safer ground with solebars and running gear, which were normally black, even on wooden-framed vehicles. Even so, there is no shortage of exceptions, and not only during the early years when livery policies were still being formulated. The ex-LNER insulated fish van with white solebars and headstocks illustrated on page 101 of Part Two is a case in point, and brakevans, especially ex-LMS ones, quite often seem to have received body-coloured solebars.

While we're talking about brakevans, the confusion over headstock colours extended to the sides of the concrete ballast blocks on the end platforms of BR standard vehicles: these are just as likely to have been body colour as black. (The surface of the concrete always seems to have been left unpainted, however.) Perhaps the most distinctive quirk of brakevan livery was the use of brick red or cream, or a mixture of both, for the cabin ends of some ex-SR vehicles.

Another, albeit minor, area where paint treatment varied on all sorts of wagons was the extension of bodyside and end ironwork over solebars and headstocks. While the 'turned-under' pattern were in all the cases I've noted the same colour as the solebar, the 'straight-down' type could be either, and I would be hard put to say which was more common. On the ends, I think that if the headstocks were black, it would be usual to expect the stiffeners to follow suit, but some medfits and plates were an exception to this rule, and no doubt there were others.

This pair of mineral wagons, one built by the Midland Railway and photographed soon after nationalisation, and the other of LMS origin and seen condemned in 1963, both appear to have been in unpainted condition except for their markings. Even then, only the second had black patches behind the lettering. Unusually, both had the end-door stripe alongside, rather than on, the diagonal brace, a feature I've only seen on ex-LMS wagons, and then only occasionally. M607072 also bore the stencilled legend 'One Journey Only Loco Coal', a common adornment of old wooden wagons at that time. ROGER CARPENTER and DON ROWLAND

Of course, we shouldn't forget that, as a matter of policy, there was a large number of vehicles that received no paint at all, or hardly any, for twenty years or more in the middle of the century. What began as an emergency measure during World War II, and applied particularly to the vast fleet of private-owner minerals requisitioned or pooled in the national interest, later extended to a much wider range of wooden-bodied, and especially wooden-underframed stock. In the case of the private-owners, repairs with unpainted timber soon led to wagons acquiring a piebald, patchwork appearance, the deterioration through wear and tear of what remained of their original livery hastening their decline into anonymity. When the former owner's identity became indecipherable, it was painted in white capitals, generally on a black ground, on the left-hand side; after nationalisation, by which time any thought of returning the wagons to their original owners had been abandoned, this was gradually replaced with a randomly-allotted P-number, though hardly ever at this stage by any more extensive livery change.

In fact, by the end of the war, even new, wooden-bodied, open wagons, both fitted and unfitted, were being turned out with only the ironwork painted and BR duly followed suit. Whilst the new undertaking did revert in due course to painting new wagons overall (although not until well into the 'fifties in some cases), older vehicles, especially unfitted ones, often continued to receive unpainted woodwork when in for repair. If they were painted at all, it was likely to be no more than a slapdash coat of paint on the ironwork, often straying untidily onto the adjacent unpainted timber.

Wooden-framed wagons fared the worst of all, and not just the former private-owner fleet: for almost a decade after nationalisation there was an embargo on the painting of all-wooden opens and minerals of whatever description. This period saw the withdrawal of the vast majority of timber-built, pre-grouping survivors as well as grease-lubricated minerals, and inevitably most of them went without having had a lick of paint for many years, except perhaps for re-numbering. The policy of neglect even extended to some covered vehicles: ex-LMS unfitted cattle vans were especially affected, and even piped and fully-fitted examples were far from immune. For some reason, however, wooden-framed ex-LNER box and cattle vans appear to have been treated with more respect.

For a few years in the later 'fifties, though, there seems to have been something of a change of heart. From about 1956 onwards we begin to see increasing numbers of wooden-framed opens and minerals appearing in a fresh (but often rather wishy-washy) coat of pale grey, generally with black solebars and headstocks. It's been suggested that the intention was to limit this treatment to steel-framed (i.e. chiefly ex-company) stock, but there's no doubt that a lot of wooden-framed wagons benefited as well, including numerous former private owners. Whatever the truth of this, repainting appears to have ceased again by the end of the decade, repairs once more being done with unpainted or second-hand timber, so that by the time the last of the wooden-bodied minerals were being withdrawn a few years later, most of those that had been repainted (which photographic evidence suggests may have made up at least a third of the final survivors) were once again in particoloured condition.

A feature of the last years of both wooden and early steel-bodied minerals withdrawn in the 'sixties was the proliferation of stencilled or crudely-painted instructions (SUBEX, COLEX, MTD, LOCO 5, etc) regarding their imminent disposal. One of the most common was 'One Journey Only – Loco Coal', or OJO, indicating that, having been unloaded at the loco depot to which the wagon was consigned, it was destined to be broken up or burnt. This phase is admirably illustrated in Len Tavender's valuable little book *Coal Trade Wagons* (published by the author in 1991).

However rough the treatment meted out to all-wooden open wagons during the early years, covered and steel-framed vehicles were for the most part looked after more considerately, especially if they were vacuum-fitted and had a reasonable life-expectancy. Modern vans and steel-bodied opens and minerals were almost

In the later 'fifties many all-wooden wagons were treated to a coat of BR grey, often rather sparingly applied, and two such examples can be seen here, both photographed in 1959. The ex-LMS 5-plank open had already had a further repair, with the new timber roughly painted in a much darker colour. P38099 was photographed in Stewarts & Lloyds sidings at Bilston in company with ex-Denaby 8-plank mineral P293199, which exhibits one of the other livery options for such wagons at this time, a particoloured mixture of unpainted timbers and the remains of its pre-war private-owner markings. The significance of the large letter K on both wagons is lost on me, though. T. J. EDGINGTON and P. COUTANCHE

In examining the Palvan conversions of ex-GWR Diagram V21 vans in Part Two, I commented on their rather surprising affinity with Kirkcudbright in South-West Scotland. Proof of this is the return instructions on each of these examples, seen at their home station in 1963. Notice the lettering variations, and the use of dark patches behind the tare weight on each van, unusual for bauxite-painted vehicles. Although vacuum-fitted, the 9ft wheelbase of these vans did not qualify them for XP rating. Compare the markings on B779569, a Palvan of standard BR design to Diagram 1/211, seen at Crewe in 1959.

DON ROWLAND

Although by the date of this photograph, taken at Carlisle in 1960, work was well advanced in retro-fitting hand-braked gunpowder vans with full vacuum brakes, these two ex-LMS vehicles clearly had yet to be attended to; moreover, the one on the right, M701020, dating from 1937, appears to have been recently repainted in unfitted grey livery. The other, rather older, van, M229085, bears the same specialised branding seen on No. 240241 in Part Two, an interesting survival of virtually identical markings across several decades and a change of ownership. DON ROWLAND

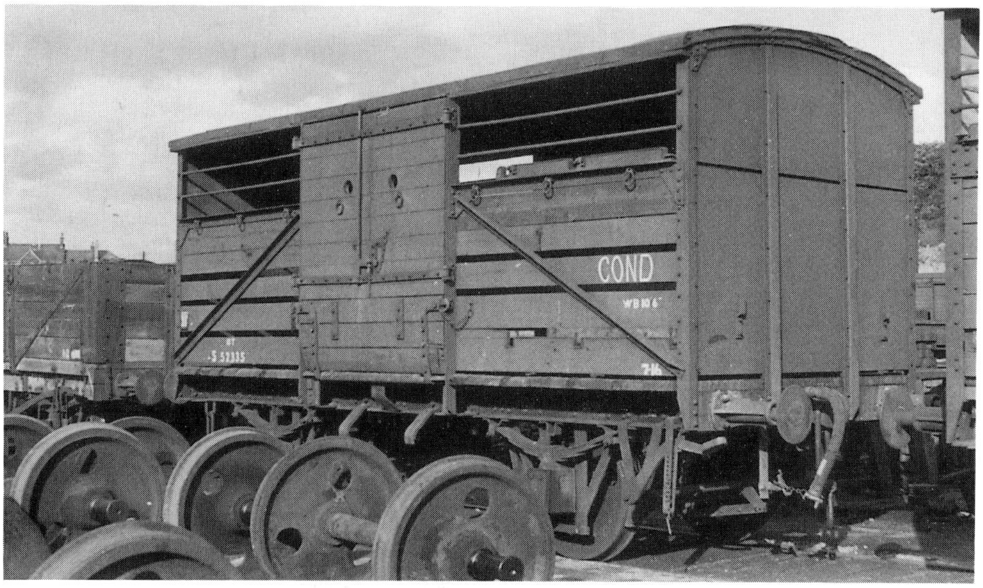

Since they were mostly either vacuum-fitted or vacuum-piped, cattle vans generally wore bauxite livery in BR days, as illustrated by one of each kind in these two photographs. The Southern van, built in 1947, is seen condemned at Carnforth in 1963, while the 1924-built ex-LMS vehicle was at Hatton in 1956. The white vacuum pipe denoting a through-piped but not fully-fitted vehicle shows up well; full vacuum-braked wagons had red pipes. Although as an all-wooden van it might not have qualified strictly for a repaint under BR ownership, it seems to have been in respectable condition with no sign of patch-painting in the area of the lettering, so perhaps as a through-braked vehicle it received more favourable treatment.
DON ROWLAND
and H. F. WHEELLER

invariably painted, not only when new, but also as they fell due for repair. All the same, economies crept in as the years went by, and older* vehicles were always the first to suffer from patch-painting or bare replacement woodwork.

No one group of wagons illustrates the variety of early BR liveries better than special purpose vans, which between them bore every colour used during this period for revenue-earning stock. As we've seen, unfitted wooden-framed cattle vans, ex-LMS ones particularly, were generally not repainted, although since there were so many (well over 4,000 including the vacuum-piped examples) and some lasted into the 'sixties, it seems inevitable that a proportion would have received a coat of BR grey. To date, however, I've found only one photograph to prove it, and that taken as early as 1953.

Grey was probably the least common colour for this group of vehicles, since the majority were vacuum-fitted. The ex-LMS slatted-side vans for the carriage of beer in barrels (at one time the subject of a Ratio kit) undoubtedly would have borne this livery, as did the unfitted gunpowder vans inherited and built by BR, at least until they were retrofitted with automatic brakes as most of them were.

The most frequently applied livery for this group of vans, on the other hand, was certainly bauxite. All fitted cattle vans were so painted, with the likely exception of some of the wooden-framed examples and many of the older steel-framed ones: vehicles such as W26040, built around 1911 and pictured on page 65 of Part Two, may well have been scrapped without repainting. Also in bauxite were fitted gunpowder vans, pallet vans, banana vans (even though they were insulated), almost all fruit vans (the GWR-designed Fruit Ds were a notable exception, reflecting their frequent use in passenger and parcels trains by being painted coach crimson, and ultimately even rail blue) and non-insulated fish vans of LNER origin. Some vans for special traffic were in fact only distinguishable from ordinary vanfits by their markings: BR margarine vans and some LNER and LMS fish vans – such as the one pictured on page 107 of Part Two – were, externally at least, no more than standard covered vans lettered for particular commodities.

*We shouldn't forget in talking about 'older wagons' that the goalposts were always on the move: wagons built in the 1920s were old by the time of nationalisation; vehicles that were modern and well-cared-for in the 'fifties were quite often run-down and neglected less than twenty years later.

Some of the variety of liveries borne by vans intended for perishable traffics in the 'fifties can be seen in these four views. (i) Insulated vehicles and containers were white with black lettering until 1964; I believe some of the surviving GWR-designed 6-wheel fish vans received the new ice-blue livery after that date, but SC3323W, seen condemned at Barry a few years later, apparently was not one of them. The coaching stock style of numbering indicates a vehicle of GWR parentage (though these vans emerged after nationalisation), transferred operationally to the Scottish Region, as confirmed by the other legends at each end. (ii) The ex-LNER insulated meat container FM459E had been condemned by the time it was photographed in the mid-'fifties. The same was probably true of the ex-SR insulated container in the background. Notice that both containers were roped onto the wagons carrying them: in the case of F695S this was quite properly because it had been loaded into a Medfit; ropes had probably been attached to FM459E, however, only because the chain bracket on the near corner was broken.
DEREK MUNDY and HMRS

Mention of GWR fruit vans and LMS fish vans brings us into difficult country: the use of red in the context of goods vehicles. I believe the former weren't alone among ex-GWR stock in receiving coach crimson: although hard evidence is in short supply, it seems that the Western Region also painted non-insulated fish vans, which had been brown before nationalisation, in this colour. The London Midland Region, on the other hand, followed LMS practice in painting purpose-built fish vans crimson lake, and used the same shade for ventilated meat vans of both pre- and post-nationalisation design (the latter represented by the venerable Airfix/Dapol kit). I use the words 'crimson' and 'crimson lake' guardedly: I suspect the LMR applied a more maroon version of red, though with a dearth of evidence

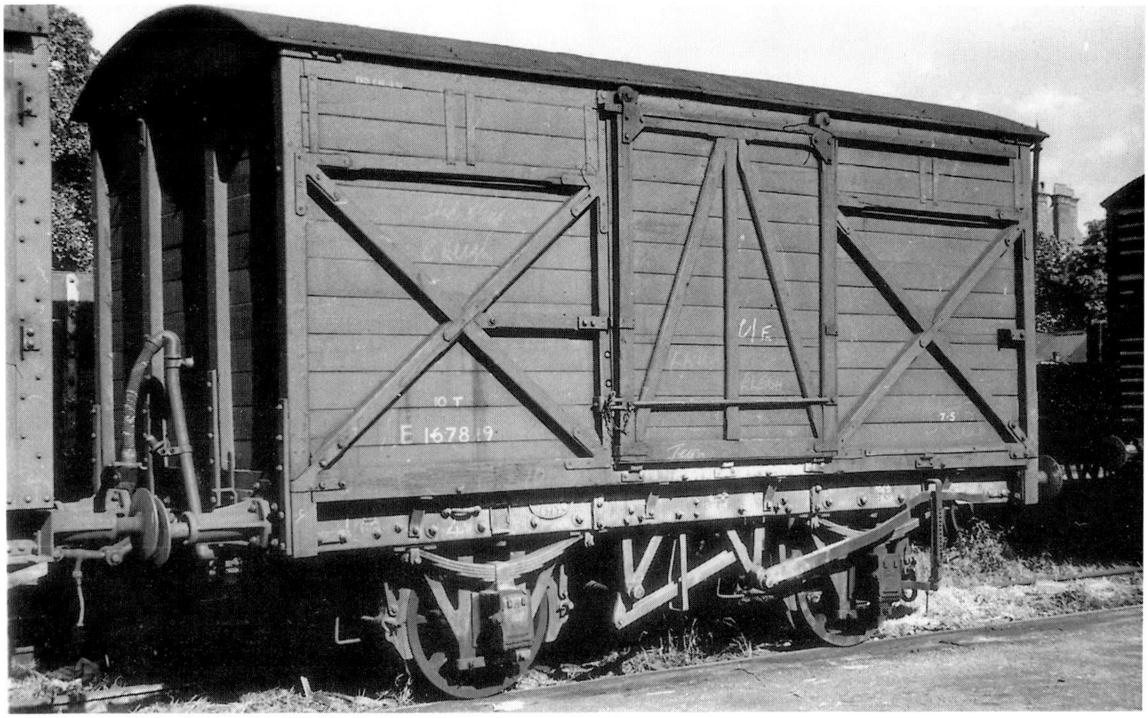

(iii) By BR days most of the first-generation LNER fish vans such as E167829 had been downgraded to general goods traffic, the louvres in the upper bodysides usually being boarded over as seen here, in which form some survived into the mid-'fifties at least. Its bauxite livery, however, was typical of all non-insulated ex-LNER designs remaining in fish traffic, whether of nine, ten or twelve-foot wheelbase. (iv) As noted in the text, the LMR maintained pre-nationalisation practice by painting its uninsulated fish vans in crimson lake. Newly-outshopped at Wolverton in 1953, M40297M (from one of the later batches actually built under BR auspices) also had black ends in full carriage style, as did the CCT beyond it. Most surviving four- and six-wheeled vans of this type eventually received bauxite livery, though not until the late 'sixties in some cases, by which time withdrawals had already begun. After passing into departmental use as stores vans, a number of the six-wheelers then appeared in olive green.
ROGER CARPENTER

from colour photographs I admit that I'm relying heavily on Don Rowland's consistent use of the term 'crimson lake' in *British Railways Wagons* and elsewhere.

Also red in the 'fifties were uninsulated covered containers. Again, the exact shade is hard to pinpoint, although there are a lot more colour photographs around to help us here, and they suggest that, latterly at least, it too verged closer to maroon than the crimson applied to passenger coaches or the road motor fleet. A good guide would seem to be the cover photograph of the recently-published *British Railways Wagons, Their Loads and Loading*, which shows part of the South Lambeth goods depot in 1959. As well as a number of insulated containers in white – some very dirty – over a dozen uninsulated B-types are visible, and all those that are clean enough for the colour to be identifiable with reasonable certainty (at least half of the total) are in maroon with yellow lettering. An added bonus is the presence of several BR road vehicles in a clearly different shade of red.

Foremost among private-owner fleets after 1948, at least in terms of numbers, were the tank wagons operated by the various oil companies. An idea of the variety to be seen can be found in the final chapter of Part Two, but pictured here and overleaf are a bitumen tanker bearing the Mexphalte brand name, and a pair of Esso fuel oil tanks, all in black with white symbols (except for the yellow commuted charge mark). DON ROWLAND

Most other pictures that I've seen taken in the later 'fifties and the early 'sixties tend to bolster this impression. However, there is some evidence that, as Roger Marsh says in his article in *Model Railway Journal* No. 43, there was a change in the mid-'fifties, a colour akin to early coach crimson (alias carmine) having been applied before that. A photograph by R. C. Riley in the September–October 1994 edition of *Backtrack*, taken at Bromsgrove in 1957, certainly shows a newly-painted container in the rather more orangey tone characteristic of coach crimson. Another by the same photographer in the August 2000 issue of *Steam World* shows (admittedly at long range) two containers at Southall in 1957 apparently in distinctly different shades of red. And yet a third of his pictures, in *Backtrack* for January–February 1994, has a freshly-painted B-type at an exhibition at Wood Green in 1958 in a colour quite similar to the BR mobile crane alongside it and the BR trailer it's sitting on, none of them very different from the Mark I coach nearby in the post-1956 maroon livery. You pays your money ...

Over and above these apparent variations, we should also bear in mind the effects of weathering and dirt. Road vehicles and passenger coaches were kept relatively clean, but containers and LMR fish and ventilated meat vans were rarely, if ever, washed on the outside, and so would appear darker as a result. And my own observations in the 'eighties of grounded containers in this livery confirmed that it weathered to a plummy, almost purple, hue in advanced old age.

Exactly when red was adopted for containers isn't clear, either. As mentioned earlier, bauxite was originally specified, and may well have been used for the first year or two. That maroon was ultimately widely applied seems unquestionable, however; witness the cover picture of *British Railways Wagons, Their Loads and Loading*. But red of whatever shade was abandoned for goods vehicles in the early 'sixties. In the case of containers this was in response to a policy decision to adopt, or revert to, bauxite, and the only area of doubt, once again, seems to be exactly when this took place. The new corporate house style announced in 1963 required uninsulated containers to bear both the new colour and the boxed arrow 'door to door' logo, but not all bauxite-painted containers did so. One that didn't was BD6457B, which has for many years sat in a field alongside the A15 in Lincolnshire. It carries a paint date of May 1963, which suggests to me that repainting of containers in bauxite started some time before the introduction of the new symbol, though perhaps not long before.

In the case of red-painted vans, the change to bauxite happened at least partly because they were being phased out of the traffics they were designed for and into general use, although the two changes didn't always coincide. The LMS fish vans were finding their role usurped by the two standard designs of BR insulated van popularly known as Bluespots, although this nickname and the mid-blue disc above the number that gave rise to it applied only to vans fitted with roller bearings. The insulated conversions of ex-LNER long-wheelbase vans, and the ex-GWR six-wheeled fish vans were also still in use, as, more significantly, was a range of insulated containers. It was these that were also responsible for ousting meat vans (both the red ventilated and white insulated kind) from their traditional role.

Until 1963 all insulated vans and containers (except banana vans) had been white, but were now undergoing their own livery change to ice blue. For the fish vans particularly the new colour was destined to be short-lived, however, since BR were to abandon the carriage of fish before the end of the decade, resulting in a further change, either to bauxite, or to rail blue for those vehicles re-allocated to express parcels traffic.

Before we leave the subject of containers, it's worth noting that quite a large number appeared in the special liveries of several companies to whom they were hired or allocated on a regular basis. The well-known Birds Eye AFP-types have been mentioned elsewhere; other organisations using traditional containers in their own colours included Raleigh, McVitie & Price, McGrouthers, Macfisheries and ICI.

Nor were these the only private-owner liveries to be seen after nationalisation. Accustomed as we are as modellers to associate such liveries largely with the coal trade, it's tempting to view the pooling of mineral wagons at the start of World War II, followed by public ownership in 1948, as the end of an era. In fact, private-owner wagons remained a feature of the railway scene, though admittedly much reduced in number and variety, until they re-emerged in more recent years as BR strove to persuade its customers to invest in their own wagon fleets. Nevertheless, for the lover of more colourful alternatives to BR's greys and browns, the 'fifties offered more scope than is perhaps generally realised, and not only in the way of surviving vestiges of the names of collieries and coal merchants on the dwindling ranks of wooden mineral wagons.

First and foremost there were the several fleets of tank wagons that had spent the war in drab grey, but regained their private

Incidentally, this second picture also illustrates the age range of tank wagons in use up to the mid-'sixties, with a pre-1927 vehicle (albeit modernised with ladders and top platforms) standing between a World War Two period wagon and a late 'fifties 35-tonner with roller bearings, vacuum brakes and Oleo buffers. HMRS

From Porthywaen in Shropshire came the lime wagons of The Steetley Co. Ltd: Llynclys Junction was just south of Oswestry on the Cambrian Railways main line. The livery is described in Private Owners on the Cambrian *by Mike Lloyd (Welsh Railways Research Circle, 1998) as overall grey with black running gear, corner plates and door catches, and white lettering shaded black, but these two wagons show some variation on this theme, especially around the headstocks. Both also bore a liberal coating of lime dust around the side doors and on the solebars and below. No. 536 seems to have lost its NON POOL marking, but this was an otherwise standard feature of all privately-owned wagons that escaped pooling at the start of World War Two.* R. STEPHENS

Wagons of the British Quarrying Company, bearing their 'Granophast' trademark, were also based mainly in the border country of north and mid-Wales, but could be seen quite far afield into the late 'fifties at least: Cheona Vol. 9 has a photograph of one at Goodrington on the Kingswear branch in 1957. According to Mike Lloyd in The Tanat Valley Light Railway *(Wild Swan, 1990), the livery was red oxide with black corner plates and white lettering, the larger characters shaded black. No. 437 does not seem to have had any black ironwork above the solebars, however. The raft of three- and four-plank wagons was photographed at Criggion Quarries in 1954.* F. W. SHUTTLEWORTH and JIM PEDEN

owner liveries soon afterwards when the pooling arrangements for these vehicles came to an end. Indeed, with the growth in oil refining and transport, these fleets were to expand dramatically, and although mergers and economies meant that their colours were less florid than they had been pre-war, there was still plenty of variety, augmented by tank wagons dedicated to the transport of other liquids such as acids and edible oils.

In addition, a good many other fleets of traditional-style wagons escaped wartime pooling because of the specialised nature of the products they carried. We've already looked in some depth at the three-box coal wagons of the Monks Ferry Company. One of the largest operators involved was ICI, who ran opens and vans in their own colours as well as their well-known bogie hopper wagons. Then there was Pilkingtons, the glass makers, who owned a fleet of wooden hoppers, and a number of salt refiners, such as Seddons and Mangers, grain merchants and brewers like Leith General Warehousing and Bass Charrington, and lime producers and quarry owners, including The Steetley Company, Derbyshire Stone Ltd and The British Quarrying Company.

Of course, the *raison d'être* of any private-owner livery was as much for advertisement as to denote ownership. An aspect of the former which has received less than its fair share of attention from the modelling fraternity is the widespread use of traders' labels on vans and containers to draw atten-

Of similar design to the peaked-roof Steetley Co. lime wagons, though without the corrugated iron roof doors, were some of the salt vans operated by ICI. The colours in this case were red with black ironwork and white lettering shaded black. The lettering above the NON POOL marking reads EMPTY TO WINSFORD & OVER CLC. JIM PEDEN

tion to the products being carried. Exactly when these came into use, I'm not sure: 1936 is the date of the earliest photograph I've come across, and the fact that railway-owned containers from the 'thirties and 'forties had the panels onto which they were pasted suggests that they were already becoming well-established by then. Their zenith came in the 'fifties and 'sixties, when most mixed goods trains would have carried a few, or at least the marks to show where old ones had been torn off.

Until recently you would have had to depend on your own artistic talents, coupled with access to the few useful colour photographs that have appeared over the years, to reproduce this feature. But a long-standing gap in the market has now been filled by Tony McSean, trading as Hollar Models, with his self-adhesive prints of a dozen of the most common labels. Alternatively or in addition, a few strokes of white paint from an almost dry brush are as effective as anything in simulating the remains of former ones that have been removed.

Three photographs showing traders' labels in use. BK-type container No. 8724B had a Spratts' dog food label, which I believe would have had black lettering on a yellow ground; it had been applied to the panel fitted to all later containers for just this purpose (the attachment of a label to the end of a container, as seen in the background, was unusual, and may have been done purely for this photograph). W104099, seen at Leith in 1962, carried a fine display of two Silcocks' labels, one for Blue Circle Cement, and a Parcels/Mails sticker as well – all now available in 4mm scale from Hollar Models. The rules required such labels to be removed as soon as the van or container had been unloaded, but, as with all such rules, compliance was often little more than a token gesture. As an alternative, one label could always be pasted on top of another.

DON ROWLAND

SCHEDULE OF EARLY BR WAGON MARKINGS

The instructions for wagon markings up to 1963 (when the typeface changed slightly, and the layout more so) were highly specific, though with hindsight they seem to have been honoured as often in the breach as in the observance. The main requirements were as follows:

1. The typeface was to be Gill Sans medium in all cases; all lettering was to be in block capitals (though see paragraph 7).
2. Letter sizes and positions:
   (a) left-hand bottom corner: capacity in 2-inch numbers and letter, above wagon number in 3-inch numerals, prefixed by 3½-inch letter denoting origin of vehicle (B, E, M, S, W or P). Additional prefix letter D signified departmental use.
   (b) right-hand bottom corner: XP in 4-inch letters (applicable only to vacuum-braked or vacuum-piped vehicles with a wheelbase of 10 feet or more), above wheelbase in 2-inch letters and numerals, above tare weight, also in 2-inch numerals. Wheelbases under 10 feet were not usually shown, and wheelbase markings were less commonly seen on unfitted stock; the solebar was an alternative position for them.
   (c) There were laid-down vertical separations between markings: in general, lettering began 3–4½ inches above the lower edge of the sides, with similar gaps between lines.

   Positional variations were authorised if the body design required it: for example, on low-sided open wagons or on vans with sliding doors opening to the left.
3. Vehicle type (e.g. SHOCKVAN, IRON ORE TIPPLER, etc): generally reserved for 'special' wagons of one sort or another at this time, though more widely applied post-1963. Letters were either 3 inches or 6 inches high, and were carried above the capacity or in the centre of the wagon side respectively.
4. End door stripes: 2½ inches wide. On wooden-bodied numerals the stripes were almost always on the diagonal braces; on steel wagons they should have vertical ends, the upper end being level with the end door hinges. No black patches were considered necessary.
5. Bottom door vees: nominally 1½ inches wide, 7½ inches high, 3 inches apart at the bottom and 13 inches at the top, and on a black ground. None of these requirements was slavishly followed. These markings were mainly intended for minerals, and were placed in the centre of the side door near the bottom, but they were sometimes seen in the equivalent position on hopper wagons.
6. Shock markings: three 4-inch wide vertical stripes; height to suit the vehicle, but generally covering almost the full height of an open wagon and a bit less than half that of a van. The position varied according to the wagon design, but was usually on the doors of vans and bracketing the doors of open wagons. The end stripes were usually spread across the full width of the body, but occasionally grouped closer together on the left. No black outlines were used on unfitted stock.
7. Containers: principal lettering (container type, number and originating company initial letter in that order, together with BRITISH RAILWAYS in full) in 3-inch letters and numerals. Subsidiary lettering 1¾ inches (Imperial measurements) or 1½ inches (Metric measurements – the only official use of lower case lettering at this time). Most of the markings were at the top left-hand corner of the side, with the number usually repeated on the left-hand end door. BRITISH RAILWAYS was central in the upper part of the side/side doors.
8. Colours: chiefly white, but yellow lettering was used with crimson and black, and black with white-painted stock.

PAINTING, LETTERING AND WEATHERING

For those of you who, having read my remarks on BR wagon liveries, are still puzzled by certain aspects, I accept that I haven't got all the answers (has anyone?), and may well have misinterpreted things to some extent along the way. However, perhaps I can offer a few crumbs of comfort.

One: Whatever the rules might have said in any context, there will always be examples of the opposite, plus all the options in between.

Two: Whatever colours those parts of a vehicle below the body may have been painted, a few weeks in traffic will make them incapable of ready identification. A few years may have a similar effect on the rest of the wagon.

Three: Notwithstanding any evidence to suggest that different works may in any case have applied different shades at different times, even colours that are consistent to start with will react differently to weathering and contaminants. As long as you don't paint your wagons sky blue pink with yellow polkadots, any approximation of the 'right' colour will be fine, and more so if they all vary a bit.

You will readily deduce from this that I regard weathering and other forms of distress (rust, dents, patching, etc) as a must for 99% of any wagon fleet. British goods wagons, certainly railway-owned ones, have never been cleaned regularly on the outside, and to see a fleet of model vehicles in pristine condition, except in very special circumstances, always jars.

First things first, however.

Much has been written over the years, and a lot of energy expended, explaining the rights and wrongs of painting finished models. Understandably, I suppose, most of this has been directed at engines and coaches, rather than wagons, although the same principles apply. A few basic points apart, it is perhaps more of an art than a science, particularly when it comes to weathering, but if you follow some simple guidelines, applying paint to a surface is a fairly straightforward exercise.

The very first thing to do is to make sure that the model is clean: no greasy fingermarks or smears of unevaporated flux. However, elaborate washing isn't necessary in my experience, even with etched brass or whitemetal models, where a rub with tissue is all that is usually required. In awkward corners wrap the tissue round a matchstick or the end of a brush handle. If the model has lain around for any length of time between completion and painting (and some of mine stay unpainted for years), it will probably want dusting with a dry, soft paintbrush first. And it helps to make sure when you start that the atmosphere is as dust-free as possible as well.

By all means prime metal surfaces if you wish. In fact, I rarely do: sooner or later some paint may wear off, or get knocked off, in use, and it doesn't seem to matter whether what you can then see is primer or bare metal. Certainly I haven't found that omitting a priming coat significantly reduces the adherence quality of enamel paint or adversely affects the smoothness of the finish. But it won't do any harm, either.

When it comes to the choice between brush- and spray-painting, I have to confess that I've never owned or used an airbrush, although for total versatility I suppose you should have both. Airbrushing is quick, even allowing for cleaning the equipment, and at its best can achieve a superb finish. It's also good at certain weathering techniques. At the end of the day, I'm not sure it can do very much that a brush can't, however, and I couldn't do without a brush for some things.

As far as the selection of brushes is concerned, I get by with only a couple of different sizes for most jobs: a number 3 or 4 for about 99% of the time and a number 00 for detail work: window frames and filling in the body of private-owner lettering and shock wagon markings, for instance. I find brushes with medium-length, tapered bristles more controllable, and consistent results are most assured with sable hair ones, though I've had a perfectly acceptable finish with less expensive brushes, such as squirrel hair. But avoid cheap brushes like the plague.

For paint, I've only ever used enamels, and I use them for everything, including lettering and lining. I've nothing against acrylics, for example, but having once got used to something, be it materials, tools or methods, you tend to stick to what you know. I'm old enough to remember when Humbrol railway colours were the only thing that was readily available, and I still have a fondness for them, even though the railway range has been virtually eliminated and other manufacturers have developed alternative products. The accuracy of colour formulations tends to be slightly subjective, but given the wealth of shades quickly assumed by goods vehicles in traffic, this isn't too much of a problem, and a degree of variety is the spice of life. So these days I don't stick to any one maker's range.

Most of the paints we use in modelling are designed to produce a matt or semi-matt finish, and I hope it's unnecessary to say that there are virtually no areas where a high gloss would be appropriate in the finish of railway rolling stock of any kind. Nonetheless, I feel we sometimes tend to overdo the flatness of, say, steel-panelled coaches, and even goods wagons had a noticeable sheen when first outshopped. Whilst they quickly lost this in service, the occasional ex-works wagon isn't out of place, and a model of such a vehicle shouldn't receive a dead matt finish. For the rest, any reflective quality in the paint used will be nullified by even a light coating of workaday dust and grime, so it doesn't really matter if they're matt to begin with.

Incidentally, I never use varnish. Since I hand-letter all my goods wagons, a protective coat of any kind isn't necessary. But even on locos and coaching stock, where I invariably use the PC 'Pressfix' range of transfers, now available through the Historical Model Railway Society, I find that these are well able to stand up to the kind of handling required under exhibition conditions, provided a degree of care is exercised, without additional protection. And if I need on rare occasions to heighten the sheen of a paint job a little, I use abrasive rubbing compound to emphasise the effect of a superficial polish.

But unless a paint is thoroughly stirred, the results can be a trifle unpredictable. Matt enamels can even dry with a gloss finish in these circumstances, and it pays to make sure that all the sludge at the bottom of a tin is properly mixed with the oily medium that rises to the top when paint is left undisturbed for even quite short periods – to the extent that it can sometimes need agitating again during use. Some modellers insist on using fresh tins all the time, but I have to say that I never throw paint away as long as it's liquid, unless the structure has broken down completely, which usually happens only as a result of repeated addition of thinners, especially to matt black and white.

Although neat paint will sometimes do for lettering, I've never found one that comes straight out of the tin at the right consistency for brushing: it's always too thick to apply successfully without adding a measure of thinners. The proportions of the mix will depend on the viscosity of the paint, and it can be as high as 50/50, though more often a combination of two or three parts paint to one part thinners will be about right. But only experience and trial and error will really show you what's needed.

For mixing small quantities of paint (and a few drops, suitably thinned, will be enough for a single van body, for example), I transfer it from the tin on a matchstick to any suitable small container, such as a bottle top; if your milk still comes in glass bottles, the foil caps make useful mixing dishes. I then add the thinners, a brushful at a time, stirring it in with the matchstick until it reaches something approaching the right consistency. What you're aiming for is a mixture that's inclined to drop off the end of the matchstick without stringing, one that will flow readily from the brush without needing to be persuaded into the nooks and crannies. Up to a point, then, the thinner it is, the better; you don't need

This Palbrick A has received only a single coat of paint at this stage. The underframe grime (matt black, matt white, earth and track colour) has covered pretty well, but the one thin coat of bauxite applied to the body allows the white plastic to show through unevenly. In the event, two more similar coats were required to provide an adequate coverage. In comparison, the shock open took two, and the three-box wagon only one coat of base colour, the Shocbar because the body was moulded in brown plastic, and the latter thanks to the generally better covering power of matt paint, even on a white styrene foundation.

Modelling the Parkside pipe wagon in its as-built, unfitted state with unpainted planking added an extra dimension to the painting process: the kit is designed to reproduce these vehicles in their later, vacuum-fitted, bauxite-liveried condition, and the body is accordingly moulded in brown plastic, which is not the ideal base for an 'unpainted' finish. So the first thing I did was to paint the body overall pale matt grey, before picking out the individual planks in differing shades of grey, intermixed here and there with traces of yellow and brown. This inevitably washed onto the ironwork in places, so this was then retouched in Railmatch 309. The final stage will be to tone down the brightness of the ironwork and the lettering panels with a wash of very thin mid grey-brown.

Two more 'unpainted' wagons, both from veteran plastic kits: Vernon Harrod built the ex-LNER six-plank open from 3H Mouldings parts, while the 21-ton loco coal wagon is an original Ian Kirk product. The timberwork of wooden-bodied (and especially wooden-framed) wagons was routinely left unpainted for a decade or more after nationalisation, and the piecemeal replacement of individual planks led to such vehicles exhibiting a haphazard range of hues from straw through fawns and browns and, most typically, every shade of grey imaginable. Sometimes the ironwork was painted, but even here rusty grey-brown was the prevailing finish.

to worry about covering the surface evenly with the first coat, because a second will probably be necessary even on plastic whose colour approximates to the final shade. On white styrene, whitemetal or brass, at least two coats will be required. Allow not less than 24 hours, preferably longer, between coats.

Use the natural divisions created by framing, doors, corners, etc, to break the vehicle up into panels or sections, and paint each one separately as quickly as reasonably possible, relying on the thinned paint to flow into crevices. Don't worry about obscuring delicate detail: the paint shouldn't be thick enough to do that when it's dried. Thinned enamels start to dry quite quickly, so don't be tempted to go back over an area you've already done or to spend too long on one patch. If you do, or if you don't thin the paint sufficiently in the first place, you risk leaving brush marks. A wishy-washy finish can always be remedied with a further coat; a model that looks as if it's been painted with a teaspoon can only be stripped and started again.

For finishes straight out of the paintshop, that's about it except for lettering. But there is one livery (or perhaps more accurately, one aspect of livery) that is rather less straightforward. Essential to the post-1940 modeller, but also relevant to those with earlier interests, we're talking about unpainted timber. This was a feature of the external appearance of a wide range of open wagons, and a sprinkling of vans, from the outbreak of World War II until the final demise of conventional wooden-bodied stock a few years ago. But in relation to the inside of all open and flat wagons with wooden sides and floors, its relevance extends throughout railway history. True, the colour of the insides of most such vehicles, once they had been in traffic for a while, could best be described as a fairly uniform grey-brown, with some variation according to the types of traffic they were designed for; but they certainly didn't start out that way.

Freshly-sawn timber in these climes is generally a pale straw colour, and left to itself would weather eventually to a silvery-grey. In practice, I suspect that these extremes would have been seen quite rarely: specifications no doubt called for well-seasoned, and perhaps treated, wood (although standards would certainly have been relaxed in war time and in the austerity period that followed), and so, even for new vehicles, a brownish yellow, or pale khaki, shade is perhaps more appropriate. Once released to traffic, wear and tear, and the effects of the goods carried, would soon ensure that the internal fabric would not be left to weather naturally. Some wagon types would be affected less than others: Conflats, for example, wouldn't see much in the way of contaminants, and might, therefore, remain a relatively pale grey-brown. Minerals, on the other hand, would soon assume a dark charcoal colour, rather lighter and with brown undertones if they were allowed to dry out for long enough (coal is often wet, and wet timber always looks darker – and don't forget that it sometimes rains in this country as well).

On the whole, darker colours are, I feel, more appropriate than lighter ones for wagon interiors, and for myself a mixture of matt mid-grey and track colour is a fair compromise; for steel-bodied wagons, try bauxite instead of track colour to suggest rustiness. In contrast to what I said earlier about mixing paint and thinners thoroughly in advance, I generally take the colours straight from the tin and mix them haphazardly with not-too-much thinners as I apply them to the model. This gives an uneven finish, and if you brush the paint out following the line of the planking, some boards end up lighter/darker than others. Oily patches can be introduced with loco black here and there if appropriate. Unpainted timber is just about the only area where brush marks are legitimate, as well: done in a fairly restrained sort of way, they can be seen as the grain of the wood.

The effect of the grain is perhaps even more relevant to the outside of an 'unpainted' wagon. Here, unless the vehicle was one of those turned out new with a bare wood finish in the 'forties and 'fifties, or had been completely re-sheeted at some time, the colouring of the individual planks would be far less consistent – anything from fresh, straw-coloured timber to a whole variety of greys and browns arising from dirt, weathering, patch-painting and make-do-and-mend repairs such as the re-use of second-hand planks from withdrawn wagons. No rules apply here, except that the timbers must be painted singly or in small groups in a range of colours in which greys predominate, but varied by the admixture of white, yellows, browns, earth colours and even greens in greater or lesser quantity. A makeshift palette such as a piece of tinfoil is useful here, on which blobs of each of these colours can be deposited and then mixed and selected randomly. A more sparing than usual use of thinners helps to suggest the grain of the bare woodwork.

The most manageable tool for small-scale lettering is for me a mapping pen. Readily available from good stationers, and not expensive, the ones pictured here are made by the firm of Joseph Gillott. The smaller ones are No. 659 'Crow Quill' nibs, shown here very close to actual size.

* * *

With the range of transfers now available from a number of manufacturers, today's wagon modellers have much less need to resort to hand lettering than their predecessors. The modeller of the post-nationalisation scene is better catered-for than most, but when I began working in 4mm scale thirty years ago, things were rather different: anyone wanting a representative range of wagon types, properly marked, had little alternative but to develop the skills necessary to letter wagons by hand.

I still do it the hard way, not because my hand lettering matches the standard of today's transfers, or anything like it, but because to change now would, I fear, point too much of a contrast with the 300-odd wagons running on 'Retford' and 'Blakeney'. To see what I mean, look at the photos on pp. 160–1 of Part Two, where one of my few uses of transfers on goods vehicles shows up the relative lack of crispness of the hand lettering accompanying it.

However, there is still some justification for the use of such skills. A glance through the pages of '*The 4mm Wagon*' will furnish ample evidence of wagon markings that don't conform strictly with official requirements in either size or shape, whereas transfers tend to obey the rules. And in addition, there is a large number of private-owner liveries that need the d-i-y touch to reproduce them accurately.

I know that some modellers achieve excellent results with a fine brush (as Paul Karau's contribution to *The 4mm Coal Wagon* amply demonstrates), but I've always used the kind of narrow-nibbed dip pen known as a mapping pen. These are available from good stationers or art shops for around the price of a pint. The nib tapers to a very fine point, no more than 10-thou across at the tip, and although designed for inks, can be used with paint as well, provided you're prepared to accept the discipline of cleaning it with a thinners-soaked tissue after every few strokes. Once again, the consistency of the paint is very important: it needs to be thin enough to flow, but not so thin that it blobs on contact. Needless to say, a steady hand is a big help, and a magnifying lens of some kind may be useful, although up to now I've got by with the naked eye in a good light.

Of course, no-one develops a skill like this overnight, but I refuse to believe that anyone who is capable of constructing a detailed scale model isn't also able to teach him- or herself to hand letter to an acceptable standard, given practice. Practice can take various forms: pencil and paper to begin with, to give yourself the confidence of writing a variety of inscriptions clearly in small scale. Then perhaps with the pen

Legible lettering down to a scale two inches or so should be achievable with practice, as shown on these two Lowfits, also built by Vernon Harrod. Anything smaller, such as the 'Not to be Loaded with Containers' legend on the left-hand wagon, tends to confirm the suggestive power of dots and squiggles – you can read it if you know what it says.

and indian ink, still on paper, moving on to paint when you've got some experience of the pen and how to obtain decent results. In principle, lighter strokes will generally serve you better than heavy ones, and in time legible letters down to a scale two inches or so should be achievable. Anything smaller can be represented with a series of dots and squiggles that suggest the shape of letters and numerals.

At some stage you'll have to take your courage in both hands and have a go on a real model. Make sure you know what you're going to write where, and if it helps, make a few light pencil marks and lines to fix positions and keep things level. And remember that mistakes can always be rectified by washing off with thinners or with a coat of base colour. Incidentally, when it comes to working on the model proper, I find I need to rest my hand on roughly the same level as the surface I'm lettering; a thickish book, or a video cassette box, with my free hand holding the model tight to the spine, are about right.

Assuming that you're working from a photograph or drawing, the key to getting the larger lettering of private-owner names or pre-1936 railway company initials to look right is to observe where they fall in relation to the planking and ironwork of the vehicle. This should help you to determine the size, shape and layout of the markings, if necessary pencilling them in lightly to guide you when reproducing them in paint. The most important dimension is always the vertical one: real signwriters weren't above tinkering with the shape of individual letters to get them to fit neatly, but the height should remain constant throughout. With straight, horizontal lettering, the planking is a good guide, but with the more florid curved or diagonal styles, light pencil lines drawn with compasses or a ruler can be used.

I begin by drawing a thin outline of the letters with the pen. As a matter of principle with any writing intended to fit a particular background shape like a wagon side, I start at the middle and work out, which reduces the scope for error in the width and spacing of the characters. The body of the letters inside the outline is filled in with a fine brush: this tends to give a more solid and uniform finish than the pen over larger areas. Although when outlining the letter I take care to get the edges as clean and as true as possible, this doesn't preclude tidying them up with the fine brush dampened with thinners or with the pen and a touch of the base colour. Where relevant, the shading can help to achieve the same end.

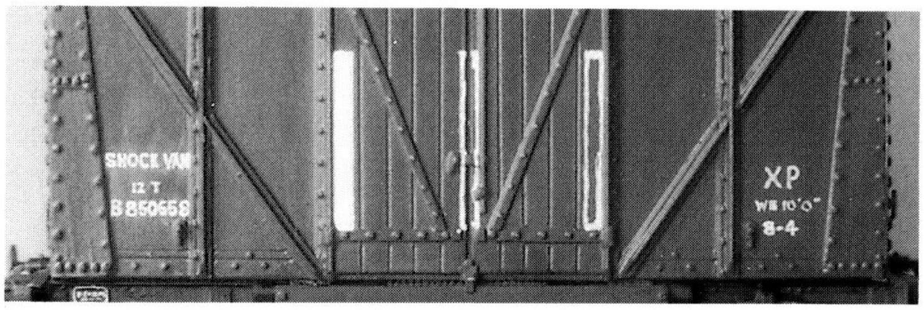

The construction of Diagram 1/209 Shock Van B850658 was described in Part Two. Here, after two coats of bauxite (needed chiefly to cover the white plastic modifications to the body), marking is under way using the mapping pen to outline the shock stripes and a 00 brush to fill them in. The unusual layout of the end symbols is taken from the 1971 photograph of B850658 in BR Standard Freight Wagons, *but it's interesting that nine years earlier B850815 from the same lot had been newly repainted in the same way – see the picture reproduced in the section dealing with liveries. The final shot shows the finished van, lightly weathered to dull the boldness of the white markings, and embellished with one of Tony McSean's traders' labels.*

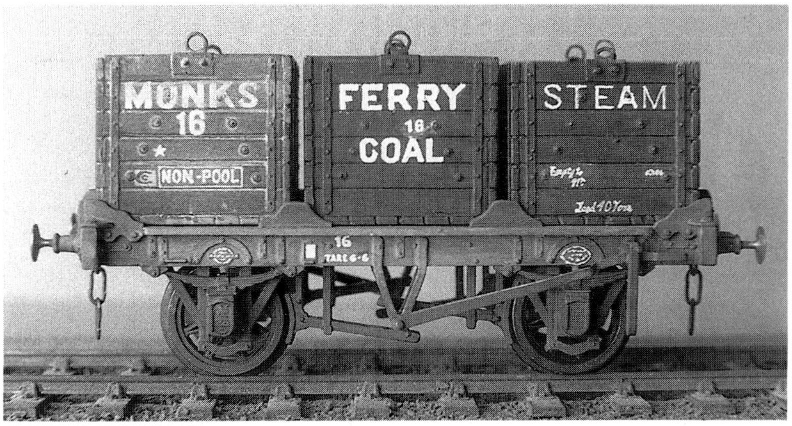

The various stages in lettering and finishing one of the three-box wagons described in Chapter 1 are illustrated here. I used pencil and paper to sketch out my interpretation of the faint return instructions on the right-hand box of No. 16; the space occupied by the IFTON plate will be filled in due course by one of the PLAS WATKIN placards drawn on the black-painted end of a scrap of 5-thou. I then reproduced the script as legibly as I could given the space available (the 'Load 10 Tons' legend is only six millimetres long in 4mm scale), before tackling the principal lettering. I started by roughly drawing this in the manner of the right-hand box. When I was satisfied that I'd got the position and proportions about right, I set about thickening the letters, as on the middle container (I had two goes at the number, hence the smudge where my first attempt was washed off with thinners). A modicum of tidying up is still called for: the F, the E, the second R and the O all need edging/filling out with a touch of base colour. The star, the yellow commuted charge mark and the NON-POOL box, each also tidied up as necessary, completed the left-hand container, leaving only the bottom plank bare for those elusive 'loaded' instructions. A wash of grime, and a little dry-brushed bauxite rust on the ironwork finished the job.

Weathering, as I said earlier, is really more of an art then a science, a fact clearly recognised by Martyn Welch, whose book in this series, *The Art of Weathering*, should be required reading for anyone tempted to dip a toe into this particular stretch of water. So, too, is *British Railway Goods Wagons in Colour*, which well illustrates the extent to which wagons that have been in traffic for any length of time can adopt a range of shades and finishes at variance with their ex-works condition.

There are several techniques that can be used, and it pays to be familiar with more than one in order to reflect the variety of the real thing. Just as a train of pristine wagons looks wrong, so stock weathered entirely by the same method and to the same degree also fails to capture this variety. However, they all use the same range of colours as each other, which is similar to those also used for reproducing unpainted wood: predominantly black, white, greys, earth, and track colour. You may notice that I haven't mentioned rust in this list. This isn't because I never use it, but because when I do I use it very sparingly. Red rust is met with far less commonly in a railway context than you might think, and whilst a touch of it around wagon brakegear for instance may not be out of place, the rust that takes hold on the iron and steelwork of bodies and underframes is generally in shades of brown, which is much more accurately represented by mid-to-dark track colour. Where a slightly redder tinge is appropriate, such as where the inside of a steel mineral wagon is regularly abraded by the loads carried, it's okay to mix a proportion of rust (or bauxite, which has much the same effect) with the darker grey and brown shades, but over-use tends to look rather garish. And remember that the very freshest rust is yellow, rather than red.

In Part One the conversion was described of the Cambrian riveted LNER steel mineral into the BR equivalent. This is the finished wagon, well-used, and with patches of rust spreading haphazardly over its steelwork. As with the sheeted mineral B216227, this was achieved by a mixture of dry-brushing and stippling.

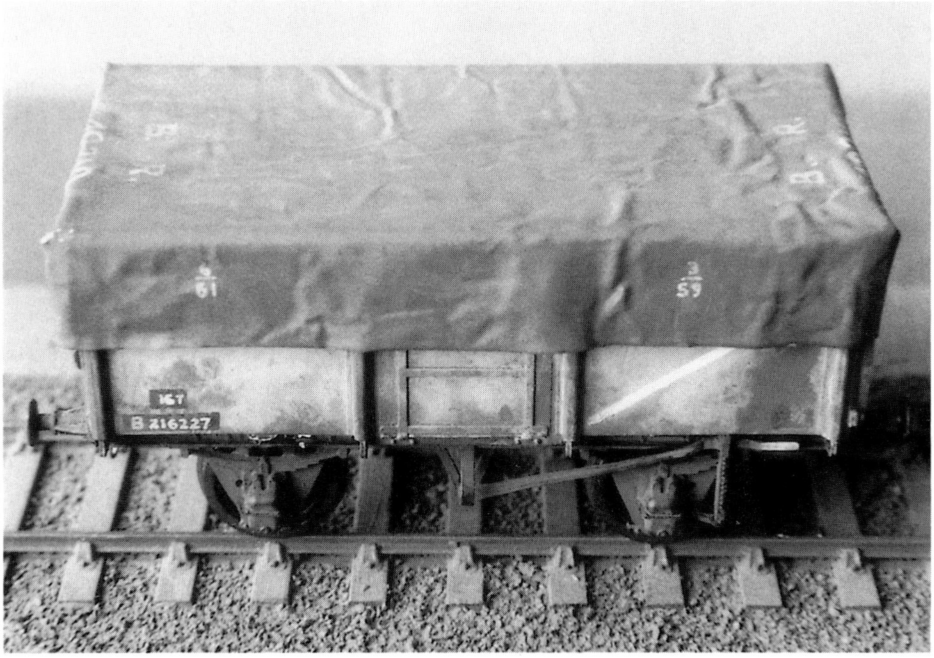

Notwithstanding what I said about metal wagon sheets taking paint well, it tends to flake off if you paint them before folding to shape. This means that you have to letter the sheet after folding as well, of course, although you don't have to complicate things by writing the number on a fold line, as here. Still, this does further demonstrate the user-friendliness of the mapping pen.

The simplest weathering treatment is to give the model a general wash over with very thin light-to-mid grey. Try to brush off the majority of this, leaving no more than a film to dull the brightness of the original paint. The shade of grey can be varied from wagon to wagon, as can the amount of paint left around ironwork, but extreme colours should generally be avoided. As a rule of thumb, weathered areas tend to be lighter in hue than you think they are. Surfaces contaminated with coal dust, for instance, are rarely black: rather, they are grey with brown undertones. For further proof, look critically at any dry, well-trafficked road surface: it won't be the colour of fresh tarmac. On the other hand, some shades may dry darker than expected: even plain matt white, applied over a grey or bauxite base colour, will seem no lighter than a pale grey, provided it isn't overdone.

Not that plain white is often usable by itself, except for wagons used regularly for lime or china clay. In the same way, charcoal grey or black are rarely appropriate for anything other than the spillage that collects on the barrels of tank wagons carrying tar or black oils. This is almost the only time that day-to-day usage can legitimately obliterate all or part of the original livery, with thick streaks of paint simulating the treacly dribbles of fluid around and below the manhole. A slightly lighter grey is a good run-of-the-mill shade for van roofs; whatever colour they started out, airborne dust and soot soon ensured their deterioration. The final appearance was usually fairly uniform, so further weathering isn't necessary, although it does look better if the shade of grey is varied somewhat from van to van.

As an alternative to using a brush dampened in thinners to remove excess grime, you might try a thinners-impregnated tissue. Because the tissue can't easily penetrate into corners, it tends to leave muck in places where it accumulates naturally: planking grooves, door framing, and around hinges and catches, for instance. With this method perhaps more than any other, it's important to make sure that the base colour has dried hard before you start so that it isn't likely to be lifted through the action of the thinners: as another rule of thumb, try to leave any newly-painted and lettered wagon for at least three days, preferably longer, before employing any weathering technique involving copious amounts of thinners.

Dry-brushing and stippling are one way round this problem. In both cases, most of the colour is brushed out onto something

A late-fifties trio of wooden minerals parked on the Quay Branch Siding at Blakeney. On the left, the Cambrian ex-PO shown earlier with a load of pit-props. In the centre, the ABS ex-LMS wagon also surveyed in Part One. And on the right a part-scratchbuilt, part-3H vehicle originally painstakingly hand-lettered in Evans & Bevan colours, and subsequently heavily distressed to leave only traces of its original livery.

I set out to paint the D1657 brake van in the manner of its unidentified sibling pictured at Northwich in the section on liveries, but in rather more tired condition approximating to the real M328337 as it appears in An Illustrated History of LMS Wagons. *Interestingly, the heavy coat of grime applied to the solebars makes it impossible to tell from a black and white photograph that they were originally grey like the woodwork above them, though this is more obvious when viewing the model in colour. Given that most of the photographs of the real thing that are available to us are in black and white and show wagons in workaday condition, it's hardly surprising that the finer points of their livery are often so difficult to pin down. The last things to be painted were the handrails, in a very pale mixture of earth and matt white.*

like a piece of card before depositing limited amounts of paint on specific areas of the model such as corner plates, headstocks and axleguards. You can afford to be fairly adventurous here: greys and earth colours show up quite strongly when wet, but generally become much less noticeable as they dry. Stippling is a good way of building up patches of colour while avoiding hard edges: sharply-defined splodges of muck and rust on otherwise plain surfaces don't usually work by themselves; even on steel mineral wagons, some effort should be made to feather the outline of most of the rusty areas to a degree. Be warned, however, that stippling isn't the kindest way to treat a paintbrush; I generally use an old one for this purpose, one that is past its best for most other jobs.

This is certainly not an exhaustive study of weathering techniques. The use of powders, and Martyn Welch's novel ideas with masking fluid are things I haven't tried, and, as I said at the beginning of this section, I don't possess an airbrush. One short cut I haven't seen described elsewhere, however, involves painting and weathering in one go. This is particularly suitable for underframes, and it can be used not only for goods stock, but for passenger coaches as well. Indeed, I've even painted a couple of engines in a single coat of rusty black. Put very simply, the method uses a range of greys, red-browns, earth and track colours applied haphazardly with a fair amount of thinners, enough to ensure that the shades blur into each other unevenly rather than staying in distinct patches. You might put a bit more black round the axleboxes, or rusty brown on parts of the brakes and the buffer spindles, but there are no hard and fast rules. As with all slants on the matter of weathering, the approach is an impressionist one, rarely a stroke-for-stroke copy of any one real-life vehicle, the objective being a wagon that may be subtly different from its neighbour, but one that doesn't stand out in a crowd, nor against the muted tones characteristic of the railway infrastructure. In short, a typical traditional goods wagon.